RETROACTIVE JEALOUSY & OCD INTRUSIVE THOUGHTS 3 IN 1 VALUE COLLECTION

THE SURVIVAL GUIDE FOR OBLITERATING OBSESSIVE-COMPULSIVE BEHAVIOR AROUND YOUR PARTNER'S PAST, POLYAMORY, DIVORCE, & OPEN RELATIONSHIPS.

RYDER WINCHESTER

STACY L. RAINIER

CONTENTS

Bonus Meditation Download	vii
PART I Retroactive Jealousy	1
Introduction	3
1. My Story	7
2. Accepting Responsibility And Coming To Terms With Your Issues	13
3. Facing Core Issues Head-On	16
4. Dealing With Triggers	22
5. Positive Action And Positive Addictions	28
6. Changing How You Feel About Yourself	32
7. Happiness Is Power	41
8. Finding Great Teachers	47
9. When Others Don't Understand Retroactive Jealousy	50
10. Clearing Up The Wreckage	53
11. Life After Retroactive Jealousy	56
PART II Book 2: Retroactive Jealousy	61
Introduction	63
12. Why You're Sitting on a Treasure Chest You Never Knew Was There	66
13. This Has NOTHING to Do With Your Partner's Past and EVERYTHING to Do With You	75
14. Retroactive Jealousy: The Gateway Into the Greatest Gift You Could Ever Imagine	87
15. Exercises You Can EASILY Do at Home to Dissolve Retroactive Jealousy	99
16. Your Jealousy Is A Hungry Monster. Starve It!	111
17. Change the Way You Think About Sex (Undoing Social Conditioning)	122
18. Why Your Mind is Locked in This Nightmarish Cycle	133
19. Your Partner is Not Your Property	145
20. Healing Your Inner Child	156

21. The Runway to Freedom and Recovery	164
22. Power-Charged Retroactive Jealousy-Crushing Guided Meditations	175
23. Destroy Retroactive Jealousy Forever; A 30-Minute Daily Ritual to Supercharge Your Existence	186
Afterword	197

PART III
Book 3: Mastering Your Thoughts	199
Introduction	201
24. Is Your Life a Self-Made Mental Hell?	205
25. An Introduction to Natural Techniques for Ending Negative Thinking	217
26. Self-Actualization and the Path to Fulfillment	226
27. Detachment: Take the By-Pass Route and Escape the Busy Freeway of Your Mind	238
28. Detachment From What No Longer Serves You	248
29. Emotional Intelligence and Healing Your Inner Child	259
30. The Beauty of Self-Forgiveness, Self-Compassion, and Self-Love	267
31. Putting Yourself First Is Not Selfish	273
32. It's Time to Reprogram Your Brain	278
33. Amazing Meditation Techniques to Master Your Thoughts	286
34. The 10 Step Daily Empowerment Ritual for Mastery of Your Thoughts	294
Afterword	297
References	301
Please Leave a Review	303

© Copyright 2021 - All rights reserved.

The content contained within this book may not be reproduced, duplicated or transmitted without direct written permission from the author or the publisher.

Under no circumstances will any blame or legal responsibility be held against the publisher, or author, for any damages, reparation, or monetary loss due to the information contained within this book, either directly or indirectly.

Legal Notice:

This book is copyright protected. It is only for personal use. You cannot amend, distribute, sell, use, quote or paraphrase any part, or the content within this book, without the consent of the author or publisher.

Disclaimer Notice:

Please note the information contained within this document is for educational and entertainment purposes only. All effort has been executed to present accurate, up to date, reliable, complete information. No warranties of any kind are declared or implied. Readers acknowledge that the author is not engaged in the rendering of legal, financial, medical or professional advice. The content within this book has been derived from various sources. Please consult a licensed professional before attempting any techniques outlined in this book.

By reading this document, the reader agrees that under no circumstances is the author responsible for any losses, direct or indirect, that are incurred as a result of the use of the information contained within this document, including, but not limited to, errors, omissions, or inaccuracies.

BONUS MEDITATION DOWNLOAD

Wouldn't it be nice to have even more motivation, inspiration and courage on your path towards freedom from Retroactive Jealousy? As a sincere "Thank you" from the bottom of my heart, i've given you access to a FREE powerful 10 minute guided gratitude meditation mp3 below. Gratitude is the key to all of your life's abundance, joy, and manifests a wealth of love and light. Practicing the meditation below has enriched my life immensely and been a major player in freeing me from the shackles of Retroactive Jealousy. I just know it will do the same for you.

Are You Sick & Tired Of Triggers & Pain In Your Relationships?

- Easily Crush negative Thought Patterns With The Power of Gratitude
- Heal Your Inner Turmoil & Experience Freedom From Retroactive Jealousy
- Enrich Your Relationship So That You Can Enjoy Life Again

Go here for your Retroactive Jealousy crushing guided meditation: bit.ly/retroactivejealousymp3

This meditation helped me immensely when I felt like Retroactive Jealousy was getting way out of hand and taking me over completely. Resting in gratitude for the beauty I already had in my life cleared the pain & created more of the same wonderful things. I know these words will help guide you towards your freedom and destiny with courage and determination!

PART I
RETROACTIVE JEALOUSY

A GUIDE TO TRANSFORMING YOUR PAIN INTO POWER

INTRODUCTION

Introduction

If you are reading this book then congratulations! You have decided you are ready for change. You are ready to become empowered and ready to get your life back into your control. This book is a completely transparent, in-depth and detailed account of my journey through retroactive jealousy, from its vulnerable innocent origins, to its ultimate epic defeat. This book is also a comprehensive guide on how I personally struggled with and eventually transformed the insidious beast into personal strength and power. At the risk of offending you the reader and retroactive jealousy sufferer, I bring you this piece of truth; Retroactive jealousy was one of the greatest things to ever happen to me. That thought may seem impossible to you at this stage. It may even anger you. But you will likely one day feel a deep sense of gratitude that you suffered through this pain once you have undergone enough of a positive transformation. My Retroactive Jealousy's healing and defeat was a physical, spiritual and mental evolution. Although its grasp caused much pain, heartbreak and despair, victory over it blossomed a more loving, strong, patient, thoughtful and confident version of myself. I was reborn anew in the ashes of Retroactive jealousy's defeat and spread my wings into a brighter future that would not have been known to me had I not suffered the way I had suffered.

What Is Retroactive Jealousy

If you have picked up this book then you likely do not need an explanation of Retroactive Jealousy. But a description of its symptoms and traits from an external being may make you feel less alone, as you have likely felt isolated in your pain in the past. Your partner, friends, and family members may be wholly confused by your affliction, leaving you further in despair. But you are not alone. There are thousands of sufferers (and ex-sufferers) all around the world that feel this pain just like you. Retroactive Jealousy is the seemingly uncontrollable obsession and curiosity regarding your partner's sexual and relationship history. This obsession often causes sufferers to become encapsulated in a trance-like state of anxiety, wherein they feel the need to extract any discover any information and details of their partner's past. These attempts at extracting information can often lead to much drama and tempestuous upsets in relationships. The obsessive thoughts associated with Retroactive Jealousy can be likened to the symptoms of obsessive-compulsive disorder. The sufferer's mind regularly enters loops of intrusive painful thoughts, usually involving a past interaction their partner had with an ex-lover. These intrusive thoughts are mostly illusory and imagined as the sufferer conjures up their mental image of these past encounters. Often the sufferers partner may mention a small detail in passing and the sufferer will take this tiny detail and either use it to slyly draw out more information from their partner, or use it as a puzzle piece to create a larger imaginary image in their head of what they thought could have happened in their partners past. These assumed or imagined past happenings are not usually based on the reality of what happened. These intrusive thoughts and seemingly uncontrollable actions are accompanied and fueled by deeply painful emotions.

Before We Begin

There are a few important points to make before you begin your journey of healing. Firstly, to speed your journey up, I will refer to Retroactive Jealousy as 'RJ' for the remainder of this book. Secondly, I have made an effort not to go into any details that may trigger you the reader and RJ sufferer. But as you know all so well, triggers have a life of their own and will appear as they please. We will look in-depth at triggers later on in our path. Should you feel triggered at any point then please follow some of the exercises found later in the book. Remember, if you can't feel it then you cannot heal it. As painful as triggers are, they are one of the secrets to healing! They are little hidden (painful) gems of growth and personal power when dealt with strategically and with conscious presence. So from here on out, if you are triggered then see it as a good thing! It's an opportunity to use the trigger to your advantage to grow. Thirdly, you may have heard that it is impossible to completely rid yourself of RJ and you may still be triggered from time to time. This may be true for some ex-sufferers, but it's still a marvelous improvement in the individual's life. I would like you, the reader to guess how much of my RJ remains. 0%! I am absolutely 100% cured of my RJ and I am never, ever triggered. I cannot promise this for you the reader as everyone is unique and will experience growth differently. But you must know and realize deeply that absolute healing has been accomplished and can be possible for you. Lastly and most importantly, you must decide **here and now** that you have had enough of this life-denying pain and you are ready to stop projecting your pain out on to your partner, friends, and family. Making the brave, empowering decision to overcome your RJ will enrich your life beyond your current comprehension. It will relieve your friends and family's lives of your RJ's negative outward projections. It will make you stronger, more compassionate and will give you the ability and tools to overcome other seemingly negative struggles that may appear in your life. In short, your overcoming of RJ will make the world a better place. It is the best thing that I have ever done and I want you to thrive from the same results. You were not brought into this world to suffer. You are a divine, unique being that exists here for a positive reason.

So you have decided that the journey towards RJ's defeat **starts now**. Read on with a sense of courage, positivity, and lust for change!

Before we begin, just take these simple truths with you and review them regularly throughout your healing journey:

1. You will be gone one day. All of your possession will eventually turn to dust. Your loved ones will eventually be gone and so will any of your accomplishments, achievements, awards, and accolades. This is not written to depress you, quite the opposite. It is written to inspire you to grasp the reality of the finiteness of all things. Life is simply too short for your RJ. You cannot allow it to remain as it is. Your life is there to be enjoyed and to share your uniqueness and love with the world.
2. Every moment of every one of your days on this earth is precious. Do not squander precious moments fighting with ungraspable, self-created demons.
3. You are a powerful, intelligent life force that is capable of manifesting almost anything into your world.
4. You are a unique human being. There is only one of you. You are the only being on the planet that has your unique fingerprints. You are a precious, powerful creation.
5. We are all connected. You have the same core fears, pains, emotions and needs as your fellow man/woman.

1

MY STORY

I seemed to destroy every romantic relationship in which I had ever been involved. Not because of infidelity or incompatibility, not even because of fights, boredom, or need for personal space. They were all destroyed because of a trance-like state that would consume my entire being on an extremely regular basis. Almost as if I were possessed by a demonic entity. I would become hyper-vigilant, as observant as a private investigator. I would become a quick and intensely sharp manipulator. Warm anxiety imbrued energy would rapidly swell up from my feet to my stomach, all the way up my throat. I would lose control of my thoughts and words. All of these symptoms were seemingly caused by my obsession with my partner's past. I would bombard my partners with personal questions about their previous relationships. No stone would be left unturned and the obsessions would fester for days, weeks, months and years at a time. A myriad of imaginary images and thoughts of my partner's past would be cycling through my mind minute after minute with no respite. And when I finally went to sleep, I would suffer an onslaught of nightmares, watching these re-imagined past encounters of my partner play out like a movie. In waking I would name, blame, and call my partners all kinds of derogatory names. I wasn't consciously aware enough to control the outward assault on the world and the people around me. I lost wonderful people from my life as a result. I would feel sick as if I had some kind of virus in my bloodstream.

It wasn't until a serious relationship in my mid-twenties that I realized that this behavior was not the norm and it didn't meet my standards and values for what was ok and right. Up until this point, I could not imagine how anyone could **not** agree with me and be okay with their partner having any kind of intimate past with anyone else. After one particularly egregious RJ triggered fight with my partner, I watched her become so upset and broken down that it forced me to see clearly for the first time that my way of thinking was fueled by my jealousy and was not of sound thought. After this epiphany, I realized that I did not want to lose another close person in my life, and I knew deep down that it was time for change.

I first met Sarah four years before we had embarked on our relationship. Meeting at a gathering at a mutual friend's house, we quickly became friends. Because the friendship lasted many years before the relationship started, I was filled in on much of her intimate relationship based history and encounters. This information would be used as ammunition in my future jealousy fueled assaults. As the relationship progressed and we became a couple, I would question her more and more about her past, filling in mental timelines and imaginary puzzle pieces to create my own personalized images of what I thought happened, with snippets of slyly and not so slyly gathered information. At the beginning of the relationship, she would easily and innocently give in to my requests for information. My newly gathered information would trigger an emotionally insecure outburst from me and she would be left confused and distraught. She learned quickly and caught on to when I was trying to pull details from her past out of her and would close up, being very careful to not escalate my jealous state. Because of this, it caused emotional walls and barriers to go up at an early stage of the relationship. These walls blocked off much of our true potential connection. Not a day went by where I was not obsessing over one of her exes. I would attempt to snoop so far back into her history that even she could not remember the details of her past. I would place the imaginary puzzle pieces together for her and create my own film reels, ready to be played on loop in the Retroactive Jealousy movie theatre in my head. Anything she said would be mentally noted down and used against her. As our fights become more frequent, they would escalate, often to the point of near breakup. The thought of breaking up offered me an intense feeling of relief, as I would no longer have to think about her past and I could let her go. In truth, I was trying to let her past that I had conjured up in my head go, not her. I was not consciously aware enough at the time to realize that if I left the relationship, the relief would be very, very short-lived. I may be free of RJ for a certain length of time. But, as I embarked on a new relationship in the future and those familiar, exciting feelings would emerge all over again, so would my RJ triggers, despair and all of the nightmarish drama to accompany it. I thank the heavens that I was matched with someone so strong to her core that she would not leave me and vowed to work with me through it no matter how bad it got. Even when I proclaimed that I would never get better (it may feel like this when you are suffering with RJ). If your partner is not this supportive then have no fear. The problem does not lie with them, you must transform yourself from the inside, regardless of any external support system or loved one's involvement. The problem did not lie with Sarah, the problem was deep inside of me. I had to get to the core of my pain. Why was I so worried about these guys from her past? Why did I care so much about the details of these men to the point of unhealthy obsession? The journey for these answers led me to discover so much about myself, including who I really was and what I truly wanted in life. But first, I needed to not only subdue the pain so I could see clearly enough to grow, but I needed to go deep into the root of my pain and rip it out with both hands. Through time, much self-reflection and hard work, I was able to get better. I have since never been happier.

. . .

My journey towards healing began with the aforementioned epiphany that the way I was acting was not okay, nor was it conducive to any kind of enjoyable life for me or my partner. This led to an extensive online search wherein I tried to scrape together any information I could on any jealousy sufferers that had similar symptoms to me. This was when I made the groundbreaking discovery that this kind of jealousy had a name; Retroactive Jealousy. Up until this point, I had simply just named my behavior as plain old jealousy. As you likely have already discovered for yourself, RJ is not just boring old standard jealousy. To find out that I was not alone was massively comforting. I found some helpful resources and even discovered a facebook group of RJ sufferers! I did, however, encounter much counterproductive, insensitive information and "help" online which obviously was not produced by someone that had suffered with RJ. The kind of articles that offer such unhelpful nonsense as "their past doesn't matter, you just need to get over it, everybody's done something". As you have likely found, this kind of advice is fleetingly relieving at best, and probably trigger inducing quickly thereafter. As I discovered more and more about RJ and the sufferers across the globe, I was overwhelmed with a new sense of fighting spirit and optimism that told me "this can be done! I can get through this!". Prior to this time, I had proclaimed the same old broken record statement of "I will never get better". As you speak, so shall you become. I began to turn this internal language around very quickly. Reversing my negative self-talk was a huge ally in my recovery. As I become more aware of my emotions and behaviors, I started questioning every aspect of my emotional states. Through much reading and study, I began to understand more about myself. One of the areas of my self that I became aware of was my intense fear and nervousness when out and about in public at night. I had always experienced these feelings but they were always under the surface and I was not consciously aware of them. As I dived deeper into why I felt this way, memories of violence inflicted upon me by older kids in my youth began to surface. I began seeing a therapist recommended by a family member. During my work with the therapist, I discovered that these feelings of fear and stress under the surface were affecting much of my life, not just when I was in public at night and felt vulnerable. I had unwittingly carried the emotional scars and fear inflicted on me as a child into my adult life. This discovery made me realize why I felt so weak and small in comparison to my partner's exes (who I had imagined and told myself were stronger, taller and overall more physically impressive then I was). It all started to come together piece by piece. My fear, my weakness, my sense of vulnerability. It all stemmed from my simple case of insecurity. Had I experienced scenarios in my youth where I had felt and appeared strong, courageous and heroic as opposed to weak and oppressed, I likely would have carried this into my adult subconscious mind and perhaps RJ would have never inhabited my being. It became clear that much of what I suffered from as an adult was a direct result of certain experiences in my youth. I had to correct these unhealthy subconscious habits that were tearing me down. I would later get in touch with my inner child.

ONE BOOK *that helped me accomplish this inner child healing was 'Healing the Shame That Binds You' by John Bradshaw.*

I HAD DISCOVERED that many of my adult insecurities were stemmed from the fact that deep inside, I felt weak, small and vulnerable. This was a huge discovery as this meant that now I knew what I was working with. I could battle my issue with its polar opposite. If I felt weak, then I had to find a way to feel strong. If I felt shame then I had to combat this with confidence. If I felt fear then I had to combat this with courage.

I PROVIDE you with this information with the hope that you will search deep inside yourself to find out exactly what it is that makes you so insecure. It is likely stemming from your youth. I recommend you seek a therapist and have them aid you in getting to know your inner child. There are likely some life experiences that have caused you to become an adult that is not comfortable in their own skin; an adult with insecurities powerful enough to conjure up a beast such as Retroactive Jealousy. I eventually worked on my weakness issues by joining a Muay Thai class (and literally became a fighter), becoming a member of a gym and re-training my subconscious mind to replace the negative self-talk with affirmations of confidence and power. With much research fresh in my mind, a wonderful therapist and a new understanding of myself, I had plenty of areas in which to begin my healing work. After about 18 months of dedicated, strategic and relentless transformative work, I was, in fact, free of RJ's insidious grip. Triggers would often continue to try and capture my attention but to no avail. I was too good at ignoring triggers. I was too good at focusing on the positive and my mind was occupied by wonderful, life-affirming thoughts and activities. Now, sometime later, I am 100% free of triggers, intrusive RJ thoughts and all of the destructive drama that accompanies them. You can be too! My relationship has also never been better. Read on with gusto!

2

ACCEPTING RESPONSIBILITY AND COMING TO TERMS WITH YOUR ISSUES

At 25 years of age, it suddenly dawned on me that it was not normal for someone to act the way I was acting. I realized that the way I had been treating those closest to me was not acceptable, and for the first time, I truly accepted that I had a problem. My RJ based past perspective was one of not understanding how anyone else didn't join me in being absolutely distraught by their partner's past. My healed perspective is a full acceptance of what is and one of spreading full love and growth. It is often quite normal for a man or woman to be slightly upset or jealous upon hearing of their partner's previous relationships. But by contrast, for the RJ sufferer, jealousy can be joy denying and agonizing when it takes over and diminishes your way of life. Being in the grips of Retroactive Jealousy can feel like an absolute nightmare.

YOU MUST ACCEPT full responsibly for your RJ. It is not your partner's problem, it is yours. It is also not your partner's fault that you are afflicted. You must own it and accept it to become set up for real change. It is neither your fault that you are afflicted with RJ, but you must own it fully. You do not necessarily need to figure out the reason why you suffer from it. That is somewhat irrelevant (although finding out the root cause can often provide clarity and may aid in healing. I recommend this highly). If you were in the wilderness and shot with an arrow, you must first heal the wound and stop the poison before searching into the foliage for who shot the arrow. Later on, we will look at digging up the roots of your pain in Chapter 3: Facing Core Issues.

WITHOUT TRULY OWNING your Retroactive Jealousy, you may continue to blame your partner for their past and outwardly express your pain in a damaging way to those around you. Their past is not a problem. Their past is not here and now; the only time we will ever have. When suffering from RJ, it may feel like you are being cheated on by your partner at this very moment. This is because your body cannot differentiate between what is real and imaginary. It reacts chemically from the thoughts you present it with. Many anxiety sufferers feel like a lion is about to attack them, or a serial killer is going to invade their home. This is the body's defense mechanism to protect you. If one closes their eyes and imagines opening their fridge door, reaching in, picking out a lemon and taking a huge bite into it, one may find that their mouth begins to salivate. We know consciously that there is no lemon there, but the body's natural mechanism still does its job regardless of tangible objects, threats or surroundings. It is important to keep this in mind on your journey toward overcoming RJ.

YOUR PARTNER'S past does not exist. When you are battling with these thoughts, you are battling with a phantom. You cannot beat RJ by battling thoughts and you can't beat it by wrestling with a ghost, or an imaginary illusion. The first step to transforming your pain into power is to take ownership of your RJ. If you own it, you can transform this painful energy into life-affirming, loving power that will change your life forever. The strength you gain after transforming this RJ energy is courage inducing and will aid you through all of your life's endeavors.

. . .

How to take ownership of your RJ

USE A WRITTEN/SPOKEN affirmation technique to fully take ownership of your RJ.

Write the following affirmations down on paper and say them to yourself twice a day for the next week while you are starting your transformative journey. Say them once in the morning as you awake and once at night before you fall asleep.

1. I, (insert name) take full ownership of my Retroactive Jealousy.
2. I, (insert name) refuse to blame others for their past.
3. I, (insert name) refuse to blame others for my suffering.
4. I, (insert name) know that I and only I am responsible for my healing.
5. I, (insert name) will not relent until I have transformed my RJ pain into powerful life-affirming energy.

FEEL the power of taking ownership of your RJ. Once you own it, you can transform it.

3

FACING CORE ISSUES HEAD-ON

You must find the positive opposite and remedy for every affliction you find shadowing over your life. For example; one of my core issues was that I felt physically and mentally weak. This insecurity gave my RJ plenty of mind food that would manifest as rapid-fire emotional triggers. This unbearable trigger ammo was based on believing that my partner had been involved with taller, more muscular and what I deemed as 'superior' men. Upon intense detective like interrogation from me, my partner would regularly pacify my OCD cycles by explaining that she was interested in me and not these taller, differently physiqued men (she was unknowingly enabling me and therefore thwarting my healing process). However, the trigger was already set, hidden under the leaves of my mind, waiting for the next upset. Then like clockwork, my mind would again be quickly caught in the seemingly inescapable bear trap.

Over time and with much work, a more conscious, positive side of my mind began to emerge whilst my RJ triggered thoughts lay struggling in the wilderness.

. . .

AFTER ONE PARTICULAR THERAPY SESSION, I went deep and discovered the root cause of my feeling of weakness and inferiority. "Have you ever suffered any violence in your past?" asked my therapist. I thought way back to when I was twelve years old. I was out skateboarding with five or so of my friends and we had traveled through an underpass leading to a field surrounded by woodland on our way to the local skate park. A rowdy group of what seemed to be at least twenty to twenty-five older kids emerged from the trees, hurling profanities at us as we walked with our heads down, scared but minding our own business. The older group seemed to be in their late teens and early twenties. As the gang closed in, my friends in front of the group were attacked with punches to their heads and faces. As they ran ahead to get away, one friend was caught in the mayhem and had been beaten to the ground. I didn't want to run and leave my friend, so I hung back for him, I was also paralyzed with fear. I watched as several of the gang stamped his head against the concrete path (he escaped with no serious injuries). After they were done with him, they turned to me. I was surrounded by what seemed like 10 of them. One punched me hard across my face. So hard in fact, that my face went numb. The sensation was similar to the sensation of a football accidentally hitting your face on the playing field. It felt like my nose was where my ear should be. I heard from the right of me "This is how you do it!" And a swinging fist caught me deliberately in the throat. I fell to my knees and could not catch my breath. I was then punched more times then I could even feel around my face and head. As the beating continued, a passerby walking his dog was crossing the adjacent field and shouted to the gang "leave him alone!". "What are you gonna do about it?" Screamed the gang's ringleader. At that moment, I saw the only adult that could have rescued me turn away and leave the scene in fear. I felt truly helpless. One of the louts proceeded to pull a thick rope with a noose already tied out of a black hefty trash bag. I looked at the slipknot, then at the surrounding trees. My pupils dilated and I was filled with survival urges and adrenaline. It was fight or flight. With tremendous fear, I could sense what was about to happen. Before any savagery could continue, I saw an opening between the gang members' legs. With nothing to lose, I hopped through their legs and ran as fast as I could while leaving a bloody trail behind me. They followed and were close behind. My legs felt like jelly, but I kept running and running. I eventually saw a house, banged on the front door and an elderly couple, seeing the sense of panic on my face, let me in. They must have been utterly shocked. I managed to call the police and I was finally safe.

Although I got away relatively unharmed physically, what was left was a deep scar that would affect me for the rest of my life. I had unconsciously and unwittingly carried this egregious terror into my adult years. I firmly believe that this violent trauma was a strong fundamental cause of my retroactive jealousy as an adult. The lack of self-esteem and feeling of absolute helplessness and fear was one of the main blueprints for my eventual retroactive jealousy's towering architecture. The scared kid being beaten so fiercely was not ever truly dealt with and led to me remaining as that scared kid well into my adult life. I had discovered the potential root of not only my low self-esteem issues but also my internalized shame. I had a hard time being in public without looking over my shoulder and any aggression from anyone else in any other scenario throughout my life would trigger a similar fear that I felt that day when I was twelve years old. The inferiority complex seed had been sown in the soil of fear and it was only a matter of time before the sprouts of retroactive jealousy would appear.

I tell you this story because the rediscovery of this trauma helped me get deep enough inside of my head to figure out why I felt so weak and why I had such an issue with my partner's ex's whom I deemed so superior to myself. Finding this trauma again was enough of an epiphany for me to realize that my feelings of weakness and low self-esteem were not pulled out of thin air and I wasn't born with them. They were learned, and as with most mental patterns, can be unlearnt! I went to the root of the problem; why I felt inferior. I ripped out the roots that lay deep in the under layers of my consciousness by learning to become strong. A powerful tool in my healing path was utilizing a wonderful therapist that I felt comfortable confiding in. Finding a fantastic therapist can be an unbelievable help, not only in the healing of your RJ but in many areas of your life. Although it is not imperative that you discover why you suffer from RJ (some sufferers may seem to have no reason at all), it may benefit you to find root causes and remove them. It helped me on my path but you **can** beat it without truly knowing why you're afflicted. Ask yourself; why do you suffer from RJ? I urge you to look far into your past, into your youth. You may just find the answer.

So how did I combat this inferiority complex that made me feel so weak? I became a fighter, in the most literal sense of the word. I felt weak, so I decided to become the polar opposite. I decided to become strong. Please pay attention to the word **decided!** I started training and studying Muay Thai in a mixed martial arts gym. I felt so shy and weak when I first walked into the gym. The sound of punch bags being aggressively kicked echoed throughout the huge warehouse, and the sounds of budding fighters being slammed to the matt in the Brazilian Jiu-Jitsu cage hit my eardrums with an excitement inducing thud. I had found a place where my shyness, strength, and fortitude would be tested. After my first training session, I felt a sense of control, power, and courage. The shy, weak boy was transforming into something completely new. I fell in love with the art of eight limbs and had found an activity that made me feel on top of the world. This time when I was being punched in the head or kicked in the face (pads included)! I welcomed it. I could feel my strength growing with every strike received and every strike launched from my limbs. I quickly found myself sparring with the kinds of men I had felt so inferior to before, and I was holding my own! This gifted me a whole new level of healthy confidence that I had not experienced before. The weak kid was not weak anymore. This new physical strength paved the way for mental strength. This newly found confidence was one of the main weapons in my arsenal in the battle against

RJ. Over the next several months of training, I would pay close attention to how my RJ would react in an environment where I would be given the tools to summon inner and outer strength. A place where I could transform my body and mind to become a more powerful version of myself. RJ could not exist here in the gym. It was being starved off from any negative mind food. I was too active and working too hard for RJ to get my attention. RJ would often strike after I had arrived home from training, but this time it was facing a far tougher opponent than it was previously used to. An opponent who's healthy self-esteem was growing rapidly. RJ's time was running out and it was becoming clear that it could not withstand many more rounds in the ring. I kept training for a while until my RJ had shrunk to the point of no return. I viewed my Muay Thai training sessions more like mental therapy sessions as opposed to just physical workouts. This helped me conjure the motivation to travel to the Muay Thai gym and train weekly, as the sessions were helping me mentally in ways I had not experienced before. With the diminishment of my RJ, I slowly stopped training periodically as other areas and goals in my life became more of a priority to me. But although I didn't continue to train as vigilantly as I once did, one thing remains; my Muay Thai training was one of the greatest and beneficial endeavors I ever embarked on. I will now live the rest of my life with more confidence, strength and personal power that I previously could have thought possible. Not to mention, it gives me great inner courage knowing that I can protect my family more than I ever could before. These positive feelings and emotions are all potent RJ repellent. Remember the beginning of this book when I told you RJ was one of the best things to ever happen to me? Well, I would not have developed these positive mindsets, physical skills and emotions had I not gone through it.

Obviously becoming a fighter is not for everyone. But the message here is that you need to find **your** Muay Thai. Whether it is yoga, weight training, making more money, painting, cycling or even cooking. It doesn't matter what it is. The fact is that there is something out in the world you can do that will combat your negative thoughts about your self and raise your self-esteem. I realized after some training that I was far stronger than I ever thought I could be. Find whatever it is that will boost your self-esteem and go for it relentlessly! This will be a major tool in your healing process. Don't wait! ACT NOW! Start today!

4

DEALING WITH TRIGGERS

If you are reading this book and are suffering with Retroactive Jealousy, then you are most likely extremely familiar with triggers. They are the ever-waiting and patient RJ's favorite tool to use against you when it is ready to feed again. If you have ever suffered from obsessive-compulsive disorder, or are familiar with the symptoms, then you will likely notice a resemblance between OCD intrusive thoughts and RJ's use of triggers. They are much the same in characteristics. Many Retroactive Jealousy resources state RJ as a type of obsessive-compulsive disorder. As I am not trained in the area of psychology or cognitive behaviors, I am not qualified to diagnose or compare symptoms. I will, however, mention that I have suffered from many OCD traits throughout my life and thought it somewhat of a coincidence that I also suffered from RJ so severely. I would regularly find myself acting out several OCD patterns such as constant checking of door locks and intrusive thoughts (not just relating to my partner's past). You may want to look further into OCD, it's traits and likeness to RJ's intrusive thoughts and triggers, as there may be some other areas of your life that OCD may have a foothold. Although, as I mention elsewhere in this book, it is not imperative that you understand the actual cause of your RJ. It is, however, imperative to a healthy life and future that you transform these painful experiences into personal power.

Triggers will appear of their own accord and will strike as if they had a life of their own. They may appear first thing in the morning and they may appear as you lay down to sleep. They may appear when you pass a bar or restaurant that your partner used to frequent with an ex, or you may hear a song on the radio from a band your partner went to see live with an ex. All triggers can be equally as painful and are ingenious and cunning in enchanting you into a trance-like panic state. You cannot control when these triggers strike, but, with practice, you can control your reaction to them!

YOU CANNOT OVERCOME or beat your triggers, but, you can starve them. They feed on your emotional reactions and thoughts. One exercise that helped me was picturing my triggered thoughts waves in a blue ocean. The thought is just a wave that will pass. All thoughts are fleeting and will pass relatively quickly when they are not powered by emotional reactions. Simply watch the wave rise and fall without getting emotionally involved with it. When you feel the emotion rise in your stomach, just let it be, breathe deeply and don't feed the thought. The mind is quick and will rapidly move on to something else. The previous negative trigger thought will be discarded until it strikes again, this time weaker, and eventually not at all. When you are not thinking about it, it does not exist. With practice, this method will starve your bombarding thoughts from negative emotional interaction, thus killing off RJ's most powerful weapon; triggers. **Don't talk about it!**

REFRAIN FROM TALKING about your triggers! You may feel the urge to discuss the jealousy infused thoughts and even question your partner about them. Don't give in! The more you talk about your RJ thoughts, the more food you feed them, and the more power you give them, lengthening their lifespan. The faster you learn to stop talking about your triggers, the faster you will overcome Retroactive Jealousy. This is by far one of the most difficult tasks to master, but extremely crucial to your recovery. Try to find some kind of engaging thought form to overtake your attention. Whenever I felt the urge to bombard my partner with questions, I would practice challenging piano scales in my mind, with my hands executing the movements in the air.

Keep a Trigger Diary

ANOTHER METHOD that helped me heal was keeping a trigger diary. I kept a notebook with me at all times. Whenever I was triggered I would write down the time and date and what the trigger inducing thought was. At first, this was a method of tracking my recovery progress. As the days and weeks went by, I would revisit my trigger diary and review the previous entries. I would be analytical of my triggers and notice that the entries were often very similar in content but sometimes focused on slightly different aspects of my partner's past. I may have been ruminating over a particular one of my partner's ex's in one week and another the next. Slowly, upon review of these entries, I started to notice that they didn't necessarily have the power to ruin my day. I survived the days in which I was previously triggered and I lived to fight another day. They were not the end of the world. I would think to myself "Oh here's that thought about that one guy again, just like yesterday, and the day before that!". I pondered the almost comical idea that I could set my watch to the times I was triggered by a particular thought. By entering my triggers into this diary, I was exposing RJ's bag of tricks and bringing them into the light of my awareness. Once you become consciously aware of RJ's tricks, they start to lose their power over you little by little. One day as I was scanning over my past entries, I came to the realization; I did not feel the same amount of grief from the triggers that I had entered previously in weeks gone by. My triggers were shrinking in power, and I was on my way to recovery.

· · ·

Meditation and Spirituality

MEDITATION IS AN EXTREMELY powerful tool that will aid you on your healing path. Meditation was one of the most valuable tools in transforming my Retroactive Jealousy and is one of the most life-altering resources you can use at any moment. At the time of writing this book, I have meditated almost every day for the past 3 years and will continue to do so for the rest of my life. The benefits are endless and I have never been so happy or been able to access such tranquil states of peace in my life. We spend so much of our time being lost and trying to grab hold of the past and we spend so much time worrying about the future, that we are rarely ever here and now; the only thing we will ever have. The past does not exist, the future is simply a thought. To access the present moment is to be free of the imaginary chains of your past and future. Meditation is a way of accessing the present moment with your focus. When you are present in the now, RJ cannot inhabit you, as it is simply brought about by a myriad of thought-forms. When you meditate and are present in the now, you transcend all thought and cut off RJ's food supply. It cannot live in the present moment if you become fully present. "Well, how do I access this presence? How do I meditate?" I hear you asking. I have outlined my daily meditation practice below.

1. Find a quiet area where you will not be disturbed.
2. Set an alarm for ten minutes from now.
3. Sit on the floor and cross your legs, place your hands on your knees with your palms facing upward in receiving mode.
4. Close your eyes and take in a deep breath for five seconds, hold for five seconds, release the breath for five seconds. Repeat.
5. Focus on your breath and listen to the silence that pervades the room. Try to not get attached to any thoughts that might appear and let them dissolve peacefully in the silence.

6. Feel the inner body by focusing on the energy pulse that you can feel naturally in your hands.

7. The mind will often creep in and try to take over. This is normal and natural. Don't scold yourself for losing focus, just gently bring your focus back to your breath and the silence.

Repeating this simple meditation daily will help you to cultivate presence and will develop your ability to tap into this peaceful silence. A space of no thought. Another benefit of meditation is the separation from your being and your mind made ego. I do not use the term ego in a derogatory way to describe an egomaniac or traits of narcissism. I use the word ego to describe that personality, character or individual which you think you are. Essentially, everything you think you are; your name, job title, political views, passions, and values were all made up at some point. They do not exist on any plain other than being thought-forms. Any physical or tangible evidence that would argue the contrary was simply manifested out of the made-up thought-forms. You may have many certificates saying that you are adept at a certain skill or have flourished in a certain career path, but none of these past accolades, trophies or endeavors are in fact who you really are. This is not to say that there are not wonderful careers and lives to be led, this is just to bring to your attention to the fact that nothing is absolutely true. This is why we are able to reprogram our subconscious minds with new thought-forms about ourselves. Everything is or was just made up at one time or another.

Starting a meditation practice and reading spiritual books gave me a whole new sense of being. I recommend it for everyone, especially if one is suffering from an affliction such as Retroactive Jealousy. Set aside 10 minutes daily to meditate starting today! I usually meditate first thing in the morning. I wake up, smile, rehydrate and immediately sit down to meditate. This has become the beginning of my daily morning ritual.

With practice, you can enter a whole new state of being. One where RJ cannot inhabit. *Two books I highly recommend in the topic of spirituality and meditation are* Eckhart Tolle's 'The Power of Now' *and* Eckhart Tolle's 'A New Earth'.

5

POSITIVE ACTION AND POSITIVE ADDICTIONS

The Myriad of harmful and potentially life diminishing addiction based scenarios we can find ourselves in is endless. Devastating addictions to drugs, alcohol, nicotine, and gambling run rampant in our world and have destroyed countless lives. We have all seen the screaming vagrant in the street or the drunk in the gutter.

But what about the positive addictions that we can invite into our lives? What about the go-getters and the winners? What about the athlete who is at the top of their game, the world-class musician or the entrepreneur whose businesses are skyrocketing? What do they have that the majority does not? I believe that their success is mostly due to an insatiable addiction to progress, gains and achieving goals.

As A KID, I would become obsessed with leveling up my character in my favorite video game. With each battle, he would become stronger and stronger, and with each victory, he would gain experience. I became addicted to my character's growth until eventually I had completed the game and destroyed the evil villain that was threatening my fictional protagonist's world! I was a relatively lazy kid outside of video games. I would sleep in late, put off homework and would study the bare minimum I needed to get by. As I grew up and became involved in different activities such as playing the piano, martial arts training, and art, I noticed that my video game positive growth addiction had actually carried over into my real-world activities. I was improving at my hobbies and endeavors because I felt the same buzz I felt when I leveled up my video game character. I realized this 'buzz' wasn't exclusive to just video games and hobbies. As an adult, the same buzz would also kick in once I had powered through a great work out at the gym, hit a financial goal, or studied a new book and expanded my knowledge. Somewhere along the line, I had become addicted to growth and progress. It may have happened naturally. It may have been passed down from hard-working parents. But it is my strong belief that no matter what your background or situation, you can train your brain to develop these positive addictions in the same way that you may have developed a buzz training up your favorite video game character as a kid or mastering a new skateboard trick.

WHEN YOU ACHIEVE, celebrate your achievement! Acknowledge it and own it. If you find that you dealt with an RJ trigger without becoming emotionally attached to it, then celebrate it. If you saw your partners ex in the street and dealt with the trigger better than you would have before, then celebrate your growth. Start associating good feelings with your achievements, you have earned it. I don't mean crack open a beer and get wild (alcohol often negatively affects RJ drastically and can inhibit your ability to cope with triggers). A little buzz of happiness is enough to push you through and continue the cycle of positive growth. Happiness breeds more happiness, and happiness is power. It is life-affirming. Happiness is a powerful tool to utilize for your healing. RJ cannot swim for long in the rushing waves of true happiness associated with progress and enjoyment of your craft, career or hobbies. Your positive addition when teamed up with your new methods of dealing with triggers will form a dynamic state altering duo to aid you on your journey towards a life without RJ.

Affirmations

Affirmations are a brilliant way to boost whatever particular state you are trying to improve. I often interchange my affirmations by which state I want to get into at that particular time of my life. For example; if I want to build confidence then I will recite ten or more confidence-boosting affirmations a day. If I am in a phase in my life where I want to overcome shyness and become better at interacting with people then I will recite ten or more affirmations that may instill bravery and courage within me. Keep repeating these affirmations day after day, week after week and month after month and see what happens. The affirmations will soak into your subconscious mind and you will train your brain to believe. This is a powerful method also used to manifest material or financial abundance. As mentioned in the previous chapter, everything is made up. So make up your own story, your own new and improved version of yourself free of RJ. You can even sleep with affirmations being played to you via recording. I often find affirmation videos I like on YouTube and will fall asleep to them. I recommend creating ten or more affirmations yourself that will boost your positive outlook on your healing process. I have created ten below for you. If you feel silly saying them out loud then just say them in your mind or quietly to yourself. If you don't truly believe the affirmations then fake it until you make it. This may sound like self-help mumbo jumbo to some readers, but if you're serious about moving on from your RJ then try it and see for yourself! Programming the subconscious mind can change your life.

Positive Growth Affirmations
1. I am powerful.
2. I am enough.
3. I am worthy.
4. I am confident.

5. I am strong.
6. I am attractive
7. I am desirable.
8. I feel inferior to no one.
9. Others look up to me.
10. Others respect me.

6

CHANGING HOW YOU FEEL ABOUT YOURSELF

How do you feel about yourself? Is your day filled with negative self-talk? Do you regularly internally mutter things like "I hate myself, I'm a loser, I can't compare to him/her" and so on. I would have a stream of this negative self-talk going on all day, every day until I became consciously aware of it. This internal negative self-talk is like a poisonous waterfall relentlessly flowing through your lifestream. You must become aware of this internal dialogue and replace these savage words with their positive opposites. "I hate myself" becomes "I love myself". "I am a loser" becomes "I am a winner". No matter how silly, arrogant or conceited this positive self-talk sounds, it is imperative to your internal uprising of happiness. Try it for yourself with an open mind and reap the benefits. Much like how a vibration of gratefulness will bring about more positive situations in your life, this internal attitude of confidence will bring about self-power and manifest positivity. The negative outburst of others will begin to roll off your back with enough self-work. You will become so comfortable in your own skin that your RJ and triggers will find this confident habitat toxic and unbearable. Your RJ will have no negative food to eat and grow from. After all, your RJ likely stems and thrives from your insecurity and not being comfortable or confident in your own skin.

. . .

IMAGINE your own personal greatest version of yourself. What do they look like? What is their primary attitude? How do they react to certain situations? Are they confident and assertive? Are they strong and centered? Are they outgoing and successful? Are they plagued with jealousy and strive to control others, or are they relaxed, calm and need no external enablers?

SPEND a few minutes closing your eyes and brainstorming your ideal version of yourself. Be as outlandish as your imagination lets you. Hold nothing back. This ideal you should have all of the attributes you aspire to have in your life. Once you have a solid image in your mind of this ideal you, you must commit to taking daily steps to become this version of yourself. Life is simply too short **not** to become this you. Write down on paper at least 10 character/physical traits that your ideal version of you possesses.

Is your ideal you in incredible shape? This is attainable for you. Is your ideal you oozing with confidence and coolness? This too is attainable for you. Does your ideal you acquire a substantially larger income than you possess right now? There has been no better time in history to build online businesses and find alternative sources of income, both passive and active. Does your ideal you possess incredible knowledge that can be used to enrich your life? We live in the digital age where you can find online courses on just about anything you can think of that will ultimately enhance and enrich your life, all available at the click of a button. You can attain any outcome you desire for yourself. We may be partially limited to changing our outer appearance (although plastic surgeons are remarkable these days!), but the inner work we can do is unbelievably transformative when practiced with gusto and enthusiasm. I was once a shy, scared adult child. I am now a confident, assertive and successful man. This was done by first imagining my ideal self, then taking a stand to become that version of myself and not wavering my gaze from the destination; a new and improved me.

Some attributes that I wished to possess (pre RJ recovery) were as follows:

Attribute 1: Confident, assertive and comfortable in own skin.

How I achieved this attribute in reality:

• Programming my subconscious mind by using confidence affirmations (usually on drives to the gym and in headphones as I went to sleep at night).
  • Getting my body into shape by daily gym workouts.
  • Learning Muay Thai and developing self-defense skills and discipline.

Attribute 2: Unaffected by RJ. Unphased by intrusive thoughts and triggers.

How I achieved this attribute in reality:

• Daily meditation work. **Practice living in the now.**
  • Breathing/meditation work to let go of triggered thoughts as they arise.
  • Practiced allowing intrusive thoughts to be without trying to stop them or getting emotionally attached to them.

. . .

ATTRIBUTE 3: A sense of strength and being able to defend myself. No longer feeling physically weak and vulnerable.

How I achieved this attribute in reality:

- Getting my body into shape by daily gym workouts.
- Learning Muay Thai and developing self-defense skills and discipline. Sparring in Muay Thai classes (holding my own against men that were physically larger than me did wonders for my self-esteem).
- Achieving higher ranks in Muay Thai over time.

ATTRIBUTE 4: Positive mood, happiness, general state of upbeat wellbeing.

How I achieved this attribute in reality:

- Daily grateful statements as part of my morning ritual (see chapter 7).
- Changing my diet. Daily juicing and smoothies to enhance my mood from the inside.
- Daily gym schedule.
- Daily reading of spiritual and self-help books.

Attribute 5: Financially better off. Not detrimentally comparing oneself financially to others.

How I achieved this attribute in reality:

- Started my own online business.

- Created new passive income streams. Increased income through a more rigorous work ethic.
  - Started investing.
  - Studied many investing and business courses/books.

ATTRIBUTE 6: A higher level of intellect and knowledge.

How I achieved this attribute in reality:

- STUDIED many online courses and books. Many to do with finances, investing and business.
  - Daily reading as part of my morning ritual.

ATTRIBUTE 7: Enhanced physical appearance.

How I achieved this attribute in reality:

- CHANGE OF DIET.
  - Implementing a weekly gym schedule.
  - Staying hydrated.
  - Implementing daily skincare routine and bi-weekly derma roller schedule.
  - Changing the products I put on my face.
  - Keeping up with hair appointments and not appearing unkempt.
  - Routine grooming maintenance.
  - Keeping up with dental appointments and teeth cleanings.

ATTRIBUTE 8: A strong work ethic. No laziness or procrastination.

How I achieved this attribute in reality:

. . .

• Listening daily to self-help teachers podcasts and audiobooks.
• Increased work ethic through determination to change.
• Daily goal setting on whiteboard (crossing out goals from your whiteboard is addicting and sparks gusto!).
• Setting alarms and reprogramming body clock to awake at an earlier time.
• Implementing a morning ritual.
• Cutting down television time and replacing this with studying, working or productive activities.**Attribute 9:** Likable, conversational and a pleasure to be around.

How I achieved this attribute in reality:

• Clearing the mind of unnecessary thoughts and emotional baggage through daily meditation practice and trigger work.
• Staying grounded in presence.
• Ceased seeing other human beings as separate entities or a threat by reading books on spirituality.
• Meeting other human beings without making any initial judgment or assumptions of their character.
• Smiling peacefully even in uncomfortable or undesirable situations.
• Listening more often than speaking. **Attribute 10:** More giving, loving and eager to share with the world.

How I achieved this attribute in reality:

. . .

• Sharing useful knowledge with others that I have gained through life experiences and studying certain subjects.
• Making my knowledge easily available to others at no cost to them.
• Giving a percentage of my newly acquired income to a needy cause.
• Helping others without expecting anything in return.

Attribute 11. Patience and kindness even when being confronted with argumentative conflict or difficult people.

How I achieved this attribute in reality:

• Daily meditation practice with a strong focus on my anger issues.
• Studying several self-help books that touch on psychology, gaining a deeper understanding of the human condition.
• Getting in touch with my empathetic side.
• Using patience and presence practices during personal relationship conflicts or situations. Working on fear of confrontation.

You may notice that I have mentioned some of the same activities aimed at improving yourself time and time again, such as working out at the gym, studying books/courses and implementing a morning ritual. This is because they work! Repetition is imperative to your success. Don't just work out once and then let your gym bag collect dust. Don't just read the first chapter of a new self-help book and stick it up on the shelf to never be picked up again. Make a habit of these attribute developing actions and they will truly become life-changing.

"I fear not the man who has practiced 10,000 kicks once, but I fear the man who has practiced one kick 10,000 times". Bruce Lee

. . .

WRITE down your own attributes that you would like to possess and start working toward them today! Your ideal version of yourself can be a reality. An RJ free you can be a reality. Once you have recovered from your RJ you can take this new work ethic with you for every endeavor for the rest of your life! Beating RJ is one of the toughest things you will have to go through. But the transformative might its recovery yields is full great power. You can achieve anything with this newfound life-affirming power, drive and work ethic. You are in control. Make your life the way you want it by first changing yourself from the inside.

STOP COMPARING yourself to others

DURING MY PRE RJ recovery years, I would regularly find myself comparing my height, body, finances, personality, looks and just about everything else you can imagine to my partner's ex-lovers. This was an absolute waste of time. Even if I temporarily felt superior in one aspect, there would be another opposing attribute my mind would conjure up to quickly tear me down and make me obsess over this particular ex. Comparing yourself to others in a mental superiority test is a futile, agonizing and time-wasting endeavor. You will never find peace from this and it will only give your mind more food for your RJ to feast on and grow. One of the only times it will be beneficial to compare yourself to others is when you are learning and growing from them.

I WOULD SCROLL through my partner's social media posts from years past to catch glimpses of her exes. I would try to see if I could compare my height or looks to them. While scrolling through these posts I would be in a trance-like state full of panic with my hands shaking and my mind super vigilant. I felt as if I were infected with some kind of virus. All these activities did was produce food for my RJ. How do you starve RJ to death? You stop serving it mind food that will sustain it. Comparing yourself to your partner's exes serves up one of RJ's favorite meals. It can feed off of this mind food for years, tormenting you day in and day out.

If you feel compelled to compare yourself to your partner's exes then try vigilantly to stop immediately in your tracks, breathe deeply, become present and remember your commitment to change. Remember the sweet benefits of change. I would often have to snap myself out of it quickly before embarking on a night of social media scrolling and the ensuing inevitable interrogation that I would dump onto my partner. They do not deserve it and it is your responsibility to change.

You are the only you in existence. You are a unique, beautiful, intelligent creation and you are worthy. You are not less than desirable. You are a magnificent creation of the universe.

7

HAPPINESS IS POWER

When you are truly happy, filled with ecstatic energy and so excited that you feel like you want to run up a wall, you are in possession of powerful life affirming energy. This happiness energy is the creative source behind much art, music, literature and just about any other outlet of passion you can think of. It will also be an important force that will aid in your recovery from RJ. You may have read the first sentence of this chapter and thought, "filled with ecstatic energy and so excited that you feel like I want to run up a wall? Who does this author think he is? I never feel like this". This is because your mind has been overwhelmed with images of your partners past and has been tormenting you relentlessly, draining you of precious life energy. In these states of torment, it is most difficult to conjure up our happiness and implement a state of healing. But it is not impossible. Think back to before you suffered from Retroactive Jealousy, perhaps when you were a child. You were not bombarded with these painful RJ thoughts. Your mind had plenty of room to focus on all of the wonderful toys, games and activities you could enjoy. When you were triggered to be momentarily sad or unhappy, it was likely because of an immediate situation bought to your direct attention such as not getting the cookie or being told to do you chores. (This is assuming you had an upbringing in a non toxic environment household. If you were bought up in a toxic environment household then there will likely be much additional work to be done with a therapist. I highly recommend seeking a wonderful therapist that will fast track your road to recovery). As adults, our minds become overactive, usually due to our daily responsibilities such as paying the bills, feeding the kids and so on. Without the necessary work on ourselves to practice clearing our mind and accessing more peaceful states of consciousness, we often get caught up in the mental rat race of relentless, anxiety ridden thoughts. We take this to be the norm in our society and most of us go through our entire lives like this. When you were a child you likely focused on one thing at a time; what was immediately in front of you. You can practice this as an adult. It is an almost meditative like exercise that helps you access the present moment and focuses you fully on the task at hand. Try it now. Take several deep breaths down into your stomach. Now focus fully on this page for 10 seconds. Other thoughts may try to distract you and come in and out, but just hold your focus and gaze on the page. As you get better at this, then try 30 seconds, then one minute and so on. You will likely find that the quality of your work benefits greatly from this practice as your mind will not be elsewhere. You have re-learnt your childhood gift of present moment focus. Now try this focus on something fun. There is a reason many adrenaline junkies and daredevils love extreme sports, racing and sky diving. It takes their complete focus for a period of time.

FOCUS ON HAPPINESS **conjuring goals**

IF YOU TAKE your focus from these intrusive RJ thoughts and replace them with happiness inducing tasks, thoughts or activities then it will fill you with the excitement, courage and life affirming power needed to recover from RJ. For me these thoughts included brainstorming my goals for the year. These may be financial, artistic or work related goals that excite me. This book you're reading right now was one of my goals. For example: this book excited me during its creation because I knew that I could help countless people suffering from RJ all around the world get better and transform their lives. What are some goals that excite you that you would like to accomplish? Write these down and keep them close to review regularly. I like to write mine out of a large whiteboard in my office. I get a huge buzz and sense of excitement when I cross an accomplished goals off of my list.

Happiness through gratefulness

One transformative tool that aided me in my recovery was developing a huge feeling of gratitude. I practice this daily without fail (usually on the way to and from the gym). I always notice a huge wave of happiness overcome me during this part of my day. I include this gratefulness practice in my morning ritual. This practice involves saying out loud how grateful I am for certain things in my life. They can vary day by day and can range from silly little things such as; "I am so grateful that the weather is great today" to more important events such as; "I am so grateful and happy that my parents are in good health and I am able to call them whenever I can". Once you start saying these grateful phrases out loud you will start vibrating on a frequency of thankfulness. You may notice that you start to attract more good things into your life. I highly recommend you try this for yourself wether you believe in the power of manifestation and the law of attraction or not. Try it with an open mind, then make your verdict. My experience was that I started attracting wonderful things into my life. My family was happy, my finances were growing and my career started to take off wonderfully, just by saying how grateful I was for what I had every day. If finances are a stress trigger for you (or an RJ trigger by comparing yourself with your partners exes) then try to remember that most of the worlds population lives off of about two dollars per day. If you are reading this book on a phone, computer or iPad, then that makes you abundant and affluent in comparison to most of the worlds population! If you show gratitude for this fact regularly, then you will start to attract more of the same into your life.

I ONCE HAD a friend who was convinced he was cursed. He would go on every day about how no one loved him, how he attracted bad luck and how he was a loser. As you can guess, his behavior manifested the equivalent outcomes of such a mindset. He was even physically beaten up two times just a few weeks apart of each other which is a horrible ordeal to go through, but it seemed as though the universe was listening to his requests. It was as if he was saying to the universe "beat me up, I'm trash". My friend soon lost his career, his friends, his home, his girlfriend and just about everything good that he had. His health was also deteriorating as he fed himself a diet of cigarettes and alcohol, and would only eat bread with ketchup day after day. He could have turned his life around and thrived had he changed his frequency to one of gratefulness and happiness. In reality he was talented, attractive, funny, kind and great to hang out with when he was not in his usual negative slump. He could have easily had anything he wanted in life, but it's not too late for him. Let's hope he learns the lessons that are in this book elsewhere and lives his life to the fullest without wasting another day. I often think of the tale of Aladdin and his magical lamp. Aladdin rubs the lamp and the genie appears. "Your wish is my command" says the genie. This is much like the universe listening to your wishes and requests. The universe is not biased and it listens to everything you send out to it. Why not try saying how thankful you are everyday for being free of Retroactive Jealousy? Even if you are not fully recovered yet, start acting as if you were and you will start to heal from the inside.

ONE BOOK that I thoroughly recommend if you have not already heard of it is *'The Secret'* by Rhonda Byrne.

. . .

SOME EXAMPLES of grateful statements I might say out loud each morning are:

"I AM SO grateful for my health".

"I am so grateful that my son is happy and healthy, and I have a wonderful relationship with him".

"I am so grateful for my career".

"I am so grateful for my work ethic".

"I am so grateful that I put healthy food into my body each day"

"I am so grateful for my wonderful relationship".

"I am so grateful for my talents".

"I am so grateful that I live in one of the most incredible places I could ever want to live".

"I am so grateful that I have great eyesight".

"I am so grateful for all of the hardships I have gone through, because they have made me strong and given me new found intelligence, power and tools".

THESE ARE JUST SOME EXAMPLES, but have fun making up your own grateful statements. Get creative and say these aloud with a smile on your face. You can watch your world transform before your eyes!

HAPPINESS THROUGH ACTIVITIES

AS I GET LOST in the enjoyment of activities, I notice that my mind is not focused on negative painful thoughts. This is a particularly helpful tool during your transformation of RJ. To be happy during an activity you love is a way to fill yourself with life affirming happiness power. The power will positively fuel your healing journey. This is not a method for merely periodically covering up your RJ. The goal is not to stick a band aid on the wound to cover it up for a while, nor distract us from the deep rooted issue. It is simply to bring more happiness and power into our life-force so that we can tackle RJ with our batteries recharged by a zest for life. Some activities I find give me happiness-strength are practicing the piano, Muay Thai, working out, reading/learning, and creating art. Notice how the activities I have mentioned help me grow either in terms of achieving new levels at an instrument, increasing my physical fitness or expanding my knowledge through reading. Growth through activities is not essential but you may find it gives you added gusto as the feeling of progress and growth often fills us with excitement. After a session of getting lost in these growth based activities, I find myself with a fresh mind and a sense of achievement that gives me additional strength and power to take on other tasks; such as defeating RJ! I am under the absolute conviction that happiness is true power. A way to be joyful is to dance amidst the external forms the universe provides and to emit the life affirming power into other forms. One activity that was personally essential to my overcoming RJ was a regular gym routine. The daily boost of endorphins was a chemical supplementary boost that often helped me access more peaceful states. This helped greatly in dealing with triggers and negative mind patterns.

8

FINDING GREAT TEACHERS

One thing I am grateful for every day is the fact that we have access to countless teachers at the click of a button. Just by picking up our smartphones we can access countless hours of free knowledge from spiritual teachers, therapists, self-help coaches and more. There is no excuse not to learn and grow in this day and age. Long gone are the days of dragging yourself to the library to borrow a book for a week or two. Although that option also still exists. I often listen to spiritual teachers' guidance, entrepreneurs podcasts, and YouTubers' helpful knowledge whilst driving in my car and working out at the gym. Although I like to enjoy music daily, I always make sure I have a steady stream of new, useful, positive information being made available to my mind and subconscious programming.

SOME SPIRITUAL TEACHERS I enjoy are Eckhart Tolle, Adyashanti, Mooji, and Sadhguru. Their teachings have helped me reach a new state of consciousness where my old negative habits find it impossible to reside. Finding a spiritual teacher you like and adding their knowledge to a daily meditation practice is a surefire way to boost your RJ recovery and give you access to a higher state of consciousness that you can primarily reside in for the rest of your life. Once you have healed your RJ, you will be able to take your transformative tools with you anywhere you go in life. It won't just be your RJ that's transformed. You can transform huge areas of your life should you choose to. You likely will once you have the gusto of transforming your RJ pain into positive life energy.

ONE BOOK that transformed my life is 'The Power of Now' by Eckhart Tolle. Eckhart's teaching states that the past nor the future exist, only now exists. The amount of truth exuded from the pages of Eckhart's book was enough to change my life forever and prevent me from going back to the way I had previously viewed the world. This was a transformative way of living that eventually withered away the power the past had over me. I had spent so much of my life living in the past and so much time worrying about the future that I had neglected that all I ever had and would ever have is right now in this very moment. A simple yet profound realization. Although not directly related to jealously or relationships, Eckhart Tolle's 'The Power of Now' remains a powerful companion by my side whenever life challenges me emotionally or mentally. This book was a must-read along my journey of RJ's transformation.

FINDING a Good Therapist

A POWERFUL WAY TO find out more about yourself and really dig to the root of your problems is to work with a therapist. It is important to find a therapist you like and enjoy your sessions with. It might take you a couple of tries to find one that you are fully comfortable with. If you like the first therapist you find then just go with it. Commit to a weekly session for a certain time period. You will likely be very glad you did. Weekly therapy sessions helped me understand certain childhood issues I was still carrying around with me as an adult. It helped me become self-aware of my many previously unconscious patterns and self-sabotage. Your RJ is likely a manifestation of unresolved childhood issues. For example; my RJ likely stemmed from a deep sense of shame I had unconsciously implemented as the default setting to how I saw myself in my youth. I also had unresolved trauma as a result of random violence inflicted on me many years ago. This was all unconscious and hiding under the surface, manifesting as negative, painful energy pulls, sabotaging my adult life. Going deep into my subconscious and remembering this violent incident helped me understand why I never felt safe out in public at night, even all these years later. It also made me realize why I felt so weak and small as an adult. I would likely have never bought these unresolved issues to the surface had I not committed to weekly therapy sessions with a wonderful therapist for a certain period of time. Once you discover these hidden issues, you must pull them out at the root. Your therapist will show you useful practices for weed pulling unresolved issues. Combine this approach with a daily meditation practice and an awakened spiritual teacher to create yourself a triple threat team ready to dissolve RJ and bring about a happier, more powerful you.

9

WHEN OTHERS DON'T UNDERSTAND RETROACTIVE JEALOUSY

At the time of writing this book, Retroactive Jealousy seems to be somewhat of an overlooked and relatively unheard of condition. There are, however, some fantastic sources to use for recovery During most of my RJ rampant years, anything I tried to look up on the subject induced many painful triggers and did not help me. Ultimately searching online did cure my RJ in the end, so the triggers were well worth it. If you are searching online for answers and are often triggered then I recommend you soldier on. The triggers are painful but will not kill you. Focus on your conscious presence and allow the triggers to be. As mentioned at the beginning of this book, use the triggers to your advantage. They are challenges tailor-made for you, telling you to grow.

YOUR RJ MAY FEEL COMPLETELY reasonable and understandable to you, but do not expect your friends, family or acquaintances to get it. They likely will not. They will offer unhelpful feedback such as "well everyone has done something with someone" or "why would you even think about your girlfriend's/boyfriend's past?". This will perhaps bring about fleeting relief at best. But don't fret. You do not need them to understand.

The only thing that matters is your own personal recovery and this can only happen from the inside. No amount of external advice from someone that does not understand is likely to bring about your transformation. Following the advice and taking action on the areas discussed in this book and other good sources will ultimately bring about your transformation. My friends and family all looked at me as though I was crazy when I would mention to them that was so distraught over my partners past. Remember, if they have not suffered with RJ themselves, then they will simply never fully understand. Just go with the understanding that they are doing their best with the information and resources that they have available to them.

YOU WILL LIKELY FEEL COMPELLED to talk about RJ regularly to friends and family. This is due to the obsessive-compulsive nature of RJ. It will try to capture your mind's attention as frequently as possible. Try to avoid this cunning RJ trap if possible. It will often end in more triggers and more mind food for your RJ to gobble up and sustain itself with. The trick to success lies in abandoning all RJ thoughts as they appear. This starves RJ and shrinks its power. When I was suffering with RJ, I often felt as if a demon was screaming in my face for attention all day and night. As I progressed with my trigger and presence work, the demon would shrink and shrink as it had no food to feed on and grow. I was no longer serving up delicious all you can eat dishes of trigger cooked, jealousy garnished intrusive thoughts on a silver platter. Eventually, the demon shrunk so much that it became more like a leprechaun trying to stamp on my toe for attention. I soon after stamped on this leprechaun and was prized with the proverbial pot of gold; my cured RJ and all of its benefits. RJ's recovery bought about my spiritual awakening, enhanced mental/physical strength, a new work ethic, and a more loving and emotionally intelligent me.Getting you to discuss RJ with loved ones is one of the cunning tricks it often pulls to get more mind food. The more you talk about RJ, the more power you give it. You becoming tiresome of the pain will push you to seek relief in many areas. Try to be strong and avoid discussing RJ as much as possible outside of therapy sessions or other past RJ sufferers. This doesn't mean you shouldn't seek solace from loved ones during a painful time. But you must simply remain aware of RJ's cunning tricks and traps to get you to feed it. You may even start to laugh at how silly its efforts become as you practice becoming aware of RJ's methods. You may also even be impressed with RJ's chess master like intellect. Just remember that this intellect is you. You cannot outsmart it because it is you. But if your RJ is that cunning and clever, then so are you, because it is, in fact, your own mind activity. Imagine a world where that cunning intellect can be put to good constructive use! Take a few moments and imagine what you could accomplish when you transform RJ's genius, energy, and relentlessness into a new positive, creative outlet. You will be an unstoppable force for good once this painful energy is transformed into life-affirming power. I believe that the true cause of RJ is the universes way to force you to evolve and grow. Looking at it in this way, your RJ becomes a gift-wrapped present from the heavens.

IN SHORT, do not worry about whether your loved ones, partner or friends understand Retroactive Jealousy. They don't need to. The answer to the cure lies deep within you. You have the power to unleash your healing life-force and work towards permanent, positive change.

10

CLEARING UP THE WRECKAGE

Saying Sorry

AN IMPORTANT PART of your journey after overcoming RJ is forgiving yourself for any damage you may have caused and for any actions that you may now regret. This does not mean that you don't accept full responsibility for your past actions. It means that you are ready for change and have eliminated your destructive patterns. You could have only acted as your consciousness allowed and at that time your consciousness was in a trigger induced trance-like state. Your being afflicted with RJ was/is not your fault, but it is your responsibly to put right any wrongdoings on your part. You must forgive yourself. You must also apologize to your partner and others for any insensitive things you may have said or done to those caught in your painful outbursts. But make sure to apologize when you are at a point when you will not be triggered again. You may cause excess unnecessary turmoil if you are not ready and your attempts to apologize are thwarted by additional triggers. We must do the hard internal work to eliminate triggers first before embarking on our forgiveness journey. You may feel a new sense of positive energy once you have apologized to those you have hurt. This is due to the closure you and those affected will gain and it will give you the added excitement of starting fresh and turning over a new leaf. Being forgiven by those you have hurt is a powerful transformative gift you can fully utilize in your own healing process. Later in life, you will be glad that you have taken the time to repair these friendships/relationships and those you have apologized to will often be grateful too. No one likes to have unresolved toxic energy residing anywhere near their aura or psyche, conscious or unconscious.

THOSE WHO DO NOT ACCEPT **forgiveness**

THERE MAY BE CERTAIN FRIENDS/PARTNERS of family members that will not accept your apologies depending on how extreme your particular struggle with RJ got, how intense your outbursts or how venomous your choice of words. This is their choice and you must respect their decision and personal healing time. But do not fret. Time can heal all wounds and eventually this important person will see your transformation with their own eyes if you allow such an opportunity. Once you let go of the steering wheel and realize that you cannot change others' opinions of you, you will leave plenty of space to give the unforgiving person time without trying to control or manipulate their verdict of you. This does not mean say sorry and disappear. It just means to allow them plenty of time and space without trying to control their feelings about you after you have made your initial apology. Periodically check in on them as long as they have not overtly affirmed otherwise. You may find over time that their efforts to cut you out and hold a grudge are more tiresome than actually giving you another chance. This can lead to their gradual acceptance of you and your reappearance in their life. On the other hand, if they portray strongly that they do not want to see you again and the damage caused is just too much, then you must accept their decision fully and take it as a life lesson and signal that you must defeat RJ fully and permanently so that you will not lose more important people during your life due to unresolved demons. Letting go and moving on can be agonizing, especially when you know you cannot right a wrong an older version of yourself is responsible for. However, you must use this pain as a fire to fuel the creation of the greatest future version of yourself. You can become this version today by making a stand and taking the right choice, right now. You must also forgive yourself. The most important relationship you will ever have is the relationship with yourself. You are the only person you will not lose throughout your lifetime. Let's make sure you are in a state of peace and forgiveness for as many of your days as possible.

11

LIFE AFTER RETROACTIVE JEALOUSY

Congratulations! If you have made it this far then you have likely absorbed lots of helpful information and practices and are well on your way to forgetting RJ for good. If you do not feel like you are gradually ridding yourself of RJ then do not despair as you will likely need to revisit sections of this book and re-read them while implementing the actions necessary to succeed. It is imperative that you take action on the exercises and practices mentioned throughout the book, otherwise, your progress may not be powered with the boost it needs to fast-track your recovery. The affirmations are presented to you to reprogram your subconscious mind. This will be one of the most transformative tools in changing the way you look at yourself. Programming the subconscious mind has the potential to improve every area of your life. It is also extremely important that you learn to deal with triggers. You must remain focussed and present when struck by a trigger and you must not get emotionally attached to them. Let them fade away in the fleeting, whizzing highway that is your train of thought.

. . .

You will likely encounter days where you feel overwhelmed by your RJ and its accompanying triggers. You may feel as though you have not made progress and are down on yourself because you are triggered again. Do not despair, as these days are opportunities to become even stronger and more proficient at dealing with triggers. Remember, if you can't feel it then you can't heal it. Be grateful for these kinds of slump days as they are pulling out the remaining RJ from your being. Power through these days as if you are cleansing yourself fully of any remnants of RJ. You may continue through your life being triggered from time to time, but just remember what I mentioned at the beginning of this book; I am 100% trigger free and suffer from RJ no more. No remnants remain and I could be (and have been) in the same room as a partner's ex and feel absolutely no trace of RJ. I believe in time and with much work that this can be possible for you too and all sufferers of RJ.

The Universe Testing You

You may find yourself encountering new situations that will challenge you and your new coping skills to boundaries never before reached. As you become stronger, the challenges the universe will offer you may increase in difficulty before you have fully transformed your RJ. This is the universes way of telling you that there is still work to be done! I will explain with an example that the universe presented to me.

In the midst of my RJ, I was suffering relentlessly and was then piling this hurt onto my partner, cunningly trying to pull information about her past from her. Whenever she even mentioned a male friend, I would immediately interrogate her and try to find out if anything had happened between them. I found out that she was involved intimately with one particular friend. The pain was excruciating. As your subconscious mind and body can't tell the difference between a thought and a real situation, This felt like I was being cheated on in real-time, which was not the case. Days passed and I was embarking on a new career endeavor and traveling the country. As I was discussing the crew members for the trip with a colleague, I discovered that I would be traveling the country by bus with none other than my aforementioned partner's ex-lover. "What are the odds!?" I miserably uttered to myself. Out of all the guys in the entire city, I ended up with my partner's ex. (I would later realize that my being placed in this predicament against unbelievable odds was the universes way of telling me I had much work left to do.) This was my worst nightmare come true, I was sharing a bus with someone my partner had been intimate with for some time in the past. His name was Tim. The fact that I would be in close quarters with Tim for an extended time almost ended my relationship with my partner right then and there. I passively aggressively passed on the information of the trip and its participants to my partner and she was overwhelmed with dread. She knew what she was in store for. Fast forward several days into the trip, I had managed to subdue my urges to ask cunning questions to my new colleague that would provide me with plenty of RJ food right from the source. I was surprised and proud of myself, although the true purpose of subduing my urges was to not embarrass myself and present myself to my peers as insecure. As I got to know Tim, I realized that he was not this macho, rough and tough, powerful, superior man that I had conjured up in my imagination. I saw on a personal basis that he was just a human being, with the same fears, insecurities, and hangups that we all seem to possess at one stage or another. It gave me tangible experience that my imagination and RJ thoughts were not based on reality. The images portrayed to me by my mind were apparitions of my own insecurity, they were not sprouted from truth. If my RJ images were this far off in this case, then how false were my assumptions of my partner's other exes and intimate encounters? I began to see the falsehood of RJ's image conjuring and started to see through the games of my own mind. There was a glaring hole in all of RJ's apparitions, one torn by tangibly triggered logic and real-life gathered information. This self-awareness was a powerful contributor to my transformation of RJ. Tim was respectful, kind and likable. He was quiet, relatively insecure himself (a thought that had never crossed my RJ infected mind) and helpful with work efforts. He was an avid gym-goer, which initially inflamed my RJ to heated temperatures and caused my insecurity much panic. I was not a gym-goer, and my body was not in particularly impressive shape. I had found a point of comparison for my RJ to latch on to. Instead of becoming hopelessly lost in despair, I chose to accompany Tim to a gym while on the road. He showed me his work out routine, how long he spent on cardio, what weight exercises he did and so on. I started incorporating these workouts into my daily life and began to feel a new sense of enjoyment I had not felt in years. The physical exercise was releasing endorphins and changing my mood and energy for the better. Over time, Tim and I became friends and I become an avid gym-goer myself. By the end of the work trip, I had discovered so much about myself, the falsities of my RJ and about compassion and empathy. I would no longer look at my partner's exes as monstrous threats, but simply as human beings, with the same core needs and desires as all of us. This was massively life-altering. I had learned so much about working out from Tim that I go to the gym everyday still to this day. This fact alone, I would not change for the world as physical fitness is now a huge part of my life. I was forced to spend several weeks coping with triggers that were physically right in front of my face, this was the ultimate challenge, but I came through the other side unscathed and my relationship with Sarah intact, with only a few RJ triggered hiccups along the way. My physical fitness and mental state was on the rise dramatically. Soon after the trip, I realized that being put into that situation against unbelievable odds was one of the greatest things that could have ever happened to me. If I could get through what I initially perceived as a nightmare situation, then I could get through anything that RJ could throw at me. I thank the universe for placing me in that situation. If you find yourself in a similar situation where your RJ coping skills are tested to all ends, then simply smile, and say thank you to the universe. Thank you for giving me exactly what I need, when I need it, no matter how painful. And thank you for showing me that there is still more work to be done! Say yes to the universe. Say yes to the intelligent flow of life that we cannot begin to comprehend. Saying yes to the intelligent life flow of the universe is one of your greatest resources. It is all within you.

In Closing

I truly hope that you, the reader are positively inspired by this book to complete your RJ work and transform your pain into power. This transformation will bring about a wonderful change in every area of your life. You will have access to so many more life possibilities that you were previously blocked from due to your emotional state. Remember, no matter how hard it may seem, no matter how much you feel like giving up into a pit of despair, no matter how impossible healing my seem, I write this book to you as an ex RJ sufferer that is 100% cured. The same is possible for you. The key to your progress and healing is in your hands. Own it fully and take control! Do not waste any more of your life confined to the nightmarish symptoms of your insecurity. It is time to thrive and live your life! Enjoy every day, enjoy every second. Be here now and breathe in the beauty that is all around you. You are a powerful force for good. I believe in you. Now you must believe in yourself. Godspeed!

PART II

BOOK 2: RETROACTIVE JEALOUSY

FROM HELLISH INTRUSIVE THOUGHTS TO BECOMING YOUR BEST SELF: GET OVER THE PAST, CRUSH OCD, & STOP BEING A JEALOUS PARTNER

INTRODUCTION

To experience retroactive jealousy is to let yourself become bothered by experiences your loved one has had in the past. This can include relationships, sexual encounters, and even talking stages. The jealousy can be enough to tear you apart, preventing you from truly connecting with your partner in the way that you desire. It can turn into an obsession, one that only causes you to feel like you are suffering. The other person will never know that you feel this way unless you enlighten them. Naturally, this can be a hard thing to do when you find it difficult to think about your partner's past. To extract this kind of information becomes a sensitive topic because your partner might feel like you are prying. There are certain things in their past that they probably wish to move on from, and opening up this can of worms with you now is likely not going to do anything positive for your relationship.

The purpose of identifying when you are experiencing retroactive jealousy is important because it will show you how effective you are at living in the present. If you are constantly worrying about your partner's past, especially when it does not even involve you, this will inevitably hold the relationship back. It will not progress because there is a lot of stress felt on both sides. Your imagination can run wild when you are left thinking about what your partner used to do or how they used to feel.

The truth is—you cannot control or influence this because it already happens. What is healthiest for you to do is to focus on the present.

You are a brave individual, and you hold the key to progress. With or without a current partner, you should already know that you are a whole person who is capable of making yourself happy. When you have this as a starting point, you will be able to acknowledge when something is bothering you and whether or not you must do anything about it. I myself have struggled tremendously with retroactive jealousy. I would always compare myself to past lovers that my partner shared connections with. I wondered if I was good enough or not as good as them.

This type of behavior really began to hinder our relationship because it put me in a position where I constantly felt unhappy. My self-esteem was lower than ever, and my partner could sense this. Even though I am not a trained professional or therapist, I did a lot of research to see if I could help my situation. I wanted to understand what I was going through from the inside out. Through my findings, I decided that it was time for me to free myself of this retroactive jealousy. I could no longer live this way if I wanted to be happy. By letting go, I realized that self-focus became my reality. I did not even know what this meant, but I knew that it was making me feel better. Truly listening to my wants and needs, I was able to make the best decisions possible for myself moving forward. I did not base my choices on whether or not my partner would find them attractive.

I looked at the goals that I had put on hold due to my relationship and my focus on retroactive jealousy. I had always wanted to start an online business, so I set forth on this process. I became my own boss in a short amount of time, freeing me from the constructs of a traditional 9-5 job. I also became much more spiritual because I was more in touch with my emotions than ever. It was clear to me that I had a lot of soul searching left to do. Pretty soon, I noticed a lot of other positive traits that followed. My diet changed, and I started to feel motivated to exercise more. I was even able to shed a few pounds that I had been meaning to lose for quite some time. Getting rid of my retroactive jealousy changed my life for the better.

You are sitting on your very own treasure chest that you must figure out how to unlock. I firmly believe that we could all do a bit of soul-searching to get back to a point in our lives where we prioritize self-care. You can still have fulfilling relationships and great connections with your partner while you get to know yourself on a deeper level. In fact, I believe this is what made my current relationship even better. When my partner realized that I wanted to improve myself and do more, it even inspired him to take on some similar actions.

Retroactive jealousy is often abbreviated as RJ, and it is something both myself and my partner practice to this day. We bond over the topic because we know how much better it makes us as individuals, which trickles down into our relationship. We can see our lives improving before our eyes, and this is very meaningful to us both. If you give yourself a chance, you too can banish RJ to prevent it from taking over your life. It is a powerful force, but you are even more powerful. You have the willpower to get ahead of this jealousy that used to control you.

You will benefit by receiving a sense of freedom from the jealousy that often ties you down. Nobody enjoys being tied down, especially when the process does not benefit them. You still have a chance to change this, no matter how long it has been! If I was able to crush my debilitating RJ, then I know you are capable of doing the same. This process is possible for anybody in any relationship. Regardless of your age, where you live, or how long you have been with your partner—your efforts make it possible. Now is not the time to sit back and relax. Good things will only come your way when you put in the effort to make them happen.

There is nothing wrong with you and no reason as to why you are being burdened by RJ. It can happen to the best of us, but what matters now is that you have the desire to change. Feel proud of yourself for acknowledging this—it is the first step toward regaining your independence. You are going to do great things for yourself, and those around you are sure to take notice. Not only will you feel more secure in your relationship, but you will also feel happy with the person that you have grown to be. Pressure creates diamonds. While this is not an easy process to undergo, it is always going to be worthwhile to try.

12

WHY YOU'RE SITTING ON A TREASURE CHEST YOU NEVER KNEW WAS THERE

Your retroactive jealousy taunts you. It tricks you into believing that you are going to be stuck with it forever, trapped by its intrusive ways. The first step toward healing is learning how to re-frame your thoughts. What once brought you down and held you back can actually become a treasure chest that is filled with unlimited potential. You might be wondering how this is possible with something so difficult. Jealousy consumes your every waking moment, so why would it ever be something that you would like to keep around? Considering this famous parable, you will begin to see that the way you are thinking about your life and your surroundings can change a lot for you.

There was once a beggar who sat on the street corner. Each day, he begged for change that passerbys had to spare. Some would deny him, while others threw some coins his way. One day, a man walking by informed the beggar that he had nothing to offer him. Taking a look at the beggar's dirty appearance and emaciated form, the man began to question him. He asked—"What is in the box?" The beggar was confused, frozen for a moment. After looking down, he realized that this stranger was referring to the box that he had been using as a chair for all of these years.

The beggar never once thought to open this box. It was dingy, almost falling apart. The only value that he could find from it was to hold him above the ground while he did his begging. Eventually, the man continued on his way, but this sparked some curiosity within the beggar. He pried open the box with his dirt-lined fingernails, only to discover that it was filled with valuable gold and silver. All along, he had literally been sitting atop his very own treasure chest. Had he taken a moment to re-frame his thoughts, he might have been able to make it out of his situation a lot sooner.

Through this example, you will find that your situation is never as bad as you think it is. While jealousy still threatens to consume you, there is still a moment where you have a choice—you get to decide how it affects you and what you are going to do about it. Based on how you perceive the threat, you can actually live a life that makes you happy and fulfilled. There is always going to be meaning in your struggle, even if you cannot see it right now. If you are miserable for no reason, you are only going to reach a point of burnout. Bringing the meaning forward will put you at ease.

The experience that the beggar went through is very similar to the experience you are going through while living with RJ. You believe that your situation is miserable and that it is unlikely to change. There are moments where you can find peace or happiness, but the underlying message is that your jealousy still has control over your existence. By learning how to look at the resources you truly have, you will see that you can unlock so many different paths for yourself. A lot of these so-called riches are not material items but different facets of yourself that you can display proudly.

If you are willing to take on this challenge, you are capable of changing your life. Soon, you will be free of your RJ and all of the ways that it binds you. Only when you can make this commitment to yourself can you truly move on with your life. Through each moment that you experience jealousy, you are being tested. These tests will always be here, but your RJ does not have to be front and center. You can prove that you are able to pass the tests while still remembering who you are at your core. By unlocking your bounty, you will see how you can become the greatest version of yourself possible. This is the version that will be loved by you and those around you.

Every single aspect of your life will improve when you are free of your RJ. Not only will you be able to have more fulfilling romantic relationships, but you will also be able to better connect with others on a platonic level. It helps to know that not everybody out there has bad intentions in mind. Your job is also going to become a lot easier because you will be able to stay focused on the tasks in front of you. Even your own self-worth will see improvement because your mind will be clear of the distractions that RJ brings. You are going to notice a major difference in the person that you are.

Do not think of your RJ as a curse, for it is actually a very big gift if you can put it into a different perspective. With your RJ, you are given the opportunity to face a big challenge in life. The feeling that you get when you can successfully overcome this challenge will prove to be thrilling and fulfilling. No matter how perfect a person or a situation appears on the outside, you never know what they are going through internally. This is why you should not doubt yourself. Just because you are dealing with RJ right now does not mean that your life cannot drastically change. There are so many inspirational stories of others who have overcome adversity that will inspire you to be better.

Real Examples of Brave Individuals Overcoming Adversity

Ram Dass and His Stroke

Ram Dass was an American psychologist, spiritualist, and teacher. He became well known for his support of psychedelics as a form of mental healing. Throughout his life, he traveled far and wide in search of enlightenment. Spending time in India, Dass trained under a guru who taught him all about Hinduism, yoga, meditation and using LSD as a way to reach a higher state of consciousness. After this experience, Dass went on to speak all around the world about what he learned in an effort to enlighten others. In 1971, he published a book titled *Be Here Now* which became known as a guide to New Age spirituality.

It is apparent that Dass lived an abundant life that was full of great accomplishments. However, he was no stranger to adversity. He suffered a stroke in 1997 that paralyzed half of his body. Now only able to move his left side, Dass still did not give up on his life. He knew that he still had many great years ahead of him. Another thing that his stroke took away from him was his ability to speak clearly. This was naturally devastating, given the nature of his work. It was after this that Dass had to relearn the basics of existence.

He had to learn how to use his body in a new way and how to communicate with the language he had left. It was a struggle, but Dass was determined. He never gave up and continued to spread his teachings to all who would listen. However, Dass had one more unfortunate health scare in 2004. Due to a life-threatening infection, his life had to change drastically once again. This infection and the healing process limited his travels—something he loved to do so much.

After this blow, you would think that Dass would surely settle down and retreat inward, but he never gave up hope. Still continuing to spread enlightenment, Dass decided to work even harder at regaining his strength and becoming a living example that would go on to be recognized around the world. Up until his time of death, Dass inspired others. He was an example of how much persistence and motivation matter in life, even when you feel you have been knocked down one too many times. There is always a light at the end of the tunnel if you are willing to look for one.

By thinking about all that Dass went through in life, you can gather that he was still ultimately fulfilled by the end. He did what he loved until he physically could not do it any longer. Through finding a passion and working toward it, Dass made a name for himself. Even if your interests differ and your goals are drastically different, you can also make your mark on the world. Your mind is unique and interesting because nobody else has it. This is why it is up to you to share your knowledge and your ideas.

The next time that you get knocked down, try not to look at it as a permanent setback. Dass nearly died on more than one occasion, and he saw each moment as a way to start fresh. A blank canvas does not have to be a negative thing. It can be one of the most inspirational moments of your life if you learn how to look at it from a new perspective. You are not a failure if you must start over. This is a stigma that is usually put into place after a setback happens. Starting over builds character, and it will showcase your strengths. You might even realize that you have much more to offer the world than you thought before.

You will truly never understand your full potential until you push yourself outside of your comfort zone. See the challenges that you face as temporary roadblocks that you will get through. Once you start to think this way, you will be able to find solutions to any problem. This is how you will adopt a growth mindset, the one that teaches you how to always become the best version of yourself possible. If you do not know what you need to work on, then you must think deeply. Go inward until you can settle on a goal or several goals.

Nick Vujicic and His Inspirational Story

Known by over 750 million people around the world, Nick Vujicic is a strong source of inspiration for many reasons. Most notably, he was born without any arms or legs. Even despite this rare genetic condition, Vujicic continued on to become a motivational speaker who continues to inspire people who come from all situations and walks of life. Given his unique perspective, Vujicic had two choices while growing up. He could either let his condition get the best of him, or he could go on to live a meaningful and fulfilling life. When he chose the latter, he wanted to make sure that others could also feel empowered in this way. This is why he decided to share his wisdom with the world.

The pain that Vujicic experienced began early on while he attended school. Children were cruel to him, bullying him for his condition. Naturally, this left Vujicic feeling very discouraged and hopeless. At times, he wondered if there was anything out there in life for him. Maybe he was not meant to amount to much at all because of this fate. These dark thoughts eventually led him to a suicide attempt that he survived. He refused to let the bad outweigh the good. While he did have to face constant torment and stares, he managed to put the pieces of his life back together.

It was after this moment that Vujicic realized he had a much greater purpose in life. He could change the world by speaking up and talking about how his condition does not define him. He is still an individual with hopes and dreams that he accomplished, just like anyone else. Through the power of his inspirational words, he became mentally stronger than ever before. After facing so many obstacles head-on, Vujicic went on to become a highly requested speaker around the world. So many people wanted to hear what he had to say.

Vujicic defines resilience. He is living proof that even the darkest moments will make way for brighter ones. Had he ended his life all those years ago, his wisdom would not have been shared with so many people. No matter how much you want to give up or how bad things are going in your life right now, things are bound to change because nothing can stay the same forever. This applies to both bad and good. You must cherish all of the great moments that you have and learn to work your way through the terrible ones. This is what Vujicic mastered, and he went on to become an important anti-bullying advocate in the process.

You must not compare your struggles to the struggles of others. Even if you are not going through what Vujicic did, you can still relate to the idea that life is very difficult at times. What hurts you the most becomes your reality, and this is what you must work on facing. Just because there are others in different circumstances does not mean you should compare yourself—they are different people, and they have different solutions to their problems. Brainstorm the best ways to improve your own life.

Just by sharing your story, you never know what great things might happen. This is exactly the route that Vujicic decided to take, and it allowed him to achieve so many great accomplishments. People love to connect with others through storytelling. It gives them a chance to feel close to one another. Speaking about things that make you feel vulnerable or that have been difficult can be a challenge, but you never know the doors that it could open up for you.

Do your best to make yourself vulnerable sometimes. While you do not have to live your life in this state, you might benefit from sharing a few of these tender moments with people who want to listen. Others care a great deal about you, and you might not even realize just how much support you have until you allow yourself to be vulnerable. It is okay to admit that you are struggling, and it is excellent to ask for help when you feel overwhelmed. Do everything that you can for yourself until the hard times pass because they will.

Travis Mills: The Injured Soldier

There are many inspirational people in the world, and Travis Mills definitely falls into this category. A retired US Army Sergeant, he is a warrior turned motivational speaker. Through his experiences on the battlefield, he has a lot to teach others about strength, courage, and determination. On April 10, 2012, Mills was on his third tour of duty in Afghanistan. A seasoned veteran, he knew what he was doing and what his mission was. Still, this could never prepare him for what was to come. This was the day that changed his life forever, the day that critically injured him to the point where many did not believe he would live to see another day.

During this tragic accident, Mills lost portions of all his limbs during an attack involving an improvised explosive device. As a result of this, he had to undergo a quadruple amputation that completely changed his life once he returned home. He is only one of five quadruple amputees from both the Iraq and Afghanistan wars combined. This is not exactly a feat that he is proud of, but he is grateful to have survived it all. After he made it back home, he had a long road of recovery ahead. Mills credits his family for helping him to regain his faith in life.

As he worked on learning how to live a normal life again, he gathered plenty of support from the men he battled with and thousands of strangers that prayed for him daily. At the Walter Reed Medical Center, where he completed his rehabilitation, he continues to work on regaining his strength. The process is going to be lifelong for Mills, but he realizes that he cannot give up hope. There is still so much life left ahead of him to live. He wants to do it for his family, but he also realizes that he can do it for himself.

In September 2013, Mills and his wife started a non-profit foundation called the Travis Mills Foundation. Its purpose is to benefit and assist

9/11 veterans who were injured during active duty. Because Mills has first-hand experience, he has a great passion for the cause. Thanks to the foundation, the veterans and their families receive all-expenses-paid vacations to Maine where they get the chance to relax in nature and participate in adaptive activities. These trips also allow other veteran families to bond with each other.

Shortly after the non-profit was founded, The Travis Mills Group LLC began. This is an organization where Travis himself speaks with companies and organizations all around the world about finding the inspiration to overcome tough challenges. Based on what he has been through in his life, it is no wonder that there are many people who are willing to listen to what he has to say. Adversity is his specialty, but he never let it completely rule his life. He turned it into a strength that eventually led him to success.

If you find the inspiration behind Mills' story, you are not alone. Any other person might have wanted to give up after what happened, but he stayed strong. He showed everyone and proved to himself that there was still so much life worth living. The next time that you face adversity, even if it seems so terrible, understand that it is not going to last forever. You can still make something of yourself if you truly have the passion to do so.

Inspirational Thoughts

You can change your life if you have dreams, but you must be willing to jump for them. Claim what you believe belongs to you, and this stems from knowing which gifts you have. The gifts that you possess should always be on your mind, keeping you awake at night sometimes. Your dream is never out of reach. It might take several steps to reach it, but this is all going to become worthwhile.

You must embrace who you are, an individual. Nobody else will understand your process or where you are coming from, and that is okay. As long as you have a purpose and a goal to work on, you will understand that you are capable of anything. You are not simply ordinary. You have so much potential, and you have many opportunities to change the world if this is something that you feel you can take on. Believe in yourself more than anyone else who believes in you. This is how you are going to get far in life. Has this chapter helped you reframe your RJ into something empowering yet?

Action Step

Sit down with a pen and a piece of paper. To begin, you are going to think of three things that you have been through in your life that have felt tragic at first but came with a silver lining. These events can be anything from any point in time, as long as they were impactful. Think carefully about which three have made the biggest difference in your life. In addition, you should make sure that you would never trade these silver linings for anything, even despite the struggles that you had to overcome to get to this point! This is how you know that the journey has been worthwhile.

The next exercise also involves writing. Make it a goal to write down your top 10 inspirational quotes that you have ever heard. You can quote literature, important figures, or even people in your daily life. These quotes should all have a similar meaning, and that is to help you focus on the riches that you have. They should inspire you to seek inner abundance, no matter what you are doing. On your journey to obliterating retroactive jealousy, you will be able to turn to these quotes as motivational pushes in the right direction. Place this list where you can see it frequently. Use it as a reminder that you have something to believe in as you are working on overcoming your RJ.

13

THIS HAS NOTHING TO DO WITH YOUR PARTNER'S PAST AND EVERYTHING TO DO WITH YOU

From the moment you met your partner, they already have a history that you were not a part of. The experiences they lived through and the people they interacted with all shaped them into the person that you fell in love with. As humans, we have a tendency to take things very personally. You might wonder if they think they can find someone better as you compare yourself to their ex. Or you might think that they find their coworker more attractive and more intelligent than you. The brain has a way of making you believe that you are far less than what you are worth.

Any RJ that you feel directly relates to how you view yourself. If you think that your partner would be quick to leave you or to cheat on you, then this says a lot about your self-esteem. You probably do not think very highly of yourself and view yourself as someone replaceable. This can all change. It is the only way for RJ to stop ruining your life and your relationships. You will learn that you are full of value and have so much to offer. No longer will you worry about who your partner spends time around or what they are thinking while they do so.

Retroactive jealousy is very powerful. Even if you were to date someone new, it would come back in full force. The insecurities that you feel surrounding your current relationship would transform into new ones that apply to your next one. This proves that the problem lies within the way that you see yourself, not the things that your partner(s) have done in the past. It is a vicious cycle that can be very hard to get out of if you are not careful. While you want to blame your partner for their past, stop to think—is this really their fault? Are they the reason why you are insecure?

Likely, it is you who puts yourself down. You determine how you feel and convince yourself that you are not good enough. You might do this beneath the surface at a very unconscious level. Comparison is one of the worst things that you can do. When you start comparing yourself to your partner's exes, it is going to consume your thoughts. RJ will flare up and make sure that you obsess over this. You must learn how to be strong and diligent when these thoughts arise. By reminding yourself that your partner has not done anything wrong and that they want to be with you, you can, and will, rise above.

Try not to punish your partner when you feel insecure. Not only is this burdensome and confusing to them, but it also will not solve the problem. The solution comes from within, and it comes from working on your self-esteem. Trigger control is something important that you will learn. There are plenty of things in your relationship that will set you off and make you feel insecure, but you get to choose whether or not to act on them. By rising above, you will allow the anger and jealousy to diminish. Your RJ comes from past conditioning, and it can even be combined with elements of OCD. This is why it is so powerful and hard to overcome at times.

Did You Create Your Insecurity?

Many of your insecurities actually come from your past, not your partner's. Starting as early as childhood, these insecurities can be placed within your brain. This is why you have such an easy time carrying them into adulthood with you. The examples of love that you had around you growing up are also big components of how you will feel about relationships. This past conditioning, what your partner has done in their past (or what you imagined they did), and OCD tendencies can all come together to make your life a living hell—it is not fun to live with intense RJ that feels way beyond your control.

You might feel an intense bout of shame or worthlessness because of your RJ, and it takes a lot of practice to get out of this mindset. Later in this book, the topic of inner-child healing is discussed in more detail. This is a crucial part for truly getting to the root of your RJ, and it can prove to be immensely helpful. There are a lot of heavy topics to be discussed, but they are necessary if you want to live a life that is not ruled by jealousy any longer.

Crushing your RJ revolves around crushing your insecurities. Once you are able to get through them, your RJ will dissolve, allowing you to live a more normal and carefree life. The two go hand-in-hand for a reason. They fuel each other, making it seem like you need both to feel okay. It takes a lot of self-reflection to work on your insecurities, but this is ultimately going to be the best way to combat your RJ. If you find it difficult to actually look at yourself, now is the perfect time to practice. Stand in front of the mirror and recite a positive affirmation. Try something like, "I am a strong, attractive, and desirable person. I am a unique creation of the universe, and I am just as spectacular as anyone else". Pay attention to your physical appearance while thinking about all of the wonderful qualities that you have to offer.

Discomfort is normal, especially when you are an insecure person. You might have a hard time making eye contact, but it takes practice to get the hang of this exercise. Do this every day until you are able to believe the positive affirmations that you are reciting. You must be able to love the person that you see staring back at you. If all you notice are your flaws, then you are naturally only going to focus on what you are insecure about. Everybody has insecurities, but there are many ways that you can deal with them, so they do not become detrimental to your life.

Overcoming Insecurity

Aside from taking a gentle approach to uplifting yourself in the mirror, there are many other activities that you can take on that will show you how amazing you are. Consider the following:

- Martial arts
- Kickboxing
- Self-defense
- Sports
- Yoga
- Working out
- Changing your diet
- Learning something new
- Starting a side business
- Improving your physical image
- Changing your personal style
- Feeling sexier (becoming a better lover)
- Speaking more clearly

These are all activities that you can do for yourself, not for anyone else. If they sound appealing to you, then you should give them a try! The best part about working on your self-esteem is that you get to choose exactly what to do to help improve it. Most of these tasks are empowering and strengthening in more ways than one. They will make you feel great physically, and they can also work on improving your mental health. Try to aim for activities like those above, the ones that will benefit you in the long run.

On a more personal level, there are other ways to build up your self-esteem so that you can finally banish RJ for good. You can try some of these things when you are on your own, paying close attention to the effort you are putting into each one.

Affirm Your Value

When you are working on your self-esteem, you need to tell yourself exactly how valuable you are. Do this every day—as often as you need the reminder! Telling yourself something enough will eventually lead you to believe it. Your value is not only what you are capable of doing for others. You have been alive for so many years, and you have been taking care of yourself for most of them. Think about what you do for yourself and why these actions matter. They are something to feel proud of, and they prove that you are a very valuable individual with a purpose in life.

If anyone has ever made you feel less, consider that this is **your** self-esteem. It is not theirs to tell you about or to instruct you on how to feel. You perceive it exactly how you want, and this is true power if you think about it. Reclaim this power by hearing what others have to say but not taking everything to heart immediately. Not everything they say is going to be true.

Embrace the Awkward

There are going to be moments when you feel awkward or just plain weird—embrace them! Nobody knows what they are doing at all times, but this is how you are going to learn. Seek discomfort on a regular basis. This should not be enough to make you upset but just enough to get you to try new things. If something happens that is awkward, ask yourself why it feels so taboo. Most of the time, it is because it has yet to happen to you. Everything awkward has the potential to become familiar the more that you do it.

One example includes going to dinner alone or seeing a movie alone. Most people go with others, but this is not a requirement. You are independent enough to do this on your own, and it might feel awkward at first. This does not mean it is inherently wrong, though. You might find that you actually really enjoy your own company. You must develop personal autonomy and take some time away from your partner for some self-reflection. This alone time is a breeding ground for exciting thoughts of what you want to achieve for your future to arise spontaneously. Future dreams and goals can trigger a new exciting urge to crush your RJ permanently.

Challenge Negative Thoughts

The negative thoughts are going to pop up left and right. This is because you are your own worst critic. You are used to putting yourself down and pointing out all of your personal flaws. Stop doing this immediately because this is what destroys your self-esteem. The next time that you want to say something negative about yourself, reframe the thought. Replace it with something positive instead.

This is also going to become apparent in the way that you describe yourself to others. Instead of pointing out what you are not good at, you will find ways to talk about the things that you are great at. This all takes a simple shift in mindset, and it can really help your self-esteem thrive. It is called a challenge because it is not the easiest thing to do. If you have been used to talking negatively about yourself for a while, this habit will be a challenge to break. You can do it, though—believe in yourself.

Stay Away From Drama

Drama fuels negativity, and this is something that you should be staying very far away from. Negativity impacts your mindset more than you realize, even if it has nothing to do with you directly. We all have friends who like to gossip and talk about other people, but are these friends adding value to our lives? Think about who you are close to right now and how enriching their friendships are. You must only keep the people close to you that are following the same positive mindset because this is how you are going to stay on track.

If you can sense drama is brewing, find a way out of it. This drama is not worth your time, and you can find other ways to satisfy your curiosity. There are many exciting and fulfilling activities to do, like the ones mentioned above, that will actually help to build your self-esteem. Remember, you cannot build yourself up by tearing someone else down in the process.

Read More Books

Reading is a great form of escapism. It can teach you so many new things that you never would have heard from a friend or a TV show. Try your best to indulge in a book every once in a while. The topics can vary, as long as you find them interesting. You can learn a lot about yourself through what you choose to read because this reaffirms your interests. It is a great way to spend time with yourself that does not take much time, energy, or money. Unlike a school assignment, you do not have a deadline for which you must complete your reading. Go at your own pace.

If there is something you have been curious about yet do not want to take a class, reading a book on the subject is the next best thing. You can do this from the comfort of your home or another relaxing place, and you can still learn about what interests you. Give it a try for yourself to see how much you enjoy reading and how it can uplift you. It also becomes a great activity to use before you are ready to fall asleep at night. Reading is proven to be much more relaxing than staring at a TV or phone screen. Self-development books helped me immensely during my period of RJ healing. You must fill your mind with empowering knowledge, not depressing trash that will further pull you down into the depths of turmoil.

Take Baby Steps

You are not going to get over your RJ overnight. Some days will be good, while others will feel a lot harder. Take the time to really focus on how you are feeling and if what you are doing is helping. It only takes a few small steps to amount to something larger. Do not force yourself to make any big leaps that you are not comfortable with because this could actually reverse your progress by causing you to revert back to your old ways. You need to do what feels right for you.

Doing small things such as treating yourself to something nice without waiting for a special occasion is just one of many examples. You can do this to show yourself that you appreciate who you are and all that you do. You do not need to wait for a partner, friend, or other loved one to fill this role. This is how you will become an independent and self-sufficient person that truly knows how to find happiness.

Reflect on the Good

There are many good things in your life that you can be grateful for. Remember to express your thanks for them often. Counting your blessings is not something that you only need to do when you are in a bad spot. Even if you feel okay, it is still a wise idea to count your blessings because you never know when your RJ is going to strike. It can make you feel worthless in no time, but having a grounding stance of gratitude is something that will truly help you overcome these outbursts.

When you feel insecure about something, see if you can find a way to turn this insecurity into a strength. While you might dislike this thing about yourself, find something that it does that helps you in life. It might make you a stronger, more resilient person. Or it might be something that others do not have. Anything that makes you feel unique will usually allow you to overcome an insecurity and move on with more positive thinking.

Are You Insecure in Other Areas of Life?

Have you ever wondered if you are as attractive as your partner's ex? Maybe you have thoughts that they are going to leave you because you are not good enough or not intelligent enough. Your RJ can impact many other areas of your life, turning you into a person who questions everything that you do and everything that you are. This is not fair on yourself because of all the hard work and progress you have made in life. Think about parts of your life that do not have anything to do with your relationship, do you often experience insecurities in these areas too?

Maybe you feel like you are not very good at your job or a terrible friend. You might tear yourself apart because you think you need to lose 10 pounds or that your haircut is ugly. These are all very negative ways to feel about yourself, and it is natural that they will develop into RJ over time. Your mind does not know how to process this much negativity at once. It cannot help but to desire what others have, others who seemingly have lives that are better than your own.

Your insecurities run deep, which is why it is important to focus on them broadly. Only addressing your relationship insecurities is not going to completely banish RJ from your life. You need to examine all of the things that make you feel bad about yourself. This process can be difficult and painful, but you will be glad once you finally get to the bottom of them all. You are going to figure out a way to be 100% happy with yourself, and this is going to show from the inside out. Your partner will take notice, and the loved ones in your life will recognize that you have been doing a lot of work on your own happiness.

How to Grow Your Self-Esteem

If you really want to be free of your RJ, you must also address the underlying causes of all of your other insecurities in life. This involves a lot of personal work, and it can be difficult to pinpoint exactly where this all stems from. A great way to begin is by completing exercises that will grow your self-esteem. Even if you still have insecurities, you will be getting closer and closer to overcoming them as you become a more confident version of yourself.

- **Be Kind to Yourself:** Negative self-talk causes low self-esteem. The way that you perceive yourself has everything to do with how you treat yourself and if you are valuing yourself in the way that you deserve. Make sure you are being kind to yourself. Imagine that you are a child, would you still treat yourself the way that you do if you were that much younger and vulnerable? This exercise could prove to be very eye-opening for you, encouraging you to be kinder.
- **Do What You Want:** As long as you are not hurting anyone in the process, do what you want! Go after those dreams and attend those classes. What you want to do is something that you should always make time for, especially if it relates to having a fun time or to learning something new. Holding yourself back in fear of judgment is one way that you are hurting your self-esteem. Any partner that you are with should understand that you want to better yourself and that you want to become an even better partner by going after the things that you want in life.
- **Get Moving:** When you do not feel your best, get up and move! It might feel like the very last thing that you want to do, but you can do it. Take a walk around your neighborhood, do a home workout, or go to the gym if you are feeling ambitious. You can do so much for your mental health by just getting your physical body moving. This is also going to increase your self-esteem because of the endorphin rush that it releases. Try your best to get up and moving at least once each day; this is going to make all the difference in the way that you feel about yourself.
- **Recognize Imperfection:** Imperfection is all around you, and

it does not only exist in your actions. Everybody has their own imperfections; this is what makes them unique individuals. What some people view as an imperfection might be an endearing quality to you. Think about it in reverse—what if your so-called imperfections are actually traits that your partner loves about you? Since you cannot see yourself from an outside perspective, you never know. Trust what others who care about you tell you. They have no reason to lie about you and about your amazing qualities.

- **Acknowledge Mistakes:** You are going to continue making mistakes in your life. Even if you have made amends for past mistakes, prepare yourself to make some more—this is how you learn. While it might not be an intentional practice, it should also be something that you should not punish yourself for. Instead, see if you can learn from them. Think about what has changed and what you might do differently if you were in the same situation again. These mistakes will help you grow, and they can help with your self-confidence by giving you newfound solutions to use in the future.
- **Focus on Change:** If you want to see a different result, then you must be willing to make a change. Even small changes can amount to huge differences in your life. From changing your habits to completely transforming your routines, this can create a lot more self-confidence for you because it breaks up the mundane routine that you are so used to. This routine makes you feel secure, but it might not be what is best for you to keep growing as a person. Think about any ways that you can change that will help you to evolve and keep learning.
- **Achieve Happiness:** At the end of the day, everybody just wants to be happy. You are no stranger to this feeling, and you deserve every ounce of happiness you can achieve. Make this a goal in life, to be happy every day. When you create an intention, it becomes a lot easier to commit to it. If you are always dreading each day and thinking that it is going to go wrong, then surely life will find a way to prove this right.

Approach life with a positive mindset and you will be surprised at where it can take you.

- **Celebrate Often:** If you complete a goal, celebrate it! This does not have to be a monumental moment or something that you have been working on for years. Anything small is worthy of a celebration of the appropriate size. When you have these little celebrations, it gives you a reason to keep going and to keep making progress. It also builds up the pride that you feel for yourself, which does raise your self-esteem. This is all going to impact you in a great way. Plus, it is a lot of fun to be acknowledged for your accomplishments. Do not be afraid to be your own biggest cheerleader.
- **Be a Support System:** Sometimes, supporting other people can do a great deal for your self-esteem. When you are seen as a valuable individual by someone else, this places a sense of importance on you. While you know you are important, this person affirming just how important you are can really help you to see how great you are. Do something kind for someone. Be a listening ear when they are in need. It does not take much to make someone's day and to make them feel like they are a little less alone in the world when they are struggling. Treat them how you would like to be treated.
- **Surround Yourself With Positivity:** Being around positive people and positive situations is ultimately the best thing that you can do for your self-esteem. The energy that you surround yourself with is the energy that you are going to feel inside. It will be the energy that you emulate back into the universe, so it matters a great deal. If you spend time around toxic people and drama, this will affect you even if it does not directly involve you. Make it a point to surround yourself with positivity at every chance you get.

Action Step

You are going to take full ownership of the retroactive jealousy that you experience. Write this down on a piece of paper, committing to the statement. Also, write down that you plan to commit 100% to not stopping until you have freed yourself from the destruction that it causes. This means that you must be willing to work hard and to do anything that it takes to get away from this terrible mindset that you put yourself in. Sign the bottom of the page, put a date on it, and think of this as a binding contract. Put it somewhere where you keep other important documents. You should be able to look at it frequently, reminding you of why you are working so hard to change your habits and to change your life.

Next, write down some insecurities that affect you. These insecurities do not have to be related to your RJ, but it is still important that you are aware of them. For now, they are considered your weaknesses. They might revolve around the way you look, how much money you have, or where you live. While anything can cause you to feel insecure, this does not mean that it has to hold power over you. After you list each one out on a piece of paper, write down an opposite statement right next to it. For example, if you said that you are insecure because you feel overweight, you would write down that your body is strong and nourished, taking you places that you want to go. This type of exercise is going to reframe your thoughts and bring you toward a more positive mindset.

14

RETROACTIVE JEALOUSY: THE GATEWAY INTO THE GREATEST GIFT YOU COULD EVER IMAGINE

You might be wondering—what good can come from retroactive jealousy? How will it change my life for the better? You will be surprised at how something so negative can transform you into a person who is motivated to become an even better version of themselves. This happens through spirituality, which differs from religion. Regardless of if you are religious or not, you can still be a spiritual person who recognizes that there is a presence out there that is bigger than yourself. You are not in control of everything in the world, not even your own feelings at times. This alone proves that you can center your energy to better ground yourself. You can transform into a person who knows how to handle situations in a calm and harmonious manner without getting upset.

To practice spirituality, it is important that you only focus on the present—there is only here and now. When you spend time worrying about the past or future, you are distracting yourself and using your energy in a wasteful way. Remain present in this moment. Think about what you can do right now to make your life better and to become a better version of yourself. What happens in the future is uncertain because it is made up of your actions. The choices that you make right now will shape your future, and that is a lot to think about.

Your ego governs your RJ, as you learned in the previous chapter. The larger that your ego grows, the worse that your RJ will become. In theory, you must bypass both your ego and your RJ to fully heal yourself. This can seem like a daunting task, but finding your own version of spirituality will help you. Through this practice, you will find a routine that makes you feel stable and secure. It will settle your worries and allow you to think logically, even when you want to explode. No situation is as bad as it seems when your ego is in check.

How to Become More Mindful

Mindfulness is not only a habit; it is a way of life. To be mindful is to be aware of what is going on around you, that your words and actions can impact others and other situations. Having this awareness is helpful because it can be extremely grounding. Having more mindful practices in your daily life will lead you to many positive outcomes. The following are a few ways to get started.

- **Start When It Is Easy:** Most people think they have to dive right into mindfulness and change their lives, but that is not the case. You can start when the moment feels right to you, but do not hesitate out of fear. In an instant your life can change if you allow it. Try to commit to the practice of mindfulness during a time when you feel ready to grow as a person. This is going to be a personal evolution that will teach you many new things about yourself. You might have to quiet down some of the external noise that surrounds you before you can begin, but this is okay. You will know when it is the right time to start.
- **Pay Attention to Daily Routines:** You can tell a lot about your current habits by observing your daily routines. Think about when you eat breakfast, if you eat it at all. How much time do you give yourself to get ready in the morning? Do you have a relaxation routine for the end of the day? Being aware of these things will help you to see that you might be lacking some of your basic needs daily. These are all very simple changes to make, and they are not going to cause you to feel

overwhelmed in doing so. This is why mindfulness is so great—you can take small steps that will amount to much larger ones.

- **Approach With Curiosity:** In life, nothing is guaranteed. You might have driven down the same road thousands of times, but you never know exactly what might happen. This is the same way you should approach everything in your life. Live curiously, questioning things that you wonder about. When you ask questions, you might end up getting answers that change your perspective entirely. The moment that you just accept what you know as the truth is the moment that you are capable of getting stuck in an unhealthy or mundane routine.
- **Remember the Four T's:** Transitions, teatime, toilet, and telephone—these are the four t's. You might be wondering what this has to do with mindfulness, and the concept is actually very simple. No matter what you are doing, take a small breath to pause between each activity. You do not have to go through your life feeling like you are running a marathon. Put your phone down, and take a breath. Enter the bathroom, and take a breath. You get the idea and soon, this will become a habit that will implement a much more easygoing and mindful way of living.
- **Breathe Frequently:** You already need to breathe to survive, but do you know how to control your breath? Breathing techniques can do a lot to promote stress relief and calmness. When you hold your breath in for four seconds and exhale for four seconds, this is like hitting a reset button. Any anger, rage, or even jealousy will begin to melt away when you control your breathing. The best part is, you can do this wherever you are. Try it the next time that you can feel your RJ flaring up.
- **Physically Ground Yourself:** You would be surprised at how much more mindful you feel when you pay attention to your posture. Starting from the way you are standing, make sure that you are upright and not slouching. This will feel good as

you stretch your muscles. Loosen your neck, shoulders, and jaw. A lot of tension is naturally held in all three of these places. Put your hands and arms in a neutral position by your side. Crossing them can actually make you feel negative or closed off. Allow your knees to remain comfortably straight, even slightly bent. By paying attention to how your feet feel on the floor, you have a reminder that you are literally grounded. You are rooted to the earth in a comforting way.

How to Meditate

Meditation can be done in many different ways. There is no right or wrong way to meditate, but having a guide to help you in the beginning is useful. When you meditate, you are being brought into the present. This will help with mindfulness and controlling your RJ. Overall, you are going to feel much better when you learn what puts you in a meditative state. This does not always have to include lying down and closing your eyes. Soon, you will be able to transform yourself to this place without even moving a muscle.

In a later chapter, there will be an in-depth explanation of how to follow a guided meditation. For now, these first few steps will get you acquainted with the practice. You can use them when you feel your RJ beginning to take over. First and foremost, get out of the current situation that is triggering you. Physically distance yourself from it as soon as possible. If you can, pick a place where you feel safe to lie down or to sit down. Dim the lighting, making sure that it is not too harsh or distracting. This place should also be quiet enough for you to focus on your thoughts.

Once you are in a comfortable position, close your eyes and simply breathe. Focus on the breath filling your lungs and leaving it. Make the breathing steady and even. You will start to notice certain thoughts filling your head. Allow them to rise to the surface, imagining that they are floating down a river. The ones that trigger your RJ get to keep floating down that river. You will meet them again, but not right now. You can let them go far away from you, being swept down by the current. Imagine that you have a net to fetch certain thoughts that you would like to explore. If something else comes up, hold onto that thought for a brief moment.

You can analyze it, thinking about what it is making you feel and why it is affecting you. Is an action step necessary? If not, you can let it go. This is a great way to figure out what is truly going on inside, and it will enlighten you as to why you feel the way that you do. Once you have sorted through all of the thoughts that come up, focus on your physical body. Notice how it feels, if any parts of it ache or are uncomfortable. Starting from the tips of your toes, relax your muscles. Work your way up in isolation until you get to the very top of your head. Each part of your body should feel at ease now.

Then, empty your mind completely. Allow yourself to just feel your body connecting with the surface it is on, entirely relaxed. Take a few deep breaths and imagine a black void that is a comfort to you. Rest here in peace, taking in all of the sights and sounds that try to enter your mind. This time, you are simply going to observe them as they pass. There will be no evaluation, no judgment necessary. Once you reach a point of full relaxation, remain here for as long as you need. Most people enjoy doing this for 10 or 20 minutes at a time. When you are done meditating, it helps to open your eyes slowly. Take a few deep breaths, and wiggle your fingers and toes. This will bring you back to reality.

Non-Judgment: Release the Chains You Cling To

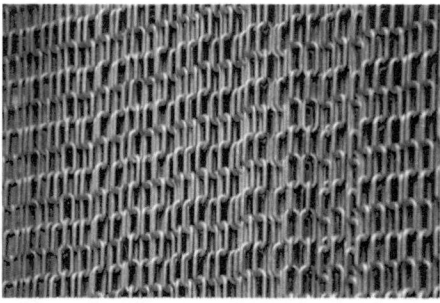

To become a nonjudgmental person, you truly need to train yourself not to care. This does not mean you do not care about anything or how it will affect you, but you have to let go enough to release the emotional chains that you cling to. This is ultimately going to help you conquer your RJ. This practice is immensely powerful, and it is deeply rooted in spirituality. When you can simply observe a situation that once bothered you without becoming reactive, this is how you will know you are being non-judgmental. You will be able to see situations at face value and this is going to help you make better decisions in the long run.

Even though being nonjudgmental is a very spiritual practice, it does not require any meditation to get there. You can work on your non-judgment abilities by simply being more mindful in your daily life. Think about what you are saying and doing. The way that you talk about others says a lot about the way you feel about yourself. It can reflect very poorly on you if you are always quick to talk about someone behind their back in a judgmental way. This shows that you have many insecurities. It is time to curb this behavior.

1. **Observe Your Thoughts:** Do your best to catch yourself thinking negatively over the next few days. If you find yourself thinking that a person "shouldn't" do something or that a situation "can't" go this way, then flag this as a judgment. These terms indicate that you think you know the person or situation better than anyone and that you are trying to take control of the outcome. You do not always need to pass a judgment to fully understand what is going on. Simply being an onlooker and getting involved if necessary will remove a lot of unwanted stress from your life.

Another interesting way that you can catch yourself in negativity is if you feel like the people around you are negative. This is you placing a judgment on them and it might be speaking more about you than you realize. The thoughts that you have about other people are directly related to how you perceive yourself, so what might you really be trying to say?

Once you get better at recognizing these negative thoughts, question yourself about them. Ask yourself why you believe you need to place these judgments and why it fulfills you. Most likely, it does not fulfill you. It might be that you are just so used to placing judgments that you do it out of habit, or maybe you just feel bored with your life. No matter the reason, you must pinpoint it if you want to take full accountability.

1. **Take Note of Your Triggers:** You understand that there are certain triggers that will activate your RJ instantly. These triggers get you heated, and they make you feel irrationally jealous or even angry. Make sure that you are paying attention to them because they will show you all of the patterns that you must become aware of. People have different triggers when it comes to jealousy. What bothers one person will not always bother you and vice versa. Your triggers are very personal and they are often based on past experiences that you have been through in life.

While it is not your fault that you are triggered by these things, it is your responsibility to deal with them properly. You do not need to take them out on other people, especially the ones closest to you, just because you feel like you cannot handle them. Instead, you must dig deeper. Think about how you can handle your triggers in a way that will make them dissipate rather than pushing them below the surface. What you suppress will always find its way back up to you.

To make the most of this step, it helps to write down your triggers in a journal or notebook. When you notice one, simply jot it down. Seeing a tangible list of what bothers you can help to pinpoint how you will avoid these situations in the future. It can also give you a better understanding of why you react the way that you do. Self-observation is a great thing, and it is a necessary part of overcoming your RJ.

You might notice that you are more judgmental around certain people because some people bring out these qualities in you. Maybe you are more judgmental in certain situations. It all becomes one big observation that you must complete on yourself to get a better understanding of what is going on. Nobody else is going to be able to do this for you, which is why it requires you to take on a lot of accountability.

1. **Practice Empathy:** In most cases, you will start to judge someone when you do not understand their behavior. What you perceive as weird or even annoying might be so because you are not coming from their perspective. To practice empathy, you are practicing putting yourself in their metaphorical shoes. You still might not be able to relate to them entirely, but this will give you a better understanding of what they are going through mentally. It is important to take this approach before you react in a judgmental way.

Nobody likes a mean person, especially one who is so quick to cast judgment. This is an ugly trait that makes you very unlikable, and it also makes you feel bad about yourself as an individual. Getting rid of this trait is going to benefit both you and the people around you. It will show you that you can still feel for somebody without actually going through what they are going through. You can empathize with their pain or their negative feelings without making them feel bad for it.

You might realize that it is hard to be empathetic on days when you are going through a lot yourself. If you are having a bad day or a rough experience, it feels natural to take this frustration out on other people. There is where you need to start implementing empathy instead. Direct all of this negative energy toward helping someone else and trying to be more understanding. While your day still might be terrible, you are going to make someone else's better in the process—this will lift your mood.

A little role reversal can help you become more empathetic. Put yourself in that person's life, imagining that you are going through what they are going through. This will really solidify their actions and maybe even their mindset. When you can transform your way of thinking into their way of thinking, if only for a moment, you will be able to relate on a more personal level. It does take a lot of energy to be an empath, but it helps to keep the judgmental side of you at bay.

1. **Reframe Judgmental Thoughts:** The judgmental thoughts will not disappear on their own. You must take proactive steps

to change your way of thinking. This is called reframing, and you can learn how to reframe your judgment. The next time that you catch yourself being judgmental, see if you can rewrite this thought into something more positive. For example, imagine that you see someone who is wearing shoes that you think are ugly. Instead of thinking that they have bad taste, you can think that you would rather wear your favorite style and that their style is different from yours.

This does not change your opinion, but it allows you to express yourself in a healthier way. There is no reason to be judgmental toward other people, especially when you can take the route of reframing your thoughts instead. This is going to prevent you from holding onto negative energy that you might accidentally unleash. It also helps your self-esteem because negative self-talk is also something that can creep into your mindset. Overall, being less judgmental is going to improve every aspect of your life.

Reframing your judgmental thoughts also helps to target any RJ that you might be feeling. Sometimes, judgment acts as a mask that hides jealousy. You might want to ridicule someone, only because you feel jealous of them or something they have. This is a common human experience that not many are willing to admit. Just as you have learned, you need to stop being controlled by your ego. Bring it down, and admit that you admire these people and things. Think about how you can use your energy to work hard and make those things happen for yourself.

Apply this step toward yourself and the way that you view yourself. If you catch yourself being judgmental about what you are saying or doing, take a pause. Think about how you can construct the thought differently in a way that will actually help you rather than hinder you. It takes practice, but you will get there.

1. **Be Accepting:** Once you have attempted to understand someone, the next step is to accept them for who they are or what they are doing. You might not fully agree, and you might not completely understand. This is normal, but the next best

thing you can do is to realize that this is their life. This is their choice to make, so you can only accept as a third-party observer. You cannot change other people no matter how hard you try. If you did, that would be one very boring life with everybody operating exactly as you predicted.

Appreciate others for who they are fully. Learn about their nuances and their strengths/weaknesses. You have them too. Other people are likely going to observe and appreciate these traits about you because this is what makes you unique. This is how you create healthy human connections that do not revolve around negativity or RJ. You must undo all of the past negativity that you have been holding onto.

Let go of the idea that you can mold someone into the ideal version of themselves. Even if you think you know what is good for them, and you could be right, they must come to this conclusion on their own. Support them on their personal journey of growth, just as you would want to be supported. Allow them to live freely and openly while you do what you can to help. Never overstep their boundaries either. If they need more from you, they will ask you.

You do not have to pretend to be somebody's best friend who you do not get along with, but you can learn to be civil through the act of being less judgmental. You should not have a list of people that you hate or have grudges against. This is a heavy burden to bear, and it will not serve you well in any way.

1. **Expand Your Social Circle:** The top five people that you spend time around are thought to influence you the most. If you think about it, these people make up parts of your personality without you even realizing. Paying attention to who you are spending your time around can have a lot to do with your judgmental attitude. If you are constantly hearing others being judgmental, then it is going to feel natural to exhibit the same behaviors. You need to think about your inner circle to determine if they are the best people to keep close to you.

If you do feel that you need more positive people in your life, now is the perfect time to expand your social circle. Try to find more people that you have things in common with and who are going to approach life with a positive attitude. These habits will rub off on you, and you will see that you can spend time around others that has nothing to do with criticism or judgment. Being judgmental is definitely a learned behavior, but it is also one that can fortunately be unlearned.

To expand your social circle, you do not need to go out and find a completely new group of friends. You can do so by taking up a new hobby or trying a class that you have been meaning to try. Through these actions, you will be bound to meet others who have things in common with you. By starting out your interactions this way, you can be sure that you are not coming from a negative or judgmental place. It will be nice to have people you can rely on who not only have the same things in common with you but who also want to spread positive energy.

Getting to know other people can be an enriching experience. Just because you live in the same place does not mean you had the same upbringing, cultural values, or childhoods. There is a lot that can be learned by simply having a conversation with someone and asking them questions about their lives. Be open-minded while you listen.

1. **Show Yourself Compassion:** One of the final steps toward becoming a non-judgmental individual is removing the judgment that you place on yourself daily. You never know how hard you are on yourself until you take the time to think about it. Since you are your own worst critic, it could come very natural to you. If you make a mistake or do something wrong, it can be very easy to degrade yourself and make you feel even worse about what you have done—this is not constructive in any way.

While you can show remorse and make amends, you need to make it a point to learn from your mistakes. Prove to yourself that you can be a better human rather than judging yourself for your behavior. When you shift this focus, you are actually going to feel motivated to change for the better instead of putting yourself down and doing nothing else.

Do your best to forgive yourself. While you might be able to move on from the things that you regret, have you really taken the time to forgive yourself? Do this from now on, making it a focus to release any resentment that you might be holding onto. This resentment can be released at any moment. As you know, it might even be directed at the wrong person through your RJ. Take it easy on yourself, and make amends in a way that feels good to you.

Action Step

You are going to read a book on spirituality to further enlighten yourself. This book can be any that you choose, one that looks interesting to you. Before you make your selection, make sure that you see all of the options that are available. If you can think of a topic beforehand, this will make it easier for you to find what you are looking for. Some great authors include Deepak Chopra, Eckhart Tolle, and others like them. These are great starting points if you have absolutely no idea where to begin. Think of the book you choose as a tool that is going to help you overcome your RJ.

Next, you are going to set aside five minutes each day to meditate. You can meditate in any style that you wish, but make this commitment to yourself. Even if you feel dumb or like you do not know what you are doing, the practice will become familiar to you. Since you were not born knowing how to ride a bike, you can see that you will learn how to meditate in a way that is conducive to your personal growth. Focus on a positive intention that you would like to manifest in your life. This can be anything meaningful to you.

The final step is to practice non-attachment daily. This means that you are going to stop taking everything so personally! Consider that not every situation or decision revolves around you. Since you do not know exactly what others are thinking, you cannot prove that you were a part of the equation in the first place. Simply observe, then act accordingly. Do not judge anything at all, including yourself or your own thoughts.

15

EXERCISES YOU CAN EASILY DO AT HOME TO DISSOLVE RETROACTIVE JEALOUSY

You need exercises that are effective and easy to implement from home. All of the exercises and methods in this book are meant to help you right here and right now. You are going to banish your RJ for good and learn to live a much healthier way of life. Mentally, you will feel rejuvenated and refreshed, no longer bothered by all of the little things that used to irk you. As you work through each of these exercises and get a better understanding of what neuro-associations are, think about them as new lessons learned—you are not going to know everything right away. This takes time, but you will get there!

Neuro-Associations

Much more complicated than they sound, neuro-associations are what happens when your nervous system links pain or pleasure to certain situations. This is very similar to word association. When you hear the word "dog," for example, you probably think of a specific dog. Your neuro-associations affect your behavior because they can get you to react both positively and negatively. Depending on what you associate with each situation, this is going to determine what you choose to do. This is why RJ can be such a familiar choice—you have made a neuro-association with it in regard to certain situations, things, places, or even people.

Neuro-associations are something that happens when you are young, usually during childhood. They are not something that you can choose to program into your brain. You were conditioned to believe in these things, and this is why it can be so hard to alter the behavior. Even though you have this set of neuro-associations in your brain, you can use them as leverage to train yourself to see the bigger picture. By choosing to associate something pleasurable with whatever it is that you need to overcome your RJ, you are training yourself to become non-reactive to the triggers that cause you to feel jealous.

To do this, you can follow these steps:

1. Define what triggers your jealousy. This can be anything, as it is something that is personal to you. Do not dissect it or place any judgment on it—that is not the purpose of the exercise. The purpose is to be able to clearly identify what bothers you and why.
2. Next, select something pleasant that you love and that makes you feel good. This can be anything in the world, as long as you can focus on it for long periods of time. This is going to become your tool to directly combat your RJ and to retrain your neuro-associations.
3. Once you have this pleasant thought to focus on when you feel jealousy brewing, you will combine it with an activity such as deep thought, meditation, EFT tapping (which you will learn more about), yoga, and even what you eat. All of these activities can be combined to completely transform the way that you feel.
4. Another option that you can take is to combat your RJ triggers head-on. If you know that something triggers you, directly fight back by using your pleasant association. Fill your mind with this uplifting thought rather than the triggering one. This takes a lot of willpower, but you will become better at it the more that you practice. Your neuro-

associations will surely begin to change no matter which method you choose.
5. If you have any negative associations that keep popping up when you are feeling triggered, you can program yourself to link the feeling of pain to these associations. This is the other aspect of neuro-associations and how they work. By associating pain with a trigger, your mind is not going to want to return to this feeling if it can help it. This will actually create an aversion to it. When you find yourself getting lost in your RJ, think about how this pains you and negatively impacts your life. It could be the motivation that you need to get out of this self-imposed rut.

Instant gratification is not going to fix your problem with RJ, though it can make it feel better for a short while. If you go out drinking with your friends or buy yourself an expensive gift, this is naturally going to give you a little rush of dopamine. You might feel like your RJ has been cured and that you can move on with your life—this is only temporary, though. You are fooling your brain into thinking that the problem is gone when it is actually only being suppressed.

There are many vices that you can rely on for instant gratification. Some of which include alcohol, drugs, sex, gambling, or food. Anything that allows you to indulge and forget why you are feeling jealous can be detrimental to your health when used improperly. Try to pay attention to what you do to fill these voids when you are feeling jealous. You must learn how to focus on the suffering that is happening as it is happening and what you can do to fix it for the long term. Ultimately, this is going to lead you to live a much better life.

Understand that your vices are holding you back from permanently healing. You can temporarily heal your RJ, but it is bound to return the next time you are triggered. This is why it is so powerful. Make sure that you are really getting to the bottom of your issues and that you want to seek help in the long run. To do this, you might have to think about your future—think about the life you want to have years from now. You no longer want to be controlled by your jealousy or ill feelings toward other people. The life that you live will be filled with the abundance that you can be proud of.

Tony Robbins and His Wisdom

In his book *Awaken the Giant Within*, Tony Robbins writes that most people strive to do the things that will avoid pain and will bring pleasure in abundance. It is not a new practice but a natural one. We all want to feel good, and we want to do so without challenges or problems. This is part of human nature, and it is easy to understand why our brains start to form neuro-associations with certain situations because of this. It can be eye-opening because it truly makes you realize why you do the things that you do. Everything from the food that you buy at the grocery store to the places you go to have fun on your days off can all revolve around neuro-associations.

You are scared to do certain things in life because you have formed neuro-associations with pain. Maybe you have had experiences in the past that caused you to feel this way, or maybe you just developed them recently. No matter how long these neuro-associations have been formed, it is not too late to change them. You can alter them to your advantage, and you can do this by simply becoming aware of when you are relying on them. They will change your behavior at times, causing you to make choices that will avoid situations or people that might cause you pain, even if the threat is not imminent. You need to be aware that this is avoidant behavior that could be holding you back.

Maybe chocolate is your favorite indulgence, but you worry about eating too much because this can lead to diabetes and other health concerns. This is a neuro-association that you have made with the food, creating an unhealthy correlation. The same thing can happen with anything that you feel jealous or strongly about. Tony Robbins reminds us that it is not only about black-and-white thinking—there is in-betweens, moderation. You can eat a little chocolate to indulge yourself without developing diabetes in the process. Learn your limits and you will succeed.

EFT Tapping

EFT stands for emotional freedom technique, and it is a method that aims to reprogram those beliefs in your brain that fuel your jealousy. There are five steps to this anxiety-reducing technique that can help to make your life a lot easier and a lot less controlled by your persistent RJ. EFT tapping will become incredibly useful to you because it is not only scientifically proven but also easy to do from the comfort of your own home. Anyone can practice this method after being given the proper steps. This is something that should absolutely become a part of your daily routine. It will help you make tremendous progress with your fight against being a jealous person.

Basically, EFT tapping is a form of psychological acupressure. It can be used to treat pain along with emotional distress, two very prominent symptoms that you experience when you are frequently jealous. This is because your body is always tensed up and your mind is racing with too many thoughts. EFT tapping will release all of this tension and stress for you, while also teaching you how to associate pleasure and pleasant thoughts with the problems that you are experiencing.

Scientifically, the healing method works by focusing on your meridian points. These are energy hot spots that your body stores energy in for later use. By placing acupressure energy into these very specific spots, it triggers your body into releasing this energy and will balance your body. With this balance in place, you will feel better both physically and mentally. This is not a new concept, as acupressure has been used in Chinese medicine for centuries. It is something that you can try in your own town, likely at a clinic that is not too far from your home.

With its rise in popularity, acupressure has become just as common as visiting a chiropractor or a dermatologist. If you have a stress problem, then acupressure is the way to go. The following are the steps necessary to complete this method and to begin healing:

Step 1

It is time to identify the issue. You will begin by thinking about the issue you are experiencing or the fear that you are facing. Try to focus on only one at a time during each EFT tapping session. This will help to ensure that you are truly eliminating all of your RJ. Your outcome will be a lot more enhanced when you can focus this way. It takes practice to do so, but try to think about it before you go in for your acupressure appointment.

Remember that the point of identifying is not to cause distress. You are not to live through the situation once again for the purpose of torturing yourself. The point is to simply identify what is bothering you and why. Leave it at that, and allow the technique to help you heal. Really focus on the issue because this is what you will be thinking about when you are going to start tapping. Make sure that you have a clear picture of it in your mind.

Step 2

Once you figure out what the problem is, you must test your intensity levels. This is basically like testing your boundaries. See how much you can think about the problem before it gets to the point where it triggers you. This means that you should be able to think about it without fully entering a point where you feel jealous. This part takes a lot of practice, as it should.

You must set a benchmark for yourself, and this is entirely personal. You can use a scale to help you from 0-10. With this scale, you can rate how difficult the problem is with 10 being the most difficult. You will use this scale to address both physical and emotional pain that you feel while you are focusing on the issue. The purpose of establishing this benchmark is to track your progress. For example, if your issue was a 10 before EFT tapping and a five after, then you will see that it is helping.

Step 3

Before the tapping begins, you need to figure out a phrase that you can use to explain what you are trying to address. For example, if you are worried that your partner is cheating on you, then you might want to make a phrase that acknowledges the issue while also accepting yourself. It could be something like, "Even though I am worried that my partner will cheat on me, I deeply and completely accept myself as a person." Your fears and your jealousy does not make you a bad person or any less of a person.

The above example is a common way to set up any phrase for your

EFT tapping sessions. No matter what situation you are facing, you can use that as a template to help you come up with an appropriate phrase each time. Again, the point of this step is not to bring back any trauma or triggers. You must simply learn how to face the issue head-on without it getting the best of you. It is great practice before the EFT tapping session begins.

Step 4

This is the most technical step of the entire process. This is how the tapping is going to take place. You do not need to necessarily memorize the sequence, you can say different phrases during each of your sessions if you would like. While there are 12 major meridian points, acupressure focuses on nine of them. The sequence begins by tapping methodically on these points in this order:

- Small intestine or "karate chop" (you will recite your phrase three times)
- Eyebrow—tapping seven times
- Side of the eye—tapping seven times
- Under the eye—tapping seven times
- Under the nose—tapping seven times
- Chin—tapping seven times
- Beginning of the collarbone—tapping seven times
- Under the arm/side of ribcage—tapping seven times

After this sequence is complete, you will finish with tapping the point at the very top of your head. As the tapping is ongoing, remember to think about your phrase and to focus on the problem that you are there to fix. You can see that it is a simple practice, but it can be too much to think about to perform on your own while simultaneously trying to heal.

Step 5

The final step is simply a test. Keeping in mind the benchmark that you originally set for yourself, judge how the problem felt before, during, and after your acupressure session. If the intensity went down, then this is a positive sign that the session relieved some of your tension.

The results are cumulative, and you might have to try it a few times before you notice a positive effect.

Once you are able to see real results, you will feel amazing. Watching the intensity scale go down is such a fulfilling feeling. Your final goal should be to reach a zero. Once you reach this point, you can switch your focus on another issue. Repeat this until you have worked through every single one. EFT tapping is a very methodical and sensical healing method, and it will benefit you greatly.

After you do all of these steps, your brain will send positive signals to the areas that control stress. It is almost like the EFT tapping is telling your brain that it is okay to let your guard down now. This can be entirely necessary when you deal with RJ, especially because you normally cannot control it on your own. By stimulating these meridian points on your body, EFT tapping can truly change your entire life and your mindset. If you are unsure of how to effectively practice EFT tapping, then please look it up on YouTube. There are countless videos you can tap along too. I recommend tapping on the subjects of Intrusive Thoughts, Triggers, and Insecurity. It is easy and free to do, in the comfort of your own home.

Meet Your Squadron

You are not alone in your fight to defeat RJ. You actually have an entire team of soldiers who are ready and able to fight for you! Think of these tactics as your team of mercenaries. They are there to protect you in case you feel like your jealousy is taking over your life. With the help of these five soldiers, you are going to have a different method of tackling your RJ and all that comes with it. This puts you in a powerful position because you will be able to release yourself from any traps or tricks that your RJ is responsible for. All you need to do is rely on the help that you have from your team.

Soldier #1—Sergeant: EFT Tapping

This is the technique that leads the squad because it is so comprehensive. As you have just learned, EFT tapping is a way for you to release both physical and mental tension. It is an impressive force to be reckoned with that will never let you down. Arguably, this is the most effective method for dealing with RJ that you will find, so make sure to use it often. The more that you practice, the better it will feel. Even if you cannot go to a professional, you can still follow along with instructional videos at home.

Because EFT tapping is designed to reprogram your brain, you will not have to worry about your RJ returning. If you practice EFT tapping enough and make it a part of your regular routine, you will see how much more difficult it is for the jealousy to get to you. Your mind is going to operate on a different level, one that is much calmer and much more positive. The jealousy that you once felt is going to completely dissolve. While EFT tapping seems very simple, there is a lot of science and logic behind it—do not underestimate its power.

Soldier #2—Second in Command: Meditation/Mindfulness

This technique is the epitome of mind over matter. You will use your thoughts and your calmness to redirect all of your negative and jealous thoughts. When you are meditating or in a state of mindfulness, picture a river before you. Any thoughts that are related to RJ can continue to float down the river, far away from you. The thoughts that are neutral or positive can stay close by. Maybe you will choose to scoop them up out of the water to take with you.

As you are meditating and being mindful, notice how you feel like you have much more control of your life. Living in a peaceful state is a much better way to live than to feel like you are constantly being controlled by jealousy. It takes a lot of willpower, but you can do this. You can completely transform your mindset to better suit your newfound peaceful lifestyle. When you are dealing with triggers, this soldier is particularly helpful because it can focus on demolishing the trigger head-on. That trigger will not stand a chance when you give yourself something else to focus on. Your intrusive thoughts might not stop for good (with only mindfulness used as a technique alone), but you can be sure to stop them in their tracks when you are in a meditative or mindful state.

Soldier #3—Affirmations

Your affirmations are all little reminders of what you stand for and who you are. They are self-guided chants that you can direct to yourself in front of a mirror or even when you are in the car while driving to work. Use positive affirmations when you need a quick boost of self-confidence. They can be anything from reminders that you are strong to how amazing you are at completing a specific task. Think about all of the things that you are good at, and speak these truths aloud to yourself often.

Since you can use affirmations at any time, repeat them to yourself when you can feel your RJ trying to creep in. While the jealousy might make its way through, it will be met directly with affirmations to shut it down. You are an astounding person, and you must keep telling yourself this until you truly believe it. The more that you practice reciting affirmations, the truer they become. You will feel empowered, like a whole new person.

Soldier #4—Trauma Release Exercises (TRE)

A TRE is very helpful because it works deep to fight against your RJ. This soldier is similar to yoga in the sense that you will be lying down on your back. Pick a comfortable spot, and use a yoga mat to support yourself. To release the trauma, you are going to be releasing the tension in your lower back, neck, and shoulders. These are the points in your body that tend to hold onto a lot of stress. By placing both arms firmly at your sides, you will gently lift your hips up into the air. Hold this position for 10-15 seconds so that you can feel the tension leaving your body.

This exercise is not meant to be too challenging or painful. The point of it is to make you feel more comfortable and to release all of that tension that you are probably unknowingly holding onto. Make sure that you do this slowly and deliberatively. This is one that you do not need to rush. Use this soldier to help you when you have a little extra time. Make sure that you have a place where you can perform your TRE that feels like a sanctuary. Also, ensure that you will have privacy. This is an act of self-care.

Soldier #5—Breathwork/Pranayama

The final soldier that can step in to help you is your breathing. Believe it or not, the way that you breathe can actually crush RJ on the spot. This is another great technique to use anywhere. When you breathe in for seven seconds and breathe out for seven seconds, this balances out your circadian rhythm. Everything in your body will feel harmonious, and you will instantly feel mentally calmer. Use this method the next time that you can feel your blood start to boil from RJ. If seven seconds feels like it is too long, you can start with four. Find the magic number that works best for you.

Pranayama breathing is a bit more complex. You can do this when you have some alone time and privacy. Begin by lying down on your back and emptying all of the air from your lungs. Using your thumb, block your right nostril. Inhale only through your left. As you do this, make sure you are filling your belly with air and not your chest. After you are full with a breath, pinch both nostrils closed completely. Hold for a moment, then release your thumb to exhale only out of your right nostril. You will complete this process using both sides of your nose.

Action Step

You are going to pick out 10 affirmations that you plan on reciting to yourself in the mirror. These all need to be uplifting and believable. You can either say them as you are getting ready for work or before you go to sleep at night. You can even say them aloud in your car to yourself during your morning commute if you feel that you do not have the time. There is always time for what is important to you, and you must make healing a priority. You do not want to be stuck in the trap of jealousy any longer. In succession with these statements, you are going to pick a power move. This can be something like envisioning yourself as the most successful and best version of you that you can imagine. The visuals and auditory affirmations will help you.

Commit to trying EFT tapping at least once a day this week. You can try it at home by following along with an instructional video on YouTube in under 5 minutes. See how the process feels and how it works out for you. EFT tapping is arguably the most powerful tool you are given in this book, so you must learn to use it wisely. Use it to your full advantage.

16

YOUR JEALOUSY IS A HUNGRY MONSTER. STARVE IT!

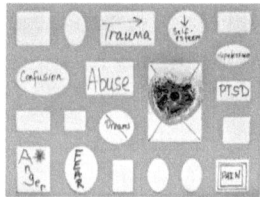

When you have RJ, you probably also have anxiety. The jealousy becomes so strong that it pushes you to the point of worrying all the time. This is a terrible feeling to live with, and it can get in the way of a lot of your goals if you do not stop it. Many who suffer from RJ not only experience anxiety but also panic attacks. These are terrible because they will literally stop you in your tracks. Panic attacks make you feel like nothing is ever going to be okay again, and it can take a while to calm yourself down if you are not experienced in dealing with them. This chapter is all about how to tame and starve the beast. You will no longer be indebted to the jealousy monster that tries to take control of you and makes you worry all the time.

When you try to poke and prod at your partner's past, you are going to hear things or discover things that you do not like—it is inevitable. This is when the jealousy monster has an opportunity for release. Stop torturing yourself! The past is in the past for a reason, and you must focus on the present if you want to find a way to be happy again. The more that you look into your partner's past, even just a glimpse, the more that you are feeding your RJ. If you think about it, this makes it stronger. You should avoid this at all costs because you are just making life more difficult for yourself.

There will be times when you are very triggered, and you must learn how to momentarily sit with this discomfort. Most who struggle with anxiety give in to their fight-or-flight response when triggered. You must teach yourself how to sit still until the trigger retreats. This moment will pass. To do this, try to get to a place where you can physically be alone. When you are alone, you will be less tempted to be reactive, like asking your partner about their ex, for example. Put your phone away for a moment, and get rid of any other distractions around you. Sit in solitude, no matter how uncomfortable it is. You need to learn how to breathe through this moment. You will prove to yourself that you can do it and that the worried feeling will go away. Also, this exercise shows you that you can challenge your triggers without getting emotionally involved.

When you are facing a trigger, picture it as an ice cube. Drop it in a hot glass of water and watch it dwindle down into nothing. As you imagine this, you might be feeling both emotional and physical pain. Allow yourself to breathe through it until the metaphorical ice cube has fully melted in the hot water. Once it is gone, write down what triggered you in a journal. Keeping a trigger journal is super useful because it will remind you of what bothers you and what you should avoid. It will also bring up any patterns that are in place, providing you with ways to stop cycles. You can mark down the date, time, and place where you experienced the trigger that you just melted away. Keep track of each instance.

How to Avoid Triggers

One of the worst things you can do is snoop around your partner's social media accounts—this is going to be incredibly triggering! Even if your partner is 100% faithful to you, there will still be messages, comments, and posts that will likely trigger you because of your sensitive nature. RJ can be ruthless when it comes to the past, trying to convince you that it is happening right now. If you were to see an old photo with your partner and their ex, what could this do to your self-esteem? You do not need to find out, which is why you should never snoop around.

Looking at your partner's phone without their permission also shows that there is a lack of trust in the relationship. It says a lot about you as a person, and this can be another issue that you will need to resolve before moving forward into healthier territory. This is a very damaging and detrimental trait because your partner is always going to feel like they are doing something wrong. You will have also taken away their privacy that they deserve. Just because you two are dating does not mean you need to know every single thing that they do on their phone or have on their phone. If there is love and trust, then the foundation of the relationship will be strong. You should not feel the need to go through it.

Think about places that might also be triggering. These places can be bars, restaurants, clubs, stores, and other locations that your partner has been with their ex. If it bothers you this much and if it is all you can think about, avoid these places. There are plenty of other locations that you can visit that will not bring up triggers. Explain to your partner why this is triggering and how it makes you feel. This should not be a big deal, and your partner should be understanding about the issue. If a memory is painful to you, this is valid. Your feelings are always valid.

It is not always going to be easy, but you need to stop questioning your partner about the past. Stop asking about their ex or what they did together. Stop asking about what their favorite things about their ex were. This information is only going to hurt you, so there is no reason for you to familiarize yourself with it. Try to focus on the present, right here and now—your partner is with you for a reason. If they still wanted to be with their ex, they would not have broken up in the first place. Remember this the next time that your RJ strikes and tries to convince you to question them.

To truly kill the beast that is RJ, you need to starve it. Asking about the past and snooping around only feeds it! These are some methods you can use to avoid being triggered and to live your life as happily and as carefree as possible:

Become Aware

The first step is to become aware that you are being triggered. When you see something that makes you feel insane bouts of RJ, do not become reactive. Pause for a moment to figure out what caused you to feel this way. Identify it, and look it straight in the eyes. This is your trigger, and this is what you are not going to give into or let control you.

Having awareness means that you have power. With this awareness, you will feel like you have many choices, which is very true. You get to control how you handle this trigger and what the next step will be. The trigger will no longer hold any of the power that it used to. There is a difference between awareness and emotional involvement—remember this. Becoming aware does not mean you need to become upset. Simply observe what is happening.

Identify Why Your Needs Are Not Being Met

When you are experiencing a trigger, there is a voice inside of you that tells you that there is something you are lacking. With jealousy, it is common to compare yourself to other people. So, what is it that this trigger is making you feel that you are lacking? Ask yourself this question, and try hard to come up with a detailed answer. This will help you to better understand why the situation, place, or person is bothering you so much.

If your needs are not being met, your brain is more willing to go to great lengths to fulfill them. This can include some of the reactive behaviors that you typically have to your RJ triggers. It is not always healthy to act on them, and it becomes a very stressful way to live. You can avoid this situation entirely by simply identifying on your own why your needs are not being met and what you can do about this.

Recognize the Illusion

A trigger causes you to think unclearly. What is normally a rational thought will be turned into something that is convoluted by jealousy. You need to recognize that this is an illusion. When you see something triggering regarding your partner or their ex, your brain might want to jump to a place that tells you that your partner is going to cheat on you, for example. This is the illusion that RJ is trying to create for you.

The more that you feed into the illusion, the more miserable you will become. Just as you have to learn to recognize your triggers, you must also learn to recognize when something is just not realistic. Think about the concrete facts. Has your partner expressed that they want to leave you? Have they verbally communicated that they want their ex back? If you can answer no to these questions, then these are the concrete facts that you are working with right now—use them to your advantage.

Avoid or Grow

You have a choice when it comes to being triggered—you can either choose to avoid your triggers entirely, or you can face them head-on and learn to grow stronger than them. There is no wrong answer here. This all depends on your current comfort level and what you feel is best for you. Keep in mind, you can avoid or grow at any point during any time you feel triggered.

This is a decision that must be made when you are feeling triggered because you will eventually need to take action. Letting a trigger fester is only going to upset you and allow the RJ monster to take over. Remember, you do not want to feed the monster—you need to learn how to starve it.

Why Social Media is Toxic

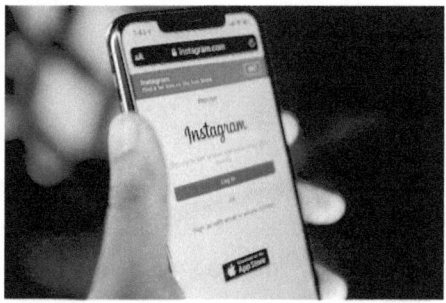

If you are on social media, then you already know how detrimental it can be to your RJ. One post or comment, and this can send you down a dark spiral of jealousy. Most of the time, social media is going to trigger you if you are not careful because people can portray their lives and themselves exactly how they want others to view them. This is not reality, and it is hard to remember this when you are seeing it all over your timeline and newsfeed. In today's society, almost everybody is engrossed in social media and posting on it. This is how we all keep up with one another, what we are doing and where we are. You do not need to indulge in social media if it is worsening your RJ.

Social Media Has Become a Marketplace

What was once a simple way to keep in touch with friends and family has now become a platform for consumerism to exist. You have noticed that social media now has advertisements left and right. Not to mention, your loved ones are also probably feeding into this marketplace by trying their hand at starting a "side gig" for additional income. There is nothing wrong with this aspect of the platforms, but this is one way that social media can actually make you feel down or even jealous. Without even realizing it, you are being pressured to make purchases and to change things about yourself subconsciously.

What is even worse is that these platforms are encouraging these marketplace aspects more and more. The people that own them are profiting off of others who are trying to sell and by collaborating with brands to form brand deals. Everyone is getting richer, and this is making you feel bad about yourself indirectly. Think about what social media actually means to you, the value that it brings to your life. It might not be as positive as you perceive it to be or positive at all. If you can only bring up negative points, it might be a sign that you should take a break from the platforms that you browse and post on.

Social Status Exists on Social Media

Even if you do not buy into the lavish lifestyles that are being portrayed on social media, there is somewhat of a social status quo that goes on underneath it all. If you do not have the latest technology, a nice car, or a wonderful home, then you get placed in a lower class. These "influencers" that try to show off their material possessions make a lot of people feel bad about themselves because it feels like they are bragging. Not everybody can afford to live this way, nor do they want to live this way. This can definitely trigger you without even realizing it.

Not knowing an influencer personally does not mean you are safe from this social status quo. Your friends and loved ones are seeing the same content. They might be trying to emulate some of it from their favorite accounts. There is nothing wrong with this if this is how they want to live, but you must ask yourself if it is negatively affecting your self-esteem. With low self-esteem comes more chances for your RJ to attack. What you must be aware of is your energy and how well you are protecting it. If something is not contributing positivity to your life, ask yourself if you really need it in your life at all.

Personal Data is At Risk

Each time that you log onto your social media accounts, your personal data is being sold to the highest bidder. No matter how careful you are, you have definitely realized by now that some ads you see on social media are specifically targeted toward your direct needs and interests. This is not happening by chance or coincidence—this is happening because your data is being sold to companies that are paid to observe and to market. There is a whole scheme that goes on beyond what people post and share on these platforms. It is much more personalized than it seems, and you are definitely a target if you use social media.

This is not meant to be a scary thought but a realistic one. Consider that what you see on your timeline is being marketed to you for a reason. When you are experiencing issues with jealousy and being triggered, this makes you weaker and more likely to make purchases that you would not normally make. This is exactly how these bigger companies suck people in—they want you to look at their ads and buy their items or services. They know that this will interest you because they already know way more about you than you think they do.

Users Are Being Sensationalized

What you see on social media creates a standard for the way that you live. In many cases, this is damaging relationships because it creates unhealthy expectations for couples around the world. You might see trends going around that portray "couple goals" and photos or videos of happy, smiling people that seem to have it all. This is very similar to the materialism fad that goes on around social media. You will see this, and there is a chance that it could make you feel bad about yourself. If you and your partner do not operate this way, your brain becomes insecure. You might start to question what is wrong with you and why you do not have this.

The images and videos that are being presented to you are influencing you all the time. Even when you are not on social media, this content sticks with you. It can decide how you act in the future and even how you look. This is a very powerful beast that almost compares to RJ in many ways if you are not careful. Think about how you are using social media and what it is currently adding to your life. You might need to do a detox with your friends' list and who you follow. This can help to make sure that you are getting nothing but positivity from the experience.

There are many other reasons why social media can become detrimental to your mental health, but these are some of the most common today. Keep this in mind the next time that you are casually browsing an app. This is not to say that you must banish all social media from your life, but it gives you a new perspective and awareness that you can use to beat your RJ monster.

RJ is Powerless

Your jealousy has no power over you, no matter how strong it can feel at times. RJ is actually powerless, and you have yet to discover this! This is not something that should be scary to you or cause you any stress because you are much stronger than you think. Your inner strength will surprise you as you take the time to work on combating your RJ for good. Think of this as a permanent step you are taking in the right direction, not merely a temporary form of instant gratification. You are going to feel better, and you are going to continue to feel this way for a long time.

One main way to take all of the power away from your RJ is to simply stop talking about it. Do not bring it up to your friends. Stop venting about it. The fewer conversations you have regarding your jealousy, the less powerful it becomes. Your words give it power, and these words can cause you great harm because they also make you feel fearful on a daily basis. You will see how much of a difference it makes when you discontinue the narrative about your RJ and focus on the things in life that are actually worth your time. Talk about the things that you want more of in abundance—this is manifestation.

It is your choice to give in to your triggers. Remember this and you will never choose to think about them or your RJ again. Make the decision to do the complete opposite by learning how to manifest what you want and need. Over time, you might even start to recognize how absurd some of your old triggers seem now. Looking back on the progress you have made, you will understand why you had to take away this power. Your RJ deserves nothing and it has nothing on you!

How to Manifest

Manifestation is a simple concept—you think about what you want, and you receive it. This sounds like magic, but it is not. All you are doing is collecting your positive energy and putting it to good use. You can manifest anything you want in your life, and this will work to combat your RJ by bringing forth more good than bad. You can single handedly bring about the manifestation of your RJ's defeat. You must have already won the fight in your mind, even if it feels impossible right now.

1. **Be Clear:** You must be very specific about what you want. Try to get as detailed as possible. You can do this by thinking about what would benefit your life the most right now. By manifesting one thing at a time, you are going to harness more power and energy. Think carefully about what you choose to manifest because the process can often happen quicker than you think it will. You not only have to be clear with the universe, but you have to be clear with yourself regarding what your priorities are.
2. **Ask the Universe:** Even if you are not a believer in a specific religion, you can still acknowledge that the universe is a great big place. It is bigger than any one person, place, or thing. Ask the universe for what you want when you manifest. This is how you are going to get what you desire. You need to ask for it and be grateful for the opportunity to ask.
3. **Work Toward Your Goals:** Just because you are manifesting greatness does not mean you can stop working hard. Keep working toward those goals that you have! Doing double duty by working hard and manifesting is only going to bring you extra positivity. Plus, you will feel proud of yourself for all of the work that you are putting toward the bettering of your life. You can do this, and you will do it with ease.

4. **Trust the Process:** When you have never manifested before, it might seem hard to believe that something like this is real. You need to trust the process before you begin. Put your belief into something unknown for once. This can feel a little scary or weird at first, but manifestation will prove itself to you every time. Trust in what you are asking for, and believe 100% that you are going to receive it. Any time you allow self-doubt to creep in, you are letting RJ win.
5. **Acknowledge What You Receive:** You might not receive what you are asking for all at once. Pay attention to the smaller gifts that you are receiving. Acknowledge that these great things are coming your way because you asked for them. You put that energy out there to attract the things that you want. When you can be grateful for the little things, reaching your end goal is going to feel like the ultimate grand prize. Keep your head up, and look around. There is so much that you currently have to be thankful for.
6. **Keep Your Vibration High:** Every human being on the planet has an energetic vibration. This is the energy that you feel when you encounter someone, the "vibe" that they put out. Make sure yours is high and functioning well at all times. When you have a high vibration, this means that you are always seeking something bigger and better. You have a positive mindset and a great attitude. It is important to keep your vibration high because this will directly correlate with the results of your manifestations.
7. **Clear Your Resistance:** You might begin to feel restless when your needs are not being met instantly. This is a bad habit that you must break. Replace this with patience. You need to clear this resistance because it will stand in the way of your efforts to manifest. Stop trying to be a control freak, and understand that the universe has its own way of doing things that you cannot always have a say in. Try your best to be open-minded and accepting of all that comes to you. There is always a lesson to be learned if you look around.

Action Step

As mentioned earlier in this chapter, you should begin writing in a trigger journal. Your action step, for now, is to purchase a journal that you will specifically use for this purpose. Make sure that you choose one that you feel comfortable using all the time. Begin entering all of the most pertinent information regarding the times that you feel triggered. Mark down the dates, places, people, and situations that relate to each trigger. This is a way for you to keep track of what triggers you and the progress that you are making. You will be able to look back on what usually triggers you and how you are becoming stronger.

Another reminder for this action step is to put up a fight when your RJ starts to flare up. Do not back down. This is not the time to ignore what you are feeling. Acknowledge the discomfort, then do something about it! You have the knowledge now to use trauma release and EFT tapping exercises to clear up any additional trauma that is still stored deep within your subconscious. The sooner you do this, the easier it is going to be to fight back against RJ. When your mind is clear of clutter, you are going to feel so much better. You will experience fewer triggers, and you will feel better able to face RJ when it tries to take over your life.

17
CHANGE THE WAY YOU THINK ABOUT SEX (UNDOING SOCIAL CONDITIONING)

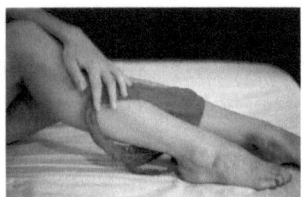

One of the most powerful tools that I have used to my own advantage was to perform a complete 180-degree transformation of the way that I viewed sex. You might be wondering what sex has to do with RJ—the connection is actually very prominent. Social conditioning and programming have you believing the way that you must feel about sex and even how often you should be having it. This conditioning happens silently, and you likely do not even realize that it is influencing you. From what you know now, you are probably aware that sex is a big cause of jealousy in relationships. Couples get into fights about sex all the time, and this is where a lot of insecurities derive from.

To change the way that you view sex, you must be willing to think about it and talk about it. In today's culture, it is almost taboo to openly talk about sex. This is something that you need to personally undo. Allow yourself to think about it, to analyze it. You need to be open to the idea that discussing sex is going to help you not only have a healthier sex life but also eradicate your RJ in the process. When you think about it, sex is simply an expression of life energy. I personally changed the way that I viewed sex by reminding myself that it is a natural act performed by most humans. No longer did I view sex as something unmentionable or dirty. I truly thought about the way that sex can be a very powerful healing force when used wisely.

AFTER LEARNING all about EFT tapping, you already know all about the benefits that you receive. You can use this practice regularly to also help to change the way that you view sex. Think about it in the most natural way possible. It is not something that you need to feel ashamed of. If you have sex, then you might as well embrace it. During your EFT tapping sessions, you can focus on changing your view of sex. This will help to eliminate a lot of the active jealousy that you are feeling.

Another way that you can use one of the techniques you have already learned is by associating sex with something positive instead of negative. Through neuro-association programming, you already know that you can change the way that you view situations by simply changing what you associate them with. Think about something incredibly positive when you think about sex. It is not something to feel ashamed of or something in your life that you need to hide. Having sex is natural. Because it is so natural, you can rest assured that the universe is not going to punish you for having sex. This can become a very healing sensation if you learn how to associate something positive with it.

The Chakras

There are seven chakras that are marked by certain points on your body. A chakra is basically just a base of energy. It is not something that you can physically see, but you can feel it if you focus. Sexual energy comes from your sacral chakra, which is located in the lowest part of your abdomen. This is where the sex organs are located, and it is applicable no matter which gender you identify with. From this chakra comes all of your sexual desire and energy. Interestingly enough, this is also the same point that your creative energy comes from. Putting this information together, you will find that sex and creativity might actually become two very useful resources that you can combine.

Many different artists and musicians often channel their sexual energy from the sacral chakra into their creative work. You have probably noticed this through pop culture over the years. It is not a new practice because it is natural. Anybody can feel this energy if they try hard enough to focus on it. From music to fashion, the sexual energy from the sacral chakra can become a huge influence. You must allow this natural energy to flow through you, as well. Even if you are not a musician or a fashion designer, you can still benefit from opening up your sacral chakra. This is going to become a very powerful move for you, and it will become yet another way for you to fight back against your RJ when it comes knocking.

No matter what sexual experiences you have had in the past, it is time to let go. Moving forward, you are only going to associate positivity with having sex. This is going to be your chance to completely transform the way you think, and it will be a powerful transformation for you. Through this, you will also notice a spark in your creativity. Everything that you say and do is going to be fueled by inspiration, and this is exactly how you should live your life if you no longer want to be controlled by RJ. Your life is going to flourish right before your eyes, and you will not even remember the way that jealousy made you feel. Your lust for life will be rejuvenated, and there will be so much positive energy for you to enjoy.

Knowledge is Power

You have been unknowingly blocking yourself from tapping into your sexual and creative energy by only paying attention to your jealousy and the negativity that comes with it. Not only does this impact you, but it also impacts your partner. If you have ever felt like there is a strain in your sexual relationship, then this could be one of the contributing factors. The good news is that you are well aware of how important the sacral chakra is now. You know that you have the power to harness this energy and to better your life. Once you do this, your partner is going to take notice. They will respond to you in a positive way once they see that you are an empowered and renewed individual.

Lately, you have actually been fighting hard against your creative energy. With RJ in your life, you have been blocking one of the most natural sources of energy that comes your way. You have been fighting against one of the main reasons why most human beings even exist—acting on sexual and creative energy. RJ creates a very huge roadblock that appears to stop you in your tracks. You might see it and feel discouraged, turning around without even trying to fight back. This stops now. You no longer need to endure the painfully exhausting path that RJ forces you on. Making your own path with the knowledge that you have is going to empower you.

To gain even more knowledge, you must learn about the opposite sex and how they view sex and relationships. This can become a massive resource for you to use against your RJ because it will give you a new perspective to view situations from. What might strike you as something negative could actually be something very positive to the opposite sex. Try to learn as much about biology as you can as well. These key differences that set you apart are actually the very same things that can bring you together. By making a commitment to learning more about the opposite sex, you are taking a proactive step toward banishing RJ from your life.

Retroactive Jealousy or FOMO?

Did you know that your retroactive jealousy might actually stem from the fact that you feel like you missed out on experiences that your partner has had? This sensation, better known as FOMO (fear of missing out), is much more common than you would imagine. Many people experience FOMO on a regular basis, but it depends on the way that you react to it that determines whether or not it transforms into RJ. You might simply be angry that your partner has different histories with people who are not you. If you have ever thought about the dates they went and gotten angry, then you are probably experiencing FOMO to a certain degree.

If you are the type of person who has not been with many sexual partners or engaged in many long-term relationships, there is a higher chance for you to experience FOMO because of your lack of experiences. This is not your fault, but it does mean that you need to learn how to control this jealousy that arises because of what you have or have not done. You have a choice here—either stay with your partner and make it work or live out your glory days and have these experiences you feel you missed out on. It really is that simple, and you need to think carefully about what you would like to do. You need to focus on your current priorities to see if your actions align with them.

When you experience FOMO, you are not always experiencing RJ. This is important to note because the way that you approach the situation can vary. When you feel like you have missed out on something but it is not detrimental to your life, this is not RJ. Remember that RJ is destructive. It causes you harm and makes you feel bad about yourself and your life. FOMO causes jealousy that you can usually bypass fairly easily. When you are in mental agony because of RJ, you will understand the difference between the two. RJ is a lot more intense, and it does not feel like something that you can initially get through.

The great news about banishing your RJ is that you will also be controlling your FOMO at the same time. All of the steps that you have taken so far and that you will take are going to combine together to get rid of your RJ and your FOMO. Because FOMO is lower than RJ in terms of how difficult it is to handle, it is also a little easier to get rid of. You will be able to live your life without living vicariously through someone else's. Above all, you should feel proud of the life you are living and happy with what you are doing.

Dating and FOMO

You are bound to experience FOMO in your relationship at some point in time. This has likely already happened to you, but what you must work on is preventing it from happening again. Through these proactive steps, you can truly get over the FOMO that you have or might have in the future. Overthinking is no longer going to be your most popular hobby. You will be able to move on from these consuming thoughts and focus on what you are doing and what you actually want from life.

1. **Ask Yourself What You Would Do if the Worst Were True:** One way to avoid becoming a victim to FOMO is something that might seem counterproductive. You should ask yourself

what you would really do if the worst thing imaginable were to become your reality. Think about your what-if scenarios, and imagine the very worst one that you can come up with. For most people, this is something like their partner cheating on them or leaving them. Whatever it is for you, capture this moment to sit with it for a moment.

What this will do is help you to realize that you have already been through the very worst moment in your life. Consider what you would categorize as the worst thing that has ever happened to you, and look at where you are now—you made it to the other side. You are still living your life, and you have moved on or are trying to move on from that issue. So, if this theory of the worst thing possible were to become your truth, you would still be okay. You would be able to move on from it.

While this is something that you do not want to happen, you can reassure yourself by encouraging yourself—you *can* get through anything that happens to you. Even if you are not in control of everything that happens, you are always in control of your actions. You get to decide how you react or if you even react at all. This should be an empowering thought that you can use to battle against FOMO.

You have coping skills that will guide you through these "worst" fears coming true. It might feel like this is really happening, but it is probably not. Regardless, you can still do your best to take note of what you can actually do to help yourself. Write all of your coping skills down to remind yourself of the power that you still hold in these situations. You can use any one of these skills or more when you are starting to feel down or when you can feel the FOMO creeping in. Surprisingly, it will help you more than you think when you can see all of the things you can do for yourself written down on paper.

1. **Reveal Your Anxiety to Your Partner:** It might feel natural to hide your anxiety from your partner because you do not want to come across as insecure or unattractive. The truth is, you need to be open and honest with them! No matter what you are feeling, they should know the truth. This is what

makes for a great relationship that allows the two of you to be closer than ever. Do not be afraid to talk about what gives you anxiety and where your FOMO stems from. Through your actions, your partner will also open up to you and feel comfortable talking about the same.

You could end up with reassurance when you hear about what your partner experiences and that they also feel FOMO. By opening up this narrative, the two of you will feel less alone in your insecurities. This will ironically give the two of you something to bond over, and it will bring you closer as a couple. Through this conversation, you will be able to talk about other personal insecurities that will help you as you work on becoming the best version of yourself.

Humor is a very important tool to use at any given time. If you can find a way to laugh at yourself about your anxiety or insecurities, then do it! You do not need to do this in a cruel or demeaning way, but you can learn to laugh at yourself by realizing that you have so much more control than you think you do. FOMO has nothing on you and neither does RJ.

You can also talk about your FOMO with others who are close to you. Having a conversation about it with your loved ones and best friends will show you that you are only human and you are not the only one who experiences these things. It is going to be okay! Bond with others who feel FOMO. You might even pick up on new techniques that they use that will help you to get over your own FOMO. You never know what might happen until you open up the floor for that conversation. Doing this, you are going to become even more comfortable facing your FOMO than before.

1. **Block Irrational; Replace With Rational:** You need to identify what you are telling yourself that is simply irrational. Write down these thoughts and worries that you have and examine them carefully. When you get the chance to see them on paper, this makes it easier for you to spot the culprits. For example, if you have a fear that your partner has

been thinking about his ex for years, you can pinpoint specific concrete facts that will prove you wrong. It can be hard to do, but you need to focus on only what is concrete and rational to banish your FOMO and RJ for good.

After each irrational thought that you write, make sure to circle it. From here, you can use a branching effect to write down all of the reasons why this is an irrational thought. Only write down clear, concrete facts. This means that if you do not have direct proof of being cheated on, then you are probably not being cheated on. This is not something that your brain needs to actively worry about or even think about. Create more rationality to balance out your emotions and to keep you in check.

Once you complete this exercise, make sure to save the page that you wrote everything down on. This is going to allow you to track your progress while simultaneously serving as a reminder of what is rational and what is not. Any time that your mind starts to wander, you can use this exercise to help you. FOMO will not stand a chance against you once you begin thinking more naturally out of habit.

Fear can create normalcy. It will be hard for you to complete the exercise at first, but do not get discouraged. You are just so used to thinking irrationally that FOMO has an easy time taking over. Soon, you will learn how to curb these thoughts by combating them with only the true, concrete facts. It takes up to three weeks to form a new habit, so you must give the exercise time to sink in. Allow it to become a part of your new routine and daily habits, if necessary.

1. **Actively Work on Your Identity and Goals:** When you have your own goals to focus on, you will be less likely to feel FOMO. This applies to relationships and otherwise. As an individual, you should have an idea of the things you want and what you are striving for in life. If you do not, now is the perfect time to explore these options for yourself! Think about what goals you currently have and how close you are to completing them. Have you taken any steps toward them

recently? This is going to become your new focus, and you are going to have an active purpose.

Keeping your mind busy is great for banishing jealousy, especially when you have a productive cause. Working toward your goals will make you feel accomplished, so you will have no reason to feel FOMO. Once you identify your goals, this is only the beginning. The next step comes with the plan of action. This is where you actually establish a deadline for each one and the steps necessary for completing them. Break each goal down into manageable steps.

You must actually start to work on the steps you outline for yourself. This becomes the next part of the process. By making sure that you are being proactive with your goals in mind, you will have a new reason to make the choices you make each day. Everything that you do will feel like it has a new purpose, and you will not even have time to consider giving in to FOMO or jealousy.

Do not forget to create both short-term and long-term goals for yourself. You can get a lot done when you plan for the near future and the far away future. This is why it is important to set deadlines for yourself. Make them reasonable, but challenge yourself to the point where you will actually be motivated to take action. Anything is possible when you have the passion and motivation to make it happen. You are going to feel like a newly energized version of yourself once you commit to your goals. Try your best to keep pushing forward, even when you want to stop and see what your partner has done or is doing in an attempt to compare your experiences.

1. **Do Not Be Paralyzed by Choices**: This step is easier said than done, but it will make your life a lot easier. When you can make decisions for yourself that are based on your own preferences, you will no longer feel paralyzed by situations that require this. FOMO tends to surface when you need to make a choice, and this is a prime chance for your jealousy to take control. You might compare your situation to one that your partner has been through, opting to make the same

decisions because of it. Think about what *you* want and need. It is not selfish to make choices that best suit your life.

You will never fully know if you are making the right decision until you make it. Through living the experience, you will discover if the choice is right for you. If it turns out to be unsuitable, make changes. This is how you grow as a person, and this is how you learn to make your own choices that are not influenced by FOMO or jealousy. It is okay to weigh your options carefully, but try not to spend too much time on this step. This is just going to give your fear a chance to take over.

Once you make your choice, commit to it. You need to believe in yourself by fully believing in the decision that you have made. Think about all of the ways it will benefit you and enhance your life. Letting doubt take over is almost as bad as letting FOMO or jealousy win—try your hardest not to let that happen! You can resist the feeling, as long as you are aware of it.

Either way, it is going to be a win-win situation for you. If it is the right choice on the first try, then you will be happy with your decision. If it feels wrong, you will get the chance to learn a life lesson that will help you make better choices in the future. Putting a positive spin on things like this really helps to put decision-making into perspective. You will learn that not all choices need to be daunting. They can be fun and exciting opportunities.

Action Step

Your goal for this action step is to complete an EFT tapping session every day for the next 30 days. This is a big commitment toward your health, both physically and mentally. It is going to benefit you by giving you the consistency that you need and the reassurance that your mind craves. Focus on changing the way that you think about sex. Remember, it is not something that you need to feel ashamed of or jealous about. Sex is an act of creation, whether it be life or energy shared with your partner. Try to adopt an attitude about sex that is healthy and positive.

Another part of your action step is to complete a sacral chakra yoga flow. You can follow along online or find a class to take locally. This will clear your mind of all the guilt and negativity that you have surrounding the topic of sex. Allow your creativity and sensuality to flow! You will see that you can live a more carefree life when you unblock this chakra and allow yourself to truly thrive the way you were meant to be. It can feel a little foreign at first, but this type of focused yoga flow will help you to embrace who you are as a person.

18

WHY YOUR MIND IS LOCKED IN THIS NIGHTMARISH CYCLE

You need more explanations as to why your mind cannot let go of the RJ that you feel on a daily basis—this is where science comes into play. RJ can be explained scientifically just as easily as it can be explained emotionally. This is because science plays a big role in the process. Your mind keeps returning to these obsessive thoughts for a reason, and that reason often seems beyond your control. Many of these thoughts likely stem from fears or worries about your partner's exes. Whether you compare yourself to them or are worried about them reappearing in your partner's life, these thoughts are unhealthy to carry around with you. It is like having dead weight with you that holds you back.

Obsessive Compulsive Disorder, or OCD, is a mental illness that causes you to feel fearful in a way that is unavoidable. For this reason, you will likely experience severe anxiety that makes you feel like something is very wrong or that something bad is going to happen. Eventually, this can result in you taking certain actions that might be destructive in a way that is detrimental to your life. As hindering as OCD is, not everybody who suffers from RJ has OCD. This is an illness that must be diagnosed by a medical professional. However, there is a lot that you can learn when you realize that you might have some OCD tendencies.

To get a better idea of what you are experiencing, here is a list of typical OCD tendencies that you can likely identify with:

- Need for extreme order/control
- Excessive doubt
- Fear of embarrassment
- Warped ideas regarding sex or sexual experiences
- Constantly checking or double-checking
- Repetitively counting
- Need for a consistent routine resulting in failure to function without one

These are only a few tendencies that you might have experienced, and they are all closely linked to OCD. These tendencies make your RJ flare up, causing you to feel worse about the situation that you are focused on. Keep in mind that your mind is very powerful. It can create thoughts that you believe are so true, but there might not be any truth to them at all. It is through a physical examination by a medical professional that you will be able to rule out any other illnesses that might be causing you to act on these tendencies.

When you have ruled out high/low blood cell count, overactive/underactive thyroid, and drugs or alcohol, a mental health professional will likely be able to diagnose you with OCD if you have it. According to the Anxiety and Depression Association of America, approximately one in 40 adults suffers from OCD. That is about 2.3% of the entire population of America. Research done by Harvard University in 2007 states that it is more likely that females will end up being diagnosed with OCD than males. The ratio is 1.8% to 0.5%. Keeping these statistics in mind, you can see that it is not out of the question that you might be suffering from OCD, but you will only be able to confirm this with a professional diagnosis. What you can confirm on your own is whether or not you experience the OCD tendencies listed above.

How to Handle Your OCD Tendencies

- Learn how to recognize what triggers you. Seeing old photos of your partner might kickstart a reminder that they were once with their ex instead of you. This is not necessary for you to remember or to even view, so prevent yourself from becoming triggered. Your OCD tendencies might try to trick you into thinking that you need to keep looking at these old photos, but you do not—you have the control to stop yourself.
- Understand that there is a disconnect between who you are as a person and your OCD tendencies. While you do feel this way, this is not the only thing that makes you who you are. You are made up of many other traits and characteristics that you can feel proud of. Do not allow your tendencies to control your entire personality.
- Realize what your triggers uncover. Subconsciously, you are holding a lot of your RJ within. When you are triggered, all of it has the potential to be unleashed. Your OCD tendencies are going to be cheering your triggers on. They want to unleash all of the obsessive thoughts and compulsive actions, but you can simply watch it unfold instead of acting on it at all. Become a bystander when you feel yourself becoming triggered. See where your mind wants to take you, but realize you still have control.
- Refocus your mind on something positive when you do not want to explore your triggers. This will work by reframing your thoughts or by simply thinking about something completely different to give your mind another thing to focus on. It takes a lot of willpower, but you can do this. The more that you practice, the weaker your tendencies will become.
- You will do the same thing with your RJ—reframe all of the negativity that it brings into your life. By transforming the experience into something more positive, you will no longer feel like you are being weighed down with jealousy. Once you fully overcome your RJ, you will feel like you can breathe again. It is very empowering to realize that you can do anything you want with the life that you are living.

Loosely based on Jeffrey M. Schwartz's process to overcome OCD, these steps will help you to battle against your OCD tendencies. They are meant to be used at any time and with any trigger that you encounter. Once you can separate yourself from your tendencies, you will see that you have been keeping an entire part of who you are locked away for far too long. It is time to embrace yourself and your wonderful traits.

Healthy Body, Healthy Mind

Your physical body gives off its own unique vibrations. These vibrations are waves of energy that interact with other waves that exist around you. Other people also have their own vibrations, as well as certain places and things. The energy that you surround yourself with is very important for keeping your own vibrations in check. One way that you can naturally release more energy from your physical body is by giving it a rush of endorphins. You are likely familiar with these happy chemicals that come from things such as exercise or movement. You need to keep your body healthy and active if you want to experience more endorphin rushes! This is the best way to naturally heal your mental state through a physical effort.

The mind and body are 100% connected. Not only is your brain telling your body how it is feeling and what it needs, but it is also relaying all of this information to your emotions to control how you feel about it all. When you think about the way that the system works, it makes sense that you should aim for a balance in both the physical and mental aspects of life. When you can include both in your lifestyle in a naturally balanced way, you are going to feel a lot better. This also means that your RJ will be less likely to flare up and ruin your good mood.

If the gym is not the place for you, do not worry—you can get your body in shape so many other ways:

- Walking
- Hiking
- Dancing

- Yoga
- Pilates
- Aerobics
- Swimming
- Sports
- Playing with your kids & pets

Any of these would make a great way for you to release those endorphins that are ready to help you feel better. If you can make a conscious effort to get up and moving more often each week, you will immediately notice a difference in the way that your physical and mental health feels. Both will increase, and you will be stronger than ever. This is a habit that sticks, and you are going to want to continue with it to maintain this newfound healthy lifestyle.

Do not forget that at-home workouts are also a great option. If you already know some exercises that you enjoy doing, put together a 20-min plan for yourself to follow. Commit to this at least three or four times per week to start. If this sounds like something that is too difficult, you can also lookup follow-along workouts online. There are countless resources for you to get these routines. The hardest part is committing to them. Once you are able to get up and do it, you will see how beneficial getting active will become for your life and for managing your RJ.

It is scientific in the sense that your body naturally releases certain hormones when you complete specific activities. When you become stagnant, you are not going to give yourself the chance to naturally release any endorphins. Staying still makes you feel worse about yourself or situations in your life because you are truly blocking all of the opportunities available for you to experience an endorphin rush. Make the most of your active time, and make it fun! You can include your family or loved ones in the experience, too.

Getting active with other people will hold you accountable for your own fitness routine. When you have an accountability buddy, no matter who you choose, you will feel like you cannot let them down. This is a great way to stay motivated and committed to getting physical more often. Do whatever you can for yourself to make the idea of working out more fun and exciting. Change it up because the same old routine easily becomes mundane. You should not be dreading your routine. If you feel this way, this might be a sign that you need to switch to something completely different.

The best part is that you are totally in control of what you do and when you do it. You get to decide what physical activity you would like to accomplish each day, and you get to plan for it around your current schedule. If something is important to you, as banishing your RJ should be, then you will make time for it. There is no such thing as being way too busy to get active. Even just 20 minutes a day can make a huge difference, and there is definitely some point in time each day where you have 20 minutes to spare. You might need to change your schedule around, but you can do this if you are committed to the experience.

You must train your brain to believe that you are worthy of all the great things that come your way. EFT tapping can help you with this, as your focus can be placed onto validating your feelings. RJ tries to take this away from you at any chance it gets. Keep in mind that you are still in control of this, as well. When you think about it, there is so much more that you are in control of, and this should be a comforting thought. You are powerful, and you are very strong. RJ has nothing on you! When you believe in this fully, you are allowing yourself to grow even stronger.

One thing that you must do each day is affirm that you are great. Use positive affirmations to validate yourself and your feelings. Look in the mirror, and make sure that you are making eye contact with yourself. It can be hard to look directly at yourself, but you need to get used to this level of acceptance. You can say something simple, such as, "You are enough." This is just positive enough to give you encouragement while also reminding you that you are worthy of anything good that happens to you. Come up with a new positive affirmation for yourself each week. This will allow you to get creative.

Stop Comparing Yourself to Exes

One of the most detrimental things that you are doing is comparing yourself to your partner's ex! This is why you should move forward from this behavior and focus on what you need in your own life to be happy again:

1. **You Are Two Different People:** Your partner's ex is a completely different person than you. No matter how similar you two might seem on the surface, underneath it all, you are individuals. It is hard to compare people because human beings are among some of the most unique and special beings on this planet. Instead of taking your anger out on them because you feel that they are prettier, smarter, or better than you in any way, work on yourself. Keep working on what you feel insecure about until you can turn it into something that makes you stronger. Think hard about the unique qualities that only you can offer your partner. Also, consider that your partner is with you currently. They have chosen you to be his partner, not anyone else from the past.
2. **The Past Should Stay There:** To your partner, their ex is in their past. It should feel the same for you. They did date this other person, but this happened before you two were together. Can you blame them for dating someone else, while you have probably also dated someone else? You both have a past, but it is there for a reason. You have learned a lot from your past, and it has helped to shape you into the person that you are today. However, your past does not define you or necessarily determine how you feel today. Values can change and so can feelings. People tend to grow over time; that is inevitable. Remember to keep the past where it belongs—in the past.
3. **Focusing on You is More Important:** When you place all of your energy into the past and into your partner's exes, you are taking this valuable energy away from yourself. This is something that you are in control of, and the way that you distribute your energy is so important. If you are constantly giving it away to other people and situations who do not even deserve it, then you are selling yourself short. You need to

remember your true value and worth. This is why you are working so hard to heal both your mind and body at once. You are working on using positive affirmations to help you truly believe that you are worthy. When you focus on their exes, this hinders any progress that you have already made—do not give them this power over you.

4. **You Will Develop an Obsession:** You already know how easy it is to become hyper-focused on a situation when you experience RJ. This tends to happen with your partner's exes. Do not allow this to take over your life or else it will make you feel miserable. You deserve to be happy at any chance you get, and by obsessing over something that happened long ago, you are taking away happiness from yourself. Think about it this way—do you want their ex to be happy or do you care more about your happiness? The answer is the latter, and that is not selfish. You might now even know them personally, so why does it matter so much? Work on your own self-fulfillment.

5. **You Will Start to Become Them:** An interesting sensation can occur when you become too focused on your partner's exes—you will subconsciously start to transform into them. Because your partner once liked or admired certain things about them, you might feel the need to change your looks or personality to match theirs. This is a detrimental action because it is setting who you truly are aside when your partner loves and respects you for who you are in the first place. Do not let your RJ fool you into thinking that you need to become him or her. You are enough as you are, and your partner picked you because you are different. Remind yourself that they picked you for a reason, and would not be with you if they did not see those great traits that you have, both inside and out.

6. **It Could Potentially Ruin Your Relationship:** When all you can think about is your partner's ex and how they used to be, this is going to start to impact your relationship. Your partner

will take notice, and they might even feel annoyed or irritated that you keep bringing it up. Their memories of the past likely hold some negativity in many ways, so by constantly bringing it up, you are reminding them of these unpleasant times. Neither one of you needs to feel stress over something that is over and done with. Do not allow the fixation to ruin what you currently have. Instead, use that energy and put it toward your relationship now. This is going to be a much more productive use of your time.

7. **It Will Not Make Your Relationship Thrive:** If you take the route of bashing their ex out of spite or jealousy, this might make you feel better about yourself at first. It gives you the instant gratification that you crave. However, think about what this will do for your relationship. It will probably do absolutely nothing positive. It will not bring the two of you closer together or closer to your collective goals. So, what are you really doing by obsessing over exes? You are only harming your mental health and actually ignoring what is right in front of you. Make sure that you are aware of how your own relationship is doing and what you can put into it to make it even better.

Their ex has nothing on you, and this is because you are two totally different people. When you can celebrate your unique traits and qualities, this further proves your worth and allows you to feel even more validated. Do your best to get out of the mindset that you need to be as good as or better than their ex.

Sobriety and Clarity

Consider your current drinking and drug habits, if any at all. Be very open and honest with yourself—what is this doing for your mental health? Scientifically, drinking alcohol and taking certain drugs will bring your mood down because they are depressants. They alter chemicals in your brain that prevent you from feeling happy and uplifted. If you are wondering why your RJ is getting the best of you and are still drinking a bottle of wine each night, it is time to reevaluate your current routines. Become aware of just how much you rely on substances to comfort you and to alter your state of mind. This is what they are great at doing, but they can easily become destructive habits that prevent you from moving forward with your RJ treatment plan.

While cutting down might be an option to take at first, the best option will always be 100% sobriety. When you know that your mind is not being altered by any foreign substances, you will be more in touch with your thoughts and feelings. You will also better understand your physical body and what it needs to feel good. Even just having a few drinks at nighttime can hinder the way that you think. It can ruin an entirely good day of progress by allowing you to slip into a state of weakness where your RJ awaits. Drinking and doing drugs will do nothing positive for you during this healing process.

Sobriety can sound like an unreasonable measure to take, but this is only because it is a big chance for most. Like any big changes in life, you are naturally going to be resistant or even avoidant of the unknown. You have to get used to something before you will fully accept it. Cutting down can be step one, but a goal of sobriety in mind will keep you on track. This is going to allow you to move onto bigger and better things during your RJ healing process. Challenge yourself to a month of sobriety, and see what a difference this makes.

What most people find is that they can continue being sober for longer than one month after they reach this milestone. The first few days and weeks will be difficult. You will have to figure out how to navigate social settings and recreational situations, but you will find other ways to cope with your feelings. Do not forget to keep your sacral chakra open and flowing with energy. Do something creative or productive to fill the void that might appear. When you can keep yourself busy with a replacement task, it will not be as difficult to stay sober.

You might find that the people you surround yourself with are not the best individuals to support you during a path toward sobriety. In this case, you will have to be careful of who you are spending your time with. It is thought that you are a mixture of the five people you spend the most time around. If your friends and loved ones are constantly drinking or partaking in drug use, this can become a temptation for you. It is not only an unhealthy influence, but it just makes the process of staying sober even harder. Consider that you do not need to banish these people from your life like you are trying to do with RJ. You just need to spend time around the right support system while you are healing.

Eventually, you might be strong enough to be around your past vices without giving in to them. This is a theory that should not be tested right away. You must make sure that you are strong in your sobriety first, and focus solely on this. When you are sober, many thoughts are going to rise to the surface. These thoughts might seem brand new because they have yet to be revealed to your clear mind. This is a good time to journal frequently and to reflect on what your brain has to say. Some interesting information might come forward that will help you heal.

You make better choices when you are sober, not only for yourself but for those around you that you care about. This is going to allow you to become a better partner, and it will keep you on track with controlling your jealous behavior and OCD tendencies. When you are sober for long enough, you eventually settle into your own thoughts and become comfortable with them. Not all of them are going to be pleasant, but this is part of growing as a person—you will learn how to navigate through the emotionally challenging ones without feeling like you have to numb yourself. You can do this, and you are going to be so proud of yourself when you finally do.

This is something that you should definitely keep track of to celebrate your milestone victories. One day of sobriety is great, and so is one week! Do not feel like any victory is too small to feel proud of yourself for. The fact that you are willing to put in so much effort toward your healing process says a lot about you and shows how serious you are about ridding your life of RJ. This is a huge decision to make, and it should already be something that makes you feel proud of yourself for. You are very strong-willed, and you can do anything you put your mind to.

Action Step

Make it a point to clear out anything in your diet that is not serving you well. This includes unhealthy foods, alcohol, and drugs that you have been taking. If it is not making your body or mind thrive, then you do not need it in your life. Take action, and be proactive at all times! Do not forget that caffeine and nicotine are also two very popular vices that tend to show up in the lives of those struggling from RJ. You have to work with what you are doing and go at a pace that is reasonable for you to manage. For the vices that are less harmful, like junk food, soda, and coffee, you can limit these to once per week or as an occasional treat. Use them as a reward to look forward to without them becoming a permanent part of your diet. Did you know that caffeine can actually accelerate triggers and anxiety? Be self-aware of this and use caffeine with caution.

Start working out! You already know that you do not need to hit the gym for the workout to count. Get your body moving in any way that sounds appealing. It is going to make a difference in every area of your life but especially toward kicking your RJ to the curb. The endorphin release that you get when you move your body will be enough to motivate you to keep doing it! This will almost feel like you are hitting a high note every single time, and you will want to keep going. Use this as motivation to create a dedicated and consistent workout routine that you can rely on.

19

YOUR PARTNER IS NOT YOUR PROPERTY

Your partner is the person that you love most in this world. You would do anything for them, and you greatly enjoy their company. No matter how close the two of you are or how long you have been together, you need to remember that you do not have ownership over your partner. They are an individual, just as you are. They have their own needs and desires, just as you do. It is a toxic mindset to go into your relationship thinking that you own your partner or control them in every aspect of their lives. In this chapter, you will learn why this behavior is unhealthy and how it can contribute to trouble for the happy couple. By letting go of this control, you are also loosening the shackles that the RJ has placed on you.

Wear Their Shoes

Your partner is not an object, and you have to think about how that makes them feel if you treat them as such. By controlling where they can go, when they can go, and who they can go out with, you are actually making their life miserable! Even if they do not realize it yet, this control is extremely unhealthy for any relationship. You have never owned your partner, and you should never make it a goal to own them in any type of way. You are two different individuals who have chosen to come together to share your lives. They will have different needs from you at times, but this does not mean that your life is falling apart or that you have to take control of the situation to feel okay.

Imagine if your partner were controlling you as much as you have controlled them. It will feel like you have no choice but to do what they say or else they will be upset—this is how it feels when you are dating something with very active RJ. When you make no effort to control your tendencies, your partner suffers because of them. You probably do not realize this because you have been so focused on your own suffering. It is time to finally take off the blinders and realize just how much RJ is affecting your relationship.

Get in touch with the empathy that you have. Try to truly put yourself in your partner's shoes and experiences. If this is difficult for you to fathom, ask them directly how your behavior makes them feel. Encourage them to be completely honest with you, even if it is hurtful. This is what you need to hear because you need to approach the situation as realistically as possible if you plan on being logical about it. Do your best to truly hear them out and not only hearing what you want to hear.

Your partner is a human being with common needs and desires, the same ones that you require to feel happy. They are a sexual being, and they have the same desires that you do. This does not take away from anything that you share with them in the present and in the future. Remember that you still have many days left to create special moments and connections with your partner. When you are too focused on jealousy, you are robbing yourself of these moments.

You are already a whole person. Whether you are single or taken, you are whole on your own. Many people believe that their partners complete them, and this can be true to a certain degree. When it all comes down to it, though, you are whole on your own. You can survive without a mate or a partner. It is just that you want to be with your partner that you feel so strongly that you would not be able to survive without them. Train yourself to think with this mindset. When you are together, you are actively choosing to be with each other every day. You do not need to be together out of survival or necessity. This will make your relationship seem even more special when you put it into perspective.

Separate your personal happiness from the things that your partner does for you. Instead of keeping track of what they are doing or not doing to make you happy, you need to figure out what it takes to make yourself happy. Without this knowledge, you are never going to feel satisfied. It should take very direct needs being met or actions being fulfilled to make you happy, and you can definitely do this on your own if you tried. Having a partner who does these things for you is a bonus that you should feel lucky to have in your life. Always express your gratitude because nothing is ever a guarantee.

You can work together to beat RJ for good. As long as you are open with your partner about the ways you are struggling, they will be able to understand where you are coming from. It is not that you want to upset them or question them about their past to be malicious; you are just tormented over an OCD cycle that you will soon overcome, and you will be so much stronger because of it. Asking for reassurance is not recommended. Hearing something reassuring from your partner can give the illusion of temporarily melting your worries away. However, it will just fuel the RJ further, it cannot be satisfied for long. When in a very self-aware and conscious state, communicate to your partner that they must not give in to your demand for answers, no matter when your seemingly uncontrollable need for interrogation strikes. You must relentlessly dedicate yourself to your healing process. Agreeing to this preconceived firewall with your partner will aid you both during those challenging moments when you are overwhelmed with RJ and feel the need to transform your bedroom into an interrogation room.

Tell your partner about what triggers you and why. When he or she is aware of these things, it is like you have an extra set of eyes helping you avoid danger. This is going to bring the two of you even closer together in the bond that you already have. It can be difficult to communicate your insecurities to your partner, but this is going to make your whole relationship better. It will feel like a huge sigh of relief when you can admit to your partner what makes you feel jealous and what that does to your mental health. Any supportive partner is going to want to help you overcome RJ. Without making the job theirs, you can still work together on the process.

Dealing With Ex Encounters

Infidelity is a huge concern in a relationship that is riddled with jealousy. You might often wonder if your partner is cheating on you or has cheated on you before. These thoughts will drive you crazy, but they can be understandable if you have been taken advantage of before, or especially, if your partner has cheated on you before. Dealing with these issues becomes a very personal matter because you need to figure out where you draw the line. If you have been cheated on, will you take your partner back or move on? This becomes a very scary and difficult thought to deal with.

There will be times when infidelity is not an issue, but your brain makes it one. You will keep wondering what if your partner decides to cheat on you. Just because they have not yet does not mean they will not later—this is a common narrative that RJ likes to plant in your mind. You need to keep these thoughts in check if they are happening frequently. They can be enough to get in between your perfectly normal relationship. Sometimes, the thought of seeing your partner's ex can send you down into a dark spiral. These worries about cheating might come at you with full force.

You do have a choice in the matter. You can either let the experience get the best of you or you can continue focusing on becoming a better version of yourself and move past it. There might be a time when you run into your partner's ex, a dreaded encounter for most. What would you do if this happened? Your brain would probably start running 100 miles per hour thanks to RJ and how it makes you worry. At the mere sight of his ex, you might worry that your partner will leave you right there on the spot. How likely is this going to be, though? It is very highly unlikely—remember, rationalize.

Even if you do not physically see their ex, you might see them on social media. You already know how triggering this can feel, but you do not need to let this experience ruin your day or even a moment in your day. Choose to acknowledge that they exist, but also choose to set your focus and energy on something more important. What you deem more important is up to you. Maybe you want to focus on your partner or your family. Maybe you have your goals and to-do list in mind. No matter what you choose, always make sure that you are focusing on something that is a better use of your time because your time is not unlimited.

Life is too short to be paralyzed by jealousy at the mere sight or mention of your partner's ex. RJ can make it feel like their ex is laughing at you or looking down at you because of who you are. These are just tricks that your mind is playing on you. Most of the time, this imaginary conflict is simply RJ trying to make you feel bad about yourself. It is hungry and trying to produce more food for itself by creating an imaginary enemy. By using these tips, you can avoid ever succumbing to this trick again. Regain your power, and realize that your relationship is so much more than who your partner had dated in the past.

Stay Out of the Past

For anything that has already happened that you were not directly involved in, keep it that way! There is no need to get involved in a situation that is long gone, especially when it was between your partner and their ex. This is only going to upset you because it will make you think of the relationship they once shared. The current reality shows you that things are different now. He or she is with you for a reason, and you need to focus on this instead of focusing on why he ever dated his ex in the first place. People change and so do circumstances.

Be Supportive When Needed

Your partner might want to talk about his ex or a situation involving his ex that happened in the past. This does not mean that he wants to get back together with her. Listen to what he has to say, and be that supportive partner that you promised to be. You might have to sit with some discomfort, but it will pass. As long as you do not allow RJ to come into the picture, the discomfort will eventually dissolve while teaching you how to be a more supportive partner in the process. He will not always want to discuss these things with you, especially if he knows that it upsets you. What will matter most is that he knows he can.

Is a Break Needed?

When couples reach a stage where they are constantly struggling, the idea of taking a break might come up. Is it the right decision, though? Taking a break can be an iffy subject because the boundaries are often unclear. There are times when a lot of people seem to get hurt because one partner thinks that they are being exclusive while the other is out talking to other people and even mingling like they are not in a relationship at all anymore. If you do decide that a break is the route that you and your partner are going to try, you need to make sure the parameters are crystal clear.

There seem to be more downfalls that come from taking a break than trying to work through the RJ while staying together. Going on a break just brings so many complicated aspects to your relationship and the bond that you have already worked so hard to create. It can feel like you are taking several steps back, which will cause you to develop new insecurities. On a break, you will truly have no idea what your partner is up to. Your RJ will have even more reasons to torment you into thinking that they are getting back together with their ex or even meeting someone completely new who is going to take your place. There are just a lot of grey areas when it comes to taking a break from a long-term relationship.

Think carefully about all of your options before you settle on this one. While it can seem like a quick solution to ease tension, it is not always going to give you the best results. It might actually end up causing more hassle than it is worth. Then, you will have to work on regaining trust and getting back to where you used to be as a couple. If you love each other and truly want to be together for the long run, then you should be able to find it in your heart to stay together. You must focus on healing from your RJ, and your partner will learn how to be as supportive to you as he can. Committing to healing will show him that you are serious about making a change for the better.

RJ is going to push you very hard in the direction of taking a break sometimes, but do not let RJ speak for your true feelings. You would likely be devastated if your partner asked you to go on a break at this point, so think about how this might make him feel if you were to propose the idea. It is a risky step to take when you are already feeling extremely insecure in your relationship. If the foundation is still good, then you need to build it from the ground up. Work with what you already have going for you. Try your hardest to take a few deep breaths before you become reactive over something that triggers you. By sitting in this discomfort, even if only for a few minutes, you will find a better solution than the one that you were originally going to choose. This works every time.

Taking a breather puts things in a new perspective for you, and it is less severe than actually taking a break from the relationship. You might just need some alone time to sort through your feelings, but you can come together at the end of the day to talk to your partner and express where you stand. It is healthy to not just spend every waking moment together, even if you both have free time. Work on some self-care objectives, and spend time with other loved ones in your life. This is going to create a balance that will banish codependency in your relationship. When you know that you would be okay with or without the relationship, this is you making an active decision to choose your partner every day.

It is more meaningful when the choice is conscious instead of something you feel you have to do because you are codependent. It is also a lot healthier for the long run. The more healthy habits you can implement in your relationship, the happier you both will feel. This will become your new focus, and RJ can be left in the dust. It will soon become a distant memory that no longer matters to either one of you. While you might still have flare ups and be triggered at times, this is a lot better than living every single day in distress or anxiety because of your jealousy. You deserve much more than that and so does your relationship.

A break is halfway to a breakup, so you might want to think twice the next time this idea is proposed. If you do not see your future with your partner, then this might be a risk you are willing to take. However, it is not recommended if it is only your RJ that is standing in the way of you feeling happy in your relationship. Your RJ will just return in your next relationship, so you may as well deal with it now. This is something that can be mended with your willingness and your partner's understanding. Make sure that the two of you are on the same page, and you will both come out of this on the other side feeling happier than ever before. It will strengthen your relationship and keep that bond strong.

Are You Single?

For those reading this book, some of these relationship-based pieces of advice might not apply because you are currently single. This does not mean that you cannot experience RJ, too. This is a monster that does not discriminate, and it can definitely cause just as much trouble for you as a single individual as it can when you are in a relationship with someone. When you are not in a relationship, now is a better time than ever to focus on yourself and to work on healing from your RJ. You can learn how to completely rid yourself of the feeling before you get into your next relationship. This is a plus because it will not even have the chance to interfere with your love life any longer.

Think about how you spend your time when you are single. Since you do not have to pay attention to another person and cater to their needs, this gives you even more of a chance to tend to your own. Being single can be a very fun and freeing time in your life. It does not need to be filled with pressure and sadness. Your next relationship will come in due time, but you do not need to rush things along by any means. What is meant to be will be, and you will have the chance to make sure that you are feeling at the top of your game before you put yourself back out into the dating world.

Explore all of the different hobbies and activities that you have always wanted to try but never did when you were in a relationship. Maybe time did not allow for this exploration, or maybe your partner then had no interest in doing these things with you. This is the perfect opportunity to create new, wonderful experiences for yourself. Do whatever it is that makes you feel happy and fulfilled! There are no rules when you are single, and this is the best part. This is why it is a better time than ever to work on ridding your mindset of all negativity that RJ tries to plant there. Tell yourself that you are stronger than this and better than RJ.

You might feel like you are getting into the habit of being selfish, but what is actually happening is that you are prioritizing yourself and your needs for once. This is healthy! Keep doing this, and understand that it is not a selfish act because you do not have a partner who needs the extra attention that you have to offer right now. Put all of this attention on yourself, making sure that you have everything you need in life. If you enter the dating world with an expectation that someone is going to fulfill these needs, you are setting yourself up for disappointment. Show yourself that you can do all of these things for yourself, and it will feel like a pleasant surprise when you finally do meet that special someone who can give you what you need because they care about you.

Develop new personal habits as a single person. What routines will you implement to feel good about yourself? You might realize that you do not exactly have routines that are set in stone, but having them can make you feel better. Once you set up some routines, you will see that they keep you motivated and focused. By continually moving forward, you will not have time to worry about what others are thinking of you or if they are thinking of you at all. This is the type of energy that you want to put out into the world. Remember, you put out the energy that you will eventually attract back into your life. Be aware of how you are presenting yourself to other people during this time. If you want a kind and caring partner in the future, then you need to be kind and caring to those around you.

Focus on any changes that you would like to make regarding yourself. Whether you want to change your appearance for fun or change some of the bad habits that you have developed over the years, now is the perfect opportunity to put in that self-work. Try your best to become someone that you could see yourself being friends with and that you feel good about when you look in the mirror. If you can see all that you have to offer, then you are going to know your worth. Other people will need to follow suit, or else they will not be good enough for you—never settle for anything less than you deserve.

It can be hard to determine what you need and what you feel you deserve, but focus on what makes you happy and allows you to feel fulfilled in life. Go for people who bring you these feelings. It should not be a struggle to find someone who is willing and able to do this for you. If they act like it is a chore, then this is probably not the right person for you. The right person is going to love you unconditionally and accept you for exactly who you are, flaws and all. There should never be a point where you must change who you are to please someone else or to make yourself seem more appealing to them. Stand your ground, and know your worth.

Action Step

Imagine that there is no such thing as RJ; it does not exist right now. Write down a list of all the incredible things that you love about your partner. It should be very easy for you to fill at least an entire page with these traits that you simply adore about them. Talk about what makes you feel proud about them and what makes you feel proud to be with them, that you get to call them your partner. Think about the path that they took that led them straight to you, and express your gratitude for them taking this path.

This action step is a very simple and positive reminder that there is so much greatness to be found within your relationship. You should never take it for granted. You have this person in your life right here and right now. RJ does not deserve to have a say in whether or not you are happy or unhappy. Make the conscious decision to be happy each day. You do have the ability to choose happiness over sadness, so make sure that you are making the right decision.

20

HEALING YOUR INNER CHILD

You may or may not feel like you have an inner child depending on how in touch you are with it, but everybody has one. When people deal with their inner child or the feelings that it brings forth, this might be because they are currently working through a difficult time. RJ certainly qualifies as a difficult time, so it is unsurprising if you feel that you can relate to the following traits that your inner child can bring forward. The problems that your inner child brings to the surface involve wounds that you experienced early on in life. This does not necessarily have to be as extreme as physical or mental abuse but can also include instances that just seemed to stick with you into adulthood. You never know what might have impacted you during your childhood and for which reasons.

For the most part, your inner child might be content. It is usually only when you are going through a distressing time that it decides to act up. RJ can definitely trigger your inner child by causing it to bring up past memories that you would probably rather avoid thinking about. As hard as it can be, you need to address and work through these experiences to really heal from your past. People from all walks of life and in all different stages of it can have experiences with their inner child. You might have one when you least expect it, and it can definitely feel foreign if you do not understand exactly what is happening.

In a sense, you are regressing back into that childlike mentality. This can cause you to feel hopeless about the situation that you are in because of any past situations that you have endured that are similar or just triggering. Do not try to resist the feelings that your inner child brings to your attention. They are being brought to you for a reason, and you now have an automatic list of the things that you must work on to be happy. Your inner child will not always make you respond in a negative or upsetting way. The inner child can often be playful and exuberant. You might feel rejuvenated in a sense because of the carefree energy that your inner child can bring out of you.

Even though your inner child is simply a psychological concept, it can feel very real at times. This is especially true when you trigger it by coming forward. Acknowledge when this is happening and what these triggers are. Just as you would with any other RJ triggers, you should write them down in your trigger notebook to keep track of them. Make sure that you specific your reaction and that it is coming from your inner child. This can say a lot about your past and how what you have been through has impacted you today. Many psychologists agree that your inner child is simply a part of who you are as an individual.

Even though your inner child is a simple concept to understand, healing it can be a whole different story. There are many steps that go into inner child work that often require the help of a mental health professional. This process can be very long, but it is worthwhile to complete because this all relates to your RJ. When you can figure out the things in your past that have contributed to who you are today, you will feel a lot more secure in our present life and situation. Having an understanding gives you more knowledge, and having knowledge is always powerful.

Ways That the Inner Child Can Be Hurt

You might be wondering what affects your inner child and what they had to go through to still be present in your daily life as an adult. The following is a list of common experiences that will influence this, but they are not limited to these situations:

- Loss of a parent or guardian
- Physical abuse or neglect
- Emotional abuse or neglect
- Sexual trauma
- Serious illness
- Severe bullying
- Natural disasters
- Broken family
- Being a victim of violence
- Substance abuse in the household
- Domestic violence in the household
- Mental illness in a family member
- Being a refugee
- Feeling isolated from family

These are just a few of the reasons why your inner child might be upset today. They are still going to feel hurt by these instances. Even if you cannot identify with any of them, there are still other reasons why your inner child might feel the need to hold on to this hurt. You need to analyze what you have been through in the past and how that might have shaped you today.

How This Damages You Into Adulthood

If you know that your inner child is appearing distressed because you have been through a lot as a child, you are going to feel this stress as an adult. It can be difficult to deal with on top of all of the other things that you are already struggling with. Be open and honest with yourself. This is a process, and it is not magically going to feel better overnight. You must be willing to commit to healing and all that it entails. It can take some time, but the ultimate reward is you feeling happy and secure again.

Some common traits that you will notice during adulthood as a result of your childhood experiences can include:

- Inferiority complexes
- Excessive toxic shame

- Self-sabotage
- Self-defeating behavior
- Self-harming
- Passive-aggressive behavior
- Violent behavior

You can see that these all have certain things in common. They are detrimental to you and to those around you. First and foremost, that is doing something negative to you and can even become severe enough to impact your life. This is likely exactly where your RJ stemmed from.

These symptoms are so common because the inner child usually still feels damaged or broken. Even if these situations happened decades ago, some things just stay with you for years and years. It is not your fault that any of this happened to you, so do not fall into the trap of that victim mentality. You will rise above.

How to Heal Your Inner Child

You know that identifying an issue you are experiencing is never the final step. What needs to happen next is real healing, and this involves getting started with the process. Take action if you want to see a real change that will make you feel better. Your first task is simple—get to know your inner child. See what they like and what they dislike. How do they act? What sets them off? Your inner child will be a lot like your childhood self, but it can differ in certain ways that regard triggers and stress.

You can use these methods to ensure that you are doing your best to address your inner child and give it what it needs to heal. Simultaneously, this is going to heal you. Do not ignore the needs of your inner child, for they will only grow more persistent to get your attention. Make a commitment to get to know your inner child. Be prepared for any difficult or negative memories that might surface during this process. The beginning is always acceptance, and then the rest will follow from this point. You can always choose to deny that you have an inner child at all, but the effects will still impact you.

Doing inner child work alone is just as valuable as doing it with a therapist. Any effort that you put toward it is going to make a difference.

Most childhood pain is identifiable, and you will start to realize what it is and where it comes from. This can be an eye-opening experience because it might show you why you have certain emotional reactions as an adult now. There are many ways that you might discover new parts of yourself. You need to realize that these feelings definitely come from somewhere and that they are not just randomly surfacing for no reason.

You must build compassion for your inner child as you work through these problems. Learn how what they went through and what they are still going through can be very difficult. If your needs were not met in the past, you might need to address them now. Figure out what it is that is lacking in your life, and learn that you can fill these voids that your inner child made you think you had to live with. There is plenty of constructive work that you can do to get to the bottom of this for yourself. You will start to feel a lot more at peace when you can address these needs that have not been met for so long.

As you work through the compassion stage, you will also reach a point where you will have the opportunity to learn how to love your inner child. You can learn to love your inner child by noticing the traits that they have that have influenced who you are today. You might have received your tenacity and strength from your inner child, and this is something to be thankful for. This bond will become strong and unconditional. Any form of self-love is a good opportunity to push RJ further away from you.

Shame: What it Means

You might feel shame about your RJ because it seems like a monster that you cannot control. It also feels like something that people in your life typically do not deal with. When you feel that you are alone, it can mess with your mind even more. You will feel trapped, absolutely unable to break free from the binds that RJ has on you. The good news is that you *can* get rid of the shame you feel. Nothing that you are experiencing is shameful or bad because jealousy is a natural human emotion, some just feel it more strongly than others. Also, you can now see that your childhood plays a huge role in how strongly you are affected. You have already made so much progress toward healing and have put a lot of work into feeling better—keep it up!

Again, EFT tapping can truly help you during the healing process when you are struggling with feelings of shame. Your inner child can bring up a lot of this shame, and EFT tapping becomes a great way to focus on what you would like to combat. Set your intention on letting go of the shame and moving toward a mindset where you love and accept yourself for who you are. No matter what terrible things you have endured in the past, this does not mean you are destined for more in the future. You can have a great life that you are able to fill with all of the things that make you happy and fulfill your needs.

With this EFT tapping method for healing, your shame will soon dissolve away. The freedom that you will feel after all nine rounds will encourage you to complete even more healing. You are one step closer to being rid of your RJ for good.

More Healing Methods

These healing methods are simpler steps that you can use daily to fully encourage the healing of pain and suffering from shame. You no longer have to live this way, feeling like you are constantly being punished for being you.

- Practice self-compassion. You can do this by using your positive affirmations. The next time that you want to punish or shame yourself for anything, past or present, quickly turn to a positive affirmation for help. This will prevent you from falling into the shame spiral. Recite a positive affirmation until you forget about the thought of shame, guilt, or fear. Over time, it will prevent you from further shaming yourself.

You can always take your shameful narrative and rephrase it to suit a more positive mindset. If you are thinking about how embarrassed you were in one instance, you can think instead that you have made mistakes and learned from them. Starting from that moment, you chose to move forward and let what no longer serves you go.

If the positive affirmation does not feel natural to you, then it is not likely going to work out. Find a statement that truly fits. You do not have to exaggerate by saying that you are perfect and amazing, but you do want to think of something positive that uplifts you. Try many different affirmations until you find a collection that feels suitable. You can use these any time that you start to feel down and ashamed.

- Come back to your body. When you sink into a state of feeling shame or guilt, you tend to internalize everything. Your thoughts become obsessive, just as they do when you are experiencing RJ. This is why the two are so closely related. You need to remind yourself to come back to your physical body. This will help to remind you that you are grounded in the present.

Imagine that you are a tree. Your body is the trunk, and your arms are the branches. This leaves your legs, the roots. Place your feet flat on the ground, and make sure that you can feel yourself standing or sitting where you are. Think about each part of your body and how you are present right now. You are physically in this space.

Getting out of your head by returning to your body is a quick way to help you avoid spiraling. You can do this from anywhere because it does not require much at all. The only thing you need to do is refocus your thoughts. When your mind tries to fight back and think about the shame, fight twice as hard. Focus on your physical body. How is it feeling today? Are there parts that feel good? Do you feel strong? You can do this.

- Try moving around. If being still is making things worse for your mind, then you need to get moving! You do not have to complete a workout routine or run around to get active. Simply standing up and walking around the room can help tremendously. Give yourself a second to move around a little, focusing on each step that you are taking. Only focus on this, and think about how your legs carry you anywhere you need to go.

This is going to completely change your mindset. From concentrating on walking to thinking about the process of walking, you will have no more room to shame yourself right now. Only allow yourself to pay attention to the fact that you are up and moving around. You do not need to focus on the shame right now. It is time to only do this and to only focus on this. Keep it simple.

When you try to do too many things at once, this is when your brain will shut down. If you keep it simple by just walking from one side of the room to the other, this will be something for you to latch onto. It is a task that you are giving yourself, and you must focus on it until it is complete. Once you reach the other side of the room, assess how you are feeling. If the shame is still trying to break through, walk to the other side of the room.

Action Step

Use meditation to get in touch with your inner child. Set your focus and your intention on getting to know this part of yourself that you have not encountered in quite some time. Their traits are always present, but how much do you really know about them? This is your chance to become better acquainted. Think about this child and what they have been through. Try to put yourself in their shoes, and then see how their experiences might be contributing to the feelings and emotions that you are having today.

Explore EFT tapping for the purpose of ridding your mind of shame. Try it out for yourself and see how this effective technique gradually melts away the shame and guilt that you have been holding onto. Even if you do not feel like you are holding onto anything anymore, these sessions can surprise you. They will show you exactly what is on your mind and what might be affecting your life. Remember, there are countless EFT tapping videos online for you to tap along to!

21

THE RUNWAY TO FREEDOM AND RECOVERY

You are almost free, and you can finally see how much your life will change once RJ is gone for good. This journey has already made you a more empowered individual, and there is much more to come along the way. This is not just a one-time process. Healing from RJ is actually a lifelong process that you will continue to navigate as you experience self-growth. It will become easier because you will be used to the new habits and techniques that you have learned. Soon, this will be the way that you automatically operate. RJ will have nothing on you, but if you are threatened by a relapse, you will also learn exactly what you need to do to get back on track.

This chapter focuses on common mistakes that are made during the healing process and how to avoid them. It also encourages you to start working on your path to self-forgiveness. With all of this useful information available to you, this will be everything you need to stay on the right path. This is your journey, and it will be as successful as you are willing to make it. You can do this, and RJ will never know what hit it! Get excited for all of the inspiration that you will become filled with. Once you see how successful you are at beating RJ the first time, any threats or relapses will simply become bumps in the road that you will learn to get over.

Mistakes to Avoid

When handling your RJ, there are several mistakes that you might be making. You need to work on avoiding them so your healing process can continue along. Each of these mistakes should be avoided at all costs. If you realize that you have been making them, then you can act now to transform your experience. The RJ does not have to win unless you let it!

Filtering

Looking at only one side of the situation is a good example of how you might be filtering. When you perceive something as bad, you tend to cling to this possibility without even considering if there are any other sides to pay attention to. Because of this, you end up in an RJ spiral that grabs ahold of you. Try to consider that there is always more than one option in any situation.

What you perceive might not be what is true, and this can be a hard concept to grasp if you have been dealing with RJ for quite some time. Your feelings are 100% valid, but consider that you might be wrong. A situation might actually have a different side to it that you have yet to consider. This will open your mind and change the way that you perceive your triggers. It will give you a more positive approach to take.

Projecting

When you start to project, you are going from 0 to 100 in a matter of seconds. If your partner looks at the cashier at the grocery store and you think that they automatically want to leave you, this is a prime example. Your brain will receive a thought from RJ and just run with it. The typically unrealistic situation is then projected into something much bigger than it truly is. Most of the time, there is absolutely no truth to these projections.

Projecting can become so damaging to your relationship because you might begin to act resentful or angry toward your partner based on these scenarios you are imagining. They will have no idea what is going on, and you will be stressing yourself out while bringing negativity into your relationship. Always remember the concrete facts. If something truly happened, you should be able to pinpoint the proof.

Relating Everything to Yourself

Not everything is about you! This can be a hard reminder to swallow, but it is true. Do not apply every situation and everything to yourself—it is that simple. If something is directly related to you, then you might be able to consider it. However, when you insert yourself into situations that are potentially triggering or negative, you are only bringing yourself down into RJ's clutches.

Stop doing this to yourself because you are making it harder than it needs to be to live your life. It is like your brain subconsciously wants to start some drama. Be very explicit with your intentions. Tell yourself that you are not going to apply anything to you or your life until it directly applies. This will prevent you from getting ahead of yourself and worrying about things that might not have anything to do with you in the first place. Just because you *can* relate to it does not mean you should.

Romanticizing

Typically, people who struggle with RJ like to romanticize certain situations or parts of their lives. If you do this, you might have thoughts like, "My partner will never leave me because I am his lover, and he has only ever had eyes for me." While this is a positive thought, it is not something that will help you heal from RJ because it is romanticized. You are stating that your partner has only ever had romantic feelings for you, which is untrue. This is what might be making it so hard for you to deal with the thought of his exes.

There is such a thing as being too positive, and romanticizing is where you must draw the line. Just as you are realistic with every other aspect of your RJ healing, you need to be realistic with your positivity. You can reframe the statement above—"My partner loves me and is with me right now." This is a true statement, and it is still positive. This is the non-romanticized version of what your brain might want you to think.

Catastrophic Thinking

This type of thinking is the complete opposite of the above. When you catastrophize, you imagine the very worst-case scenario as being true. Your brain cannot help but to go to the most negative place it can think of and then proceed to torture you with these thoughts. If your partner is late coming home from work, you might wonder if they stopped by another woman's house to cheat on you. The worry does not stop there—what if he has been doing this your whole relationship and has a secret family that he visits every day?

This is an example of catastrophic thinking. It is an extremely unrealistic narrative that your brain follows because it gets sucked into the idea. With one small catastrophic thought, you can be in a lot of trouble. You need to work on squashing these thoughts the moment they arise, or else they will definitely turn into something a lot worse and harder to handle.

Negative Self-Image

You have been working on your self-esteem for the duration of this book. It is so important to continue working on it because any type of negative self-image that you have will become a setback to you on your healing journey. RJ loves to look for weaknesses. Even if you talk poorly about yourself in a joking manner, this is still a negative projection that you are expressing—stop doing this to yourself.

You need to work on always being positive. Like you have been taught, without anything nice to say, do not say anything at all. Reserve your thoughts and words about yourself until you can figure out how to put a positive spin on them. Be realistic with these positive affirmations, but make sure that they are uplifting in some way. You are going to retrain your brain and get rid of all of that negative self-talk that you have been putting up with for far too long.

The Wrong Cause

When you are a jealous individual, you might try to justify your jealousy by making up a narrative that is not true. You will try your best to rationalize your behavior to others and to yourself, but this is not helping you. This is fighting for the wrong cause. You do not want to mask the reasons why RJ is challenging you. Instead, you want to address them head-on. Do your best to be completely open and honest about the way you are feeling and why.

RJ does not have to get the better of you, and it will if you keep covering up for it. When you can come up with a narrative for your behavior, you will eventually start to believe it. This is not RJ's fault, it is simply explained by the situation you are creating in your mind—this will be your thought pattern when you are trying to make excuses for RJ. Remember this, it is always RJ's fault. You are here to fight back and to reclaim your life.

A Relapse: How to Deal

So, you have been free of RJ for quite some time, but you are experiencing a relapse—what do you do? The first step is to make sure that you are not punishing yourself for this. Relapses will happen, but treating them with negativity is not going to make things any better for you. The most important thing is that you need to acknowledge that you have relapsed and identify what you are feeling. Try to pinpoint what triggered the relapse and why you were not able to fight back. Do not shame yourself because this is only going to cause guilt. Just observe what you are feeling and what behaviors you exhibited that have shown you that you have relapsed.

It is all going to be okay. You already know how it feels to live your life removed from RJ, so you know that you can do it again. You will get back to that freedom with a little hard work. There are techniques that you can rely on to help you get back to your path of recovery. Because healing is not linear, it is not uncommon to experience a relapse or a few. After admitting and acknowledging what it is happening, it is time to dig deeper. You need to think about the root of the cause of this relapse. What was the person, place, or situation that triggered you into this old way of thinking?

Because it made you feel this way, you can be certain that there are still some parts of yourself that need to work through the issue. Just because it is still unresolved does not mean you cannot fix it now. It is the best time to continue working on fixing it! As long as you are putting in an effort, you are automatically winning this fight against RJ. You are taking a proactive stand against it by saying that you will not give in. It may have brought you down, but you can get right back up if you choose. Always remember that you have this power over RJ and that you have this control.

Stay grounded by focusing on all that you have accomplished since your last relapse or the last time that you felt your RJ. How have you made it this far? Rediscover the coping mechanisms that you have been relying on to get you through even the toughest moments. Going through a relapse can feel similar to going back to the beginning of your healing process, but the clock is not reset. You still get to hold onto all of the wonderful moments you created for yourself. Take note of the tips that worked well for you and the healing methods that worked. You will be using them again.

Try to focus on one of your healing methods first. See if this changes the way that you feel. Work through the ones that you know, going one at a time. This will ensure that your brain does not get too overwhelmed and starts running back to RJ. If none of them seem to work, do not panic. This could be a sign that you are ready to try something new. This book is full of so many different techniques that will help you and different angles that you can take to view your RJ. Choose one that you would like to focus on, and begin going through these steps. Remind yourself that you are still empowered. You still have the ability to fight back, and you have new tools to do so.

Breathing is very important. Whether you are going through an active moment of relapse or trying out a new coping skill, make sure that you are breathing steadily and evenly. Try to inhale through your nose and exhale through your mouth for four seconds each. This is going to regulate both your mind and body. It will put you in the correct mindset for healing by reminding you that you are still grounded. Do not forget how important it is to physically ground yourself, as well. By planting your feet firmly on the ground, you are setting your roots deep into the soil. RJ cannot make you budge because you are so strong.

Choose to focus on a saying or a positive reinforcement as you begin to get back on track. Your RJ tried to pull you down, but you are not going to let this happen. Select something that makes you feel strong and resilient. It can be anything that speaks to you. Say it aloud if you can. This will solidify the positive reinforcement and ensure that you truly believe what you are telling yourself. Your brain might try to stray, try to wander back to what is bothering you. Do not allow it to do so.

This is just RJ trying to distract you. Remain focused on the positivity you are creating.

Now, you are going to manifest something for yourself. Think of something that you want or need right now. This can be anything at all, as long as it is positive and will make you feel happy and uplifted. You need to focus on this thought for the rest of your day and the rest of the days to come. Use this manifestation to boost your self-esteem all the way back up, even further than it was before. You can transcend any level that you were on before just by staying as positive as possible. Your mindset is the key to getting through a relapse.

This relapse is only temporary, a small roadblock. Once you get through it, do not dwell on it or feel bad that it happened. You need to keep your eyes straight ahead or else you will miss what is going on in your life. You have so much to be grateful for. Remind yourself by writing down a few things that you currently feel grateful for. This is going to show you that you still deserve to be happy and far removed from RJ. The times have changed for the better.

You might feel like a different person than you were and, in some ways, you are now. This is a good thing. It shows that you have evolved and grown. You no longer feel like you are RJ's personal victim. Now, there are many things that you can point out about yourself that you love. You should be able to recognize that you have so many desirable traits both inside and out. This is what matters far more than what RJ wants you to believe and what anyone else might be saying or doing. Focus on you and bettering yourself.

Forgiving Yourself for Good

Forgiveness is one of the most challenging actions a human being can take. It requires you to step down from any platform you have put yourself on by reminding you that it is okay to say that you are sorry, especially to yourself. You are now ready to forgive yourself for good, not just for a temporary feeling of happiness or contentment. This time, it is for real. If you are ready to live your life without these qualms, use the following tips to help you reach a point where you can feel proud of the person you truly are.

Focus on Your Emotions

When you set your focus on your emotions, you will be able to identify any lingering negativity. If something is still bothering you, this is going to make it hard for you to forgive yourself. Work on processing these feelings and getting through this part of the journey first. Then, you can move forward with forgiveness. It takes courage to truly identify the emotions that you are feeling and what you need to do to settle them.

Acknowledge the Mistake Out Loud

This is another step that requires bravery, but it helps to take the power away from any mistakes you have made. Say it out loud. Tell yourself what it is that you did that you are trying to forgive. See how this makes you feel and if it helps to make the problem feel less severe. This is also a great way to acknowledge that you have made a mistake but that you are working on forgiveness as an end result.

Identify the Learning Experience

With every action you are not proud of comes a learning experience. Identify what that is and how it can help you in the future. Before you work on total forgiveness, it helps to determine what exactly it is that you learned from the experience. Think about how this is going to benefit you by making similar situations easier in the future. You will know how to handle them. You did the best that you could at that time; now you can work on becoming even better.

Give Yourself Permission to Go On Hold

When a mistake is being relentless in your mind and causing you to experience negative symptoms, you might need to take a little break. This is okay. Give yourself permission to relax and unwind before you return to the process. It can feel incredibly taxing if you jump straight from a mistake to the process of forgiveness and healing. Teach yourself that it is okay to put a pause on this until you are in the right headspace to deal with it.

Have a Conversation With Your Inner Critic

You need to confront your inner critic when it tries to stand in your way. With this conversation, you will write it down in a notebook to refer back to in the future when you need it. Tell your inner critic that you are moving on and that you have no more room for negativity or self-hatred right now. It is onto bigger and better things for you and for your life.

Notice When You Are Being Self-Critical

There are going to be moments when you will spot yourself being critical. Take note of all these moments. You need to recognize when you are being hard on yourself and why this happens. If you ignore these things, you are giving yourself permission to keep doing them. Acknowledge when you are being self-critical, and try to correct the behavior on the spot. This will help you forgive yourself. It will show you that your mind just wants to naturally work against you because this is how RJ taught you to think.

Quiet the Negative Self-Talk

Negative self-talk will commonly pop up at any given time. It acts like a distant reminder of the RJ that you used to struggle with daily. You need to find ways to quiet this negativity for yourself. Clear your mind of negative self-talk by either reframing your thoughts or focusing on something else altogether. When you have goals that you are actively working on, this helps you to focus on something more purposeful. Use your goals and motivation to combat negativity and negative self-talk.

Get Clear About What You Want

Be specific! What exactly are you hoping for from this forgiveness? Do you want to be relieved of your shame and guilt? Do you want the overwhelming thoughts to stop keeping you awake at night? Get very clear about what you want from the experience and how you are going to obtain it. Recognize that forgiveness is the starting point that will get you on the right path. If you are too general with your goals, then you will never know when you have made any progress.

Take Your Own Advice

You need to practice what you preach. If you are the type of person who is quick to uplift others, why not take your own advice and apply it to yourself? You deserve just as much kindness and happiness as anyone else in the world. You need to level the playing field for yourself by recognizing this. Remember to never give any advice that you are not already taking yourself. Identify times that you have helped people and consider if you are helping yourself by doing the same.

Quit Playing the Tape

The tape is an obsessive reel of thoughts that force you to look back on the mistakes you have made. This is not constructive. It will not lead you to any kind of healing or progress. Stop allowing this to happen, and only focus on your mistakes when it pertains to what you have learned or what you can do from this point going forward. Always keep your eyes forward; do not look back.

Show Kindness and Compassion

It can help you to be kind and compassionate, even to other people, when you are trying to work on forgiving yourself for something. These actions make you a more positive person in a very natural way. They will uplift you and remind you that you can treat yourself this way, too. If you are struggling with your forgiveness journey, do something nice for someone else. This will put you in a better headspace.

Seek Professional Guidance

Getting professional help is something that is generally stigmatized but can be incredibly beneficial. Seeking counseling will give you someone who is there to support you and help you through your hardest moments. They will be able to guide you through the process of letting go and teach you even more steps you can take to apply toward forgiveness. Seek professional help if you ever feel like you are too overwhelmed to function. This is not something to be ashamed of—it shows that you are serious about getting better.

None of these tips are particularly hard to practice or remember, but forgiveness itself is not always an easy task. Be gentle with yourself as you try to reach a point where you can forgive yourself and all that has occurred during your battle with RJ. This is a very important step to take because it will give you the peace of mind you deserve.

Action Step

Make it a point to practice a lot of self-compassion this month. Any time that you fall off the wagon, get right back on with the notion that you already forgive yourself. This will make the transition a lot easier for you if you do experience a relapse with your RJ. Remember not to use catastrophic thinking—it is not the end of the world if you relapse. It is just going to become a lesson that will make you even stronger in the end. Do an EFT tapping session on self-forgiveness. This is going to solidify in your mind that you can forgive yourself and that you deserve to forgive yourself.

Now, focus on moving forward. After you have forgiven yourself for everything that you once held close, you can look forward to your future. Consider all of the wonderful things that you currently have going for you and all of the great things to come. You have created this life for yourself, and you should feel so proud of all the progress you have made on your journey thus far. Success will never be a straight line, but you have so many resources to help you stay on track!

22

POWER-CHARGED RETROACTIVE JEALOUSY-CRUSHING GUIDED MEDITATIONS

Meditation is one of the most useful tools for healing that you will find. RJ likes to control your mind and make you focus on intrusive thoughts that become bothersome. When you meditate, you focus on doing the exact opposite. With an intention set, you will be able to concentrate on a much more positive end result. All of your worries, fears, and anxieties will melt away after you complete these step-by-step guided meditations. Each of them places a focus on getting you back in control and making your mind strong enough to defeat RJ for good. Follow one of these meditations when you feel like you need a reset or when you feel like RJ is trying to come back into your life. All of them are designed to help you and make you stronger.

Meditation One: Letting Go

Begin by setting aside 10 minutes of your day that you can spend in this guided meditation while remaining uninterrupted. Pick a location that you feel comfortable in, most likely your bedroom or living room. Make sure that you can be alone for these few minutes, as the silence will become a very important part of your practice. Before you begin, check in with yourself. See where your headspace is and how you are feeling. You can probably tell that RJ is trying to threaten you, so you might feel worried or stressed out by the thought of this. Do your best to remain calm, as this mediation will send RJ on its way.

Before you get started, focus on your breathing. Breathe in for four seconds through your nose and out for four seconds through your mouth. Practice this breathing exercise for a few moments before you start to meditate. This will ground you. When you are ready, lay down in a comfortable position with your legs uncrossed and your arms resting naturally by your side. Make sure that your fists are not clenched and that your toes, jaw, and neck are relaxed. It helps to do this barefoot and in comfortable clothing that you feel you can move in.

Set a timer for ten minutes with a gentle alert sound, and close your eyes. Focus on your breathing exercise again—in for four and out for four. You will find that certain thoughts will begin to arise. Welcome them. See what is truly on your mind, examining one thought at a time. During this whole meditation, you will be breathing at a steady and even pace while making sure that your physical body is relaxed. When an uncomfortable thought pops up, acknowledge it. You do not have to find a solution or do anything further, just sit with the thought for a moment.

Imagine a vast river before you. After you have examined a thought, you will carry it over to the water's edge and send it along. Watch it float down the current, far away from you. Keep doing this for each negative thought that comes up. If a positive thought arises, hold onto this. Cradle it in your arms, metaphorically. Allow yourself to feel all of the benefits of this goodness and all of the great emotions that this brings you. Continue to observe the thoughts that arise. It will be an interesting lesson because your most subconscious thoughts tend to arise during a meditative state.

Once you find a break in the thoughts, focus on your breathing again. Check-in with your physical body. Take note of whether or not you feel more relaxed and calm. If you are holding onto any tension, now is the time to let go. Just let go. As you let go of the negative thoughts that were fueled by RJ and watched them float down the river, you are also working on relaxing your physical body until it feels good. The entirety of this meditation is healing and will work on relaxing you from the inside out. Do not forget to keep breathing, in for four and out for four.

Focus on an intention that you would like to leave the meditation with. This intention can be anything, as long as it pertains to letting go and to freeing yourself from RJ for good. Once you have this in your mind, hold onto it tightly. Imagine it burning brightly, surrounded by a protective white light of energy. This represents that RJ cannot touch your intention. This is yours to keep and to manifest. Nothing bad will happen to it, as long as you honor it by protecting it and practicing it when you complete your meditation. Think about this intention, observing the calming glow of its light. Think about how many good things it will bring into your life.

It is time to come back now. Start by wiggling your toes, bringing life back into your feet. Remember where you are, the room you are in. Move your legs around a bit, followed by your torso. Open and close your hands while gently shaking your arms. Turn your head from left to right a few times. Finally, take a big inhalation of breath, and on your exhale you will open your eyes slowly. The calmness should remain with you, and you will understand that you have let go of your negativity. You no longer have room to house it within. Sit up slowly, observing how grounded you feel.

Meditation Two: Tension Release

Allow yourself 15 minutes for this mediation. If you are feeling particularly stressed out or frustrated, this is a great one to use. This tension-release guided meditation will allow you to feel better physically while also reframing your thoughts. Much like the other mediation, pick a safe location and a comfortable outfit to wear. Set a timer with a gentle alert tone that will remind you when 15 minutes have passed. Always start by focusing on your breathing before you lay down. Make sure that you are taking steady and even breaths, leveling out any shaky or shallow breathing.

Lie down and close your eyes, this time with your legs crossed and your arms crossed. Close off your physical body as much as you can. You will need ample room for this mediation, so make sure that you can spread out during the process. For the first few moments, focus on all of the worries that RJ has brought into your life. Think about how much RJ wants to ruin you and make your life more difficult. Direct this anger and frustration into your meditation right now. Allow your body to naturally tense up as you think about how terrible it has been dealing with RJ.

As your tension rises, allow your toes to curl and your fists to close. Hold as much tension inside of your physical body as you can while thinking about this negativity. Next, take a large inhalation and hold it for 10 seconds. Count slowly in your head, backward from 10. You are going to have a big release of tension at the end of your countdown. Get ready to send RJ out the door and to reclaim your life. Think about how RJ has no control over you because you are powerful and strong. There is nothing that you cannot complete when you put your mind and energy behind it.

Once 10 seconds have passed, release your breath with an audible sigh. You can even groan if it feels right. Uncross your arms and your legs while you simultaneously open your fists and uncurl your toes. Relax every single muscle in your body, freeing it from the tension you were holding onto. You can spread out like a starfish, getting completely comfortable and basking in this feeling of relaxation. This is what your body feels like now with the stress alleviated from it. You do not have to carry these burdens with you any longer. Acknowledge how much better you feel.

This is what your mind feels like when it is free of these bothersome thoughts that RJ brings. It should now be emptier than ever, cast aside are the negative thoughts that left when all of the physical tension was released. You might feel a little drained after this process because you were holding so much tension inside for so long. Think about how this is what you are doing to yourself when you let RJ control you. By living with so much stress and tension, you are hurting your mind, body, and spirit. Try to take a mental snapshot of this feeling, pure relaxation. This is what you must return to every time.

You are empowered now, stronger than before. You can take on anything that comes your way. When you open your eyes shortly, the RJ cannot come back to you because you have banished it. Focus on your breathing. Is it still steady and even? Make sure that you get it back to that steady place, and become aware of your physical body. Release the stress in your neck and jaw that likes to return out of habit. You no longer need to hold on tightly to these things.

Once your 15 minutes is up, slowly open your eyes. Sit up when you feel ready. Take a look around the room, and realize where you are. You have just released all of your tension, and it is nowhere to be found. You can continue with your day or end your night in peace while knowing that your RJ will not return to you. Now, you are protected from its negative ways. As you place your feet on the ground, make sure that you are sturdy and stable. After standing up, stretch your body out as much as you can. Feel all of the tension-free movement that you now have. Remember this feeling and how you can return to it in as little as 15 minutes the next time that you are stressed out.

Meditation Three: Deep Healing

For this meditation, you will be focusing on one specific issue or trigger that RJ brings into your life. Before you lie down, think about what your focus is. Feel all of the negativity that it brings to you and how it makes you feel powerless. You do not like this feeling, and you are ready to take your life back. RJ has been in control for far too long, ruining moments and opportunities for you. If a little anger builds up inside, this is okay. It is time to heal yourself deeply, and you are now ready to begin. Set a timer for 10 minutes with a gentle alert tone. You will be seated for this mediation, so find a comfortable and quiet place to sit. When you take a seat, place your palms down on your thighs while resting them comfortably.

Close your eyes, and think about the way that your feet feel on the ground. Are you grounded right now? Imagine the roots of your tree coming out from the bottoms of your soles. Make sure that each part of your feet is firmly planted. This is your strength, where you stand. RJ cannot rip you from the ground and rip you away from your life because you are strongly rooted in your beliefs and values. Remind yourself of some of the amazing qualities that you possess. Think about the qualities that your partner loves most about you, the ones they tell you about.

Move up to your legs, thinking about the way that they carry you through life. Acknowledge that you can walk away from negativity and toxicity at any time. The situation that you were focusing on before is something that you can react to. If you choose to react in a way that is going to upset you more, then this is not the right approach. Imagine yourself walking away from this choice. Cycle through your mind while considering some other approaches. Think about how you can handle this without disrupting your peace.

Your torso holds a lot of power. Think about all of your bodily systems and how they work to keep you healthy. Your heart beats for you to keep you alive, and your heart has many feelings. The situation you are focusing on hurts your heart and causes you to act out of jealousy. You no longer need to put this much stress on yourself. Acknowledge your worth and that you deserve better. Your body deserves better, for it carries you through each day without any complaints. It is something that happens naturally, and it is something to be thankful for.

The way that your arms can pull you back up gives you strength. When you have spiraled in the past, you pull your way up and out of that dark place. You are going to do this again with this situation. Think about how you have made it this far, always pulling yourself back up. You do not need anybody to give you permission or validation to feel better. You can do this for yourself, reminding yourself that you are a lot stronger than you think.

Lastly, your mind becomes the focus. The way that you think is so unique and special. Even despite what RJ does to your mind, you are still capable of coming up with some great thoughts and ideas. Think about the last time that you felt happy. Think about what you were doing and what was going on around you. Imagine that you are currently in those surroundings, about to experience this happiness again. You can recreate a specific moment if you would like.

You are here now, in this moment for the last part of your guided meditation. Imagine that a bad situation is trying to disrupt your moment. You gently turn your back to RJ, and you continue to focus on this great memory of being happy. This is the feeling you are left with as the timer goes off and alerts you to come back to the present. You are now rejuvenated and strong. The situation that you started off your mediation thinking about has no place in your life any longer.

Meditation Four: Transformative Space

This is going to be the longest of the guided meditations, so make sure that you set aside 20 minutes of uninterrupted time for yourself. Pick a quiet and safe space where you can lie down before you begin. During this meditation, you will set your timer like you normally do but will also play some calming music. Any music that is slow-paced and instrumental only will do. Put on your music, lie down comfortably, and close your eyes. Feel yourself sinking into this vibration. Consider how this music makes you feel, what it makes you think of. Certain thoughts that are fueled by RJ might rise to the surface, but that is okay—observe.

The moment is yours to guide, not RJ's. See what it wants, then decide what you are going to do about it. Depending on the thought that comes up, either cast it away from you or bring it in close to you. Focus on the music while also paying attention to your steady and even breaths. Feel how grounded you are right now, strong and confident. You do not need anything else to complete you or to make you feel good about yourself. You can do this on your own because you have this kind of power—tell yourself how powerful you are if the doubts start to creep in.

Keep observing your thoughts, paying attention to the ones that come up. After a few moments of this, you will notice some quiet space. Grasp onto this quiet space and fill it with the music that is playing in the background. Imagine a bird that is soaring in a clear, bright sky. It is flying directly above you and circling around to the music that is flowing through you. This is a symbol of peace and resilience. You are going to feel like this bird, free and able to spread your wings.

Now, you are going to think about yourself at your very strongest. Think about who this person is and what makes them strong. If you feel like it, you can even create an alter-ego that is stronger than you have ever been. Even though you have yet to reach this point, you can vicariously live through your alter-ego. Consider what they would do if RJ tried to ruin their life. Would they stand for it? Imagine how effortless it is for them to banish RJ and to continue living the best life possible while surrounded by only positive things.

Become this strong being, manifesting that you are going to feel this power when you are finished with your mediation. Do not forget about the music, creating a wonderful tune to fill the background. How would your strong alter-ego feel when looking up and seeing the bird? They would not have a feeling that is wishful or worried. Instead, they would feel just as strong and just as free. Maybe they would look up and smile, acknowledging that they know how the bird feels and what it is like to be free. They would understand that it is empowering to live their life while being free of any binds or vices.

You are this person. Tell yourself again—this is you. While you envision someone so strong and powerful, it is coming from a place deep down that is actually who you are. You just need to work on bringing this version of yourself to the surface when RJ tries to threaten you. Since you created this all in your mind, recognize how powerful you are and that these thoughts are your own. You are transformative because you can become this strong representation of freedom. Since you did it now, you can do it again.

End your mediation with this thought, feeling empowered and proud of yourself. Tell yourself why you are proud, thinking about some positive affirmations that will make you feel great. Begin to focus on the music again, allowing it to fill your ears with the tune. Steady your breathing if it becomes unsteady. Relax all of the muscles in your body, still keeping track of the music and how it sounds. When your timer goes off, you are going to open your eyes and realize that you are the strongest version of yourself. You have transformed into this powerful being, and nothing can bring you down.

Meditation Five: An Emotional Purge

RJ makes you feel many different emotions when you least expect it. By making you feel like you are not in control of your emotions, this can bring up some pretty strong negative feelings. You do not need to live this way, and you can emotionally purge all of this negativity from your life now. Set aside 10 minutes for this guided meditation, and complete it in silence. Lie down in a place that is comfortable and quiet. Once you feel steady and secure, close your eyes. You are going to think about all of the emotions that are currently in your mind and in your body. Every single emotion will rise to the surface now, from the good to the very bad.

Breathe steadily as all of these emotions come to you. The more difficult ones to deal with are going to challenge your breath, but you will be prepared to steady it. Keep calm as you cycle through all of these different emotions. You must allow them to all rise to the surface before you can purge them. Imagine that they are all in a bowl, swirling around together. Let them mingle; observe which ones play off of each other. Some of them are closely connected; this is RJ's doing. They want you to feel bad about yourself and upset about your life. Jealousy threatens you, acting as the most powerful of all.

While it can be overwhelming to feel them all, you have them contained now. All of them are in this bowl, and you can take the bowl into your hands now. Imagine that you are towering over the bowl, looking inside of it. With one hand, you can pick out any of the positive emotions that you want to fill yourself with. Let them back into your mind, uplifting your spirit. As for the negative emotions, keep them contained in this bowl. Watch them swirl around, hopeless and in your hands now. You get to decide what you would like to do with them.

Picture that you are walking through a dense forest. All of the trees, shrubs, and plants are surrounding you as you walk along the path. You are still holding onto the bowl, placing any new emotions that come your way inside of it. By the time you reach the end of the trail, you encounter a huge sinkhole. It is deep enough to take several people down into its depths, but it is not a threat to you—it wants your negative emotions. Survey the bowl one final time, plucking out any of the stray positive emotions that have since filled its vessel.

Now, it is time for the purge. Pour out all of your negative emotions with a forceful hand. Watch them get eaten away by the sinkhole, taking RJ along with it. They can no longer touch you because they are going down, down, and even further down into the earth. Place the bowl on the ground, imagine turning around, and walk away back out of the dense jungle. You are free from these negative emotions now. Imagine that you have selected a peaceful place to rest on the surface of the forest floor. The grass is lush and warm on your skin.

You are fully at peace now, fully relaxed and at ease. Allow your physical body to relax as if you were really there right now. Become in tune with the moment that is unfolding before you. Notice that your mind has a lot more space for thinking and for positive emotions. Think fondly of the ones that you held onto. This is true peace, and this is what you deserve. Remain here, breathing steadily until it is time to open your eyes and come back. You are going to have a great rest of your day or a great evening. Nothing can bring you down now.

Action Step

Your step for this chapter is to commit to meditating every day this week! It is not a lot to do, as you can see that some of these meditations range in length. If you can find even just 10 minutes to set aside for yourself, you will be able to feel all of the wonderful and powerful benefits that these guided meditations bring. At any point, you can refer back to them to help guide you away from the negativity that RJ wants you to feel. You now have these meditations as additional tools to help you when you feel like you are about to be stuck in the darkness. You are never as alone as you think you are, and these meditations will prove it to you.

When you meditate, you are sitting in a state of pure mindfulness. By acknowledging how you are feeling and why, you will gain a better understanding of what exactly RJ is doing to your mind and body. This is going to make you even more present in your daily life. After each meditation session, you are going to feel invigorated and powerful, like you should. Nothing will be able to stop you now, and this is just the beginning. As you continue on your healing journey, make sure to include plenty of meditation. Commit to it, just like you committed to healing from your RJ.

23

DESTROY RETROACTIVE JEALOUSY FOREVER; A 30-MINUTE DAILY RITUAL TO SUPERCHARGE YOUR EXISTENCE

This is your step-by-step guide to supercharging your day. By committing just 30 minutes of time being extra mindful each day, you will learn how to completely rid your life of jealousy for good. This is not a temporary fix. It is something that you can do continually and become great at. These habits will form a new routine for you that will work hard to keep you protected from RJ and any of its other symptoms. In general, each of these habits is great to keep because they are all going to positively benefit many aspects of your life. Those without RJ would even benefit from adopting them, but you will find them to be extra helpful as you continue with your RJ healing journey.

The 4-Step Ritual

This practice is meant to be quick and easy for you to follow. Because it involves techniques that you have become familiar with throughout this book, you should find it especially easy to jump right in. Now is the best time to begin crushing RJ for good because each moment that you do not, it has the potential to grow even stronger and to ruin your life. You want to stop RJ in its tracks without giving it any further opportunities to take power away from you. This is your life, and you should be able to live it freely. This ritual will help you reclaim your freedom and empower you to become an even better version of yourself.

1. Gratitude Meditation

You will begin your ritual with a brief meditation. Fit this in sometime between waking up and leaving your house for the day. This should be one of the very first activities that you do because it will leave you feeling charged and ready to take on anything! You only need to commit five minutes of time to this first step, so there are no excuses—you have five minutes to spare each day, so find them! It would be best to do this upon waking up in the morning because you are already in a quiet and comfortable space. Before your mind starts wandering, you will be able to clear your head.

Close your eyes, then focus on something that you are grateful for. Whether you decide to focus on one thing at a time each day or all that you are thankful for, make sure that this is the only thing on your mind as you complete this short meditation. Make sure that your eyes are closed, your body is resting comfortably, and your breathing is steady. This is a standard approach for most meditations, and it should be the one that you take daily as you complete your gratitude meditation. It is simple because you do not have to focus on anything else, only what you are grateful for.

At the end of your mediation make sure to smile. Smiling can actually release endorphins and make you feel happier. It is a way to uplift your spirits and ensure that you are going to get your day off to a great start. While you smile, think about what you feel grateful for that day. Really try to make this your main focus so that you can leave your meditation still thinking about it. This is going to raise your vibration in both a way that you can feel internally and a way that people will notice externally. The vibration that you put into the world is going to manifest what happens to you daily.

If you wake up feeling grumpy and dreading the start of your day, imagine what that does to your vibration. It is going to feel very negative and low. This might actually inspire others to start conflicts or disagreements with you because they will be able to feel this negativity coming off of you. While the practice of performing a gratitude meditation daily supercharges you, waking up in a negative mood can do the complete opposite. It can cause a lingering feeling of disdain that will make everything seem harder than usual and more frustrating.

So many people roll out of bed and sigh at the thought of what they must tackle at the start of their day. Your goal is to get out of bed feeling inspired. Get ready for what is to come and how you will handle it with ease! You can do this, and your meditation is going to get you started on the right path. When you give yourself this kind of structure to start your day, the rest of the positivity will follow naturally. It becomes a lot easier to look on the bright side when you are already starting there.

You cannot live your life trapped in your fears and anxiety. This is what RJ wants for you, and this is how you become prey. Being deeply immersed in a feeling of gratitude is a great way to banish jealousy from your life. When you are so involved with a feeling that is consuming and positive, there is absolutely no room for RJ to insert itself. Your focus is going to become even stronger and more powerful each day that you complete step one. As you get used to this new routine, it will even become comforting to you. This is something you will start to look forward to each day.

Having a guaranteed moment of peace is so important in today's world. With all of the chaos that is always going on around you, it makes sense that you are just craving some time to breathe and to be. You are only human, and you can only take on so many stressors at once. There is no need to push yourself to the point of burnout by trying to juggle them all. Instead, you will rid your body and mind of them. Soon enough, you will be able to rid your life of them. With step one alone, you will be able to see major improvements in your life and in your mindset.

1. Sending Love

The second step can be done while you are getting ready in the morning. You might usually spend this time thinking about what you have to do that day and about all of the tasks that you are dreading. You might even be focused on what your RJ wants you to think about, causing your anxiety to feel like it is through the roof. This is not a great way to begin your day, and you do not have to feel this way on a regular basis any longer. You are going to set your focus on sending love and putting out good intentions now.

While you get ready, think about three people that you want to send love to that day. There are probably many more people that you want to set this good intention for, but selecting three each day will make it more meaningful. You can plan to send love to the same people every day or change it up—this part is up to you. Once you have these people in mind, take a moment to think about who they are and what they mean to you. Are they your friends, family, and loved ones? These people came to your mind first because they matter a great deal to you.

For each person, think of a different intention that you would like to send their way. It can be something as simple as hoping they have a good day to something more specific and tailored to the individual. Experiment with the intentions that you send and the way that you express your love. Even though they will not be able to hear the intentions directly from you, believe in your higher vibration and the way that the energy will carry it toward them. This is why your meditation is step number one. You will be fully prepared to send out this mass amount of love.

Much like expressing gratitude for the things that you have in your life, continuing down this kind path to start your day is going to uplift you even further. When it feels difficult to be kind to yourself, you can probably find it easier to be kind to other people. Saying something nice to someone you love feels more natural because RJ has conditioned you to treat yourself poorly. When you practice both forms of kindness each day, this is going to show RJ that you are no longer playing by these rules —you can do both and feel great about doing so.

This step should take around 10 minutes, but you do not necessarily have to time it. You always take at least 10 minutes to get ready for your day anyway, so you might as well put this time to good use. You can send out love and great energy while preparing yourself for the day ahead.

This routine is meant to mesh flawlessly with your current lifestyle by becoming something that does not require much change at all. You should not feel very overwhelmed by beginning this ritual because it works in line with the activities that you are already doing anyway. This is just a more efficient way to start your day.

Imagine all of the good energy that you are putting out into the world after completing this step for a week, even a few weeks. This thought should make you feel good and feel proud of yourself. It is definitely an accomplishment, and the energy that you put out is going to mirror the energy that you receive in return. You know that your loved ones cannot hear you sending love and good inventions their way, but they will likely be sending them right back to you. It is amazing how this can foster an even stronger bond and connection with someone that you care about without even directly contacting them.

Starting your day in a loving and caring mindset puts you in the right headspace to interact with other people. This is important for those who have jobs that require socialization. You need to feel prepared to handle all of the interactions that you will have each day, and some are going to feel challenging. This is okay because step two will help to remind you to send out positive energy at any chance you get. Just because you do not get along with someone or if someone complains to you at work does not mean that your entire day will be ruined.

1. **EFT Tapping Routine**

This is the second to last step of your new daily ritual. After you have gotten ready for the day, you are going to take 10 minutes to practice an EFT tapping routine. This is going to be simple yet effective. It will help you by reminding you that you will stay strong during moments that trigger you or past memories that try to intrude upon your day. By performing an EFT tapping routine daily, your nervous system will learn that it does not have to enter fight-or-flight mode each time that a trigger is encountered. You will be able to look it in the face and go around it.

Take a seat, and begin with the karate chop that you are now familiar with. Think about your triggers and how they used to upset you so much, potentially even ruin a perfectly good day for you. This is the power that they once had over you, but this is in the past. Tapping the side of your eye, you will remind yourself that RJ has nothing over you, no control over you. By tapping under your eye, you are acknowledging that you are filled with positivity and good energy. Under the nose will signify that you have overcome so much and worked very hard to get to where you are.

Continuing forward, the tap on the chin will remind you that you have a voice to use and that you should use it wisely. Your words and thoughts have so much power. Your collarbone tap will teach you that you are strong-willed and able to take on anything. Under the arm is your reminder to go for your goals and aspirations. The final tap on top of your head is you putting on your suit of armor. RJ cannot reach you now, and you will do everything in your power to deal with it in a way that no longer disrupts your life.

As you stand up, feel that you are firmly rooted in place. You are a strong, courageous being. You have come so far and have already accomplished so much. All of these triggering moments in the past and outbursts caused by RJ have allowed you to learn many lessons that are going to be useful to you for the rest of your life. While you once felt like you had to live under RJ's control, you can now see the light at the end of the tunnel—it is you who holds all the power and control. This is your life to make what you will of it. You can choose to do anything and be anything that you set your mind on.

If at any point throughout your day you feel that there is something triggering or relating to RJ trying to stand in your way, you can remind yourself of this EFT tapping session that you had in the morning. This will keep you strong and allow you to keep bettering yourself. It can be very difficult to unlearn how to be triggered by certain things because of your past history. It has shaped you, and there is nothing wrong with that. Without your past, you would not be the amazing person that you are today. You must understand that there is a difference between your past shaping you and your past controlling your life in the present.

RJ will do everything that it can to encourage you to live in the past, but you will not give in. You will use EFT tapping as a scientific approach to banish it from your life for good. By tapping these acupressure points, you are physically and mentally healing yourself in a way that avoidance cannot compare. You have probably just tried to avoid or ignore triggers before, and this will not always work. RJ can be strong when you are not in the right mindset. It sneaks up on you when it knows that you are feeling weak.

Remind yourself that EFT tapping is one of your strongest soldiers. It always has your back, and it will be there for you at any time that you need it. When you feel incredibly triggered, EFT tapping is one of the best ways to bring yourself back to the present and to remind yourself not to live in the past or these past worries. You have already made it so far, and these moments do not have to cause you to have any setbacks.

1. Powerful Affirmations

The final step in your new daily ritual is a short one. This step only takes five minutes, and you can complete it before you walk out the door to start your day. You are going to stand in front of a mirror and take a good look at yourself. Make sure that you respect yourself by making eye contact and really observing the person standing in front of you. If any negativity tries to pop into your head, banish it. Remind yourself that you are an amazing individual who is working so hard to channel more positivity into your life. You have no room for anything that tries to bring you down.

You are going to recite 10 positive and powerful affirmations to yourself with conviction. Take this step very seriously, as it is going to become the foundation of your day. You are about to get started on a day that will have its ups and downs, but you will not falter. No matter what happens to you, this process is going to encourage you to stay strong and to remain positive. Affirmations hold a lot of power behind them, especially when you can come up with them on your own. Earlier in the book, you learned how to create your own, so you should have a few that you use regularly already. You can say any 10 affirmations that you would like to yourself as you stand in front of the mirror.

If you find it hard to focus or to take yourself seriously, imagine that you were saying each of these affirmations to someone that you love and care about very much. You would be genuine with them, would look them in the eyes with honesty. This is how you deserve to treat yourself, and you will practice this until you are able to get to this point. Many people find it difficult to be kind to themselves because RJ has completely destroyed their self-esteem, but this is no excuse to hold onto —you can reverse this feeling by taking a proactive approach to being much kinder to yourself on a regular basis.

This step is part of your daily ritual because it is meant to become habit-forming. You will learn how to say these kind words to yourself without having to imagine that you are saying them to someone else. Eventually, you are going to believe yourself and believe all of these kind words. Take them to heart, and truly listen to each affirmation carefully. These are the thoughts that you want to randomly have in your head throughout the day. You can learn how to reprogram your entire brain to think more positively by keeping up with your affirmations and closing out your daily ritual in a fantastic way.

When you make it a point to regularly recite positive affirmations aloud, this encourages your inner critic to become less harsh. RJ has trained your inner critic well. It has used your inner voice against you many times in the past, but now you are the teacher. You get to tell your inner critic how it should behave and why it should respect you. This is something that you deserve because you are a great person with many redeeming qualities. By changing up the affirmations on a regular basis, this step will never get mundane or boring. There are always so many great things that you can find to say about yourself, as you are a person who is constantly healing and growing.

Bonus: Nighttime Ritual

At the end of your long day, you will probably feel a little different than you felt when you were supercharged and positive in the morning—this is natural. Each day is going to take a different emotional toll on you. Some will be great and positive, allowing you to remain mindful of the ritual that you completed. Others will completely challenge you and drain you, but this is okay because you can create a nighttime ritual that mimics the one that you started your day with. By having two rituals in your life, you will always be sure to start and end each day on a good note. This is going to impact your mental health in a positive way and make it even more difficult for RJ to return.

After you have spent time with your family, eaten dinner, and relaxed a bit, you can unwind for bed while completing a positive nighttime ritual. This ritual will become just as beneficial to you as the first one. With this ritual, you can make it fit the actions that you already take when you end your day. You might like to relax in bed or spend some quality time with your partner. No matter what you are doing, you can always set a focus on gratitude. As soon as your head hits the pillow, you will begin by thinking of what you are grateful for. Compare these things to what you thought of earlier in the day. Observe how similar or different they are. This can teach you a lesson about what might be bothering you or what might be helping you get through your tough moments.

As you close your eyes, you can have a short meditation session that will allow you to flow gently into your sleep state. Focus on your day and all of the most memorable highlights. If anything positive happens to you, hold onto these moments. Think about why they made you happy or why they uplifted you. These are the moments that you will want to strive for during the next day and the days to follow. See if you can pinpoint anything that you chose to do that made these positive moments possible.

For the negative moments, you will use visualization to help you rid your mind of them so you can sleep soundly. After observing the thoughts that arise and taking the lessons that you need from them, send all of the negative moments down the river. Watch as they float far away from you, unable to pair up with RJ and hurt you as you sleep. You are going to have a very good night's rest so that you will be ready for the day to come. No matter what you have planned, this is going to get you off to a great start and put you in a good mood when you wake up.

Your nighttime routine can be just this simple, but it will make a huge impact on your life. You will no longer have to worry about RJ and when it might strike because you are in control now. You are the one who gets to decide what kind of energy is allowed in your life and what kind of energy is going to be cast far away from you. This is a very powerful thought to observe, and it should make you feel great and so much stronger than you were when you first started reading this book. Take a moment to look back on how much progress you have made already. This is only the beginning for you and your healing journey.

Action Step

Your final action step of the book is to write out your daily ritual and place it on your wall, or someplace you will see it frequently. This will serve as a constant reminder that you can do this and that you have a life that is structured to defend you against RJ for good! Mark off each day on a calendar that you complete your daily ritual, and watch as you see yourself making ample amounts of progress. This will keep you going and allow you to stay motivated. The way that you choose to motivate yourself says a lot about how far you have come already. RJ cannot touch you anymore, and you are choosing a better life for yourself.

Even if it tries to reenter your life, you now have a daily routine that you can use to banish RJ at the sight of it. You know all of the signs to look for and the ways it can make you feel. You also have plenty of tools and resources to help you get through potential relapses and tough times. No matter what happens, you are going to be solid and resilient. You are not the same person that you were before, helpless against RJ. Now, you can rise above it and feel proud of who you are and where you stand.

AFTERWORD

Now, you must go off on your healing journey by using the practices that you were taught in this book. As you do so, think about light and love surrounding you every step of the way. You are now being guided by positivity and a higher vibration that will encourage you to not only become a less jealous partner but a better person as a whole. You can do anything! Banishing RJ is definitely one of those things that you have already taken great strides toward accomplishing. It is one gigantic monster to face, but the bravery and courage that you have is seen by your willingness to change your life for the better. By using this book and the tools within, you are already expressing that you do see hope for your present and future.

You have already transformed your life in so many ways, and you will continue to do so. Not only are you a powerful individual, but you are a wonderful human being who can use your good intentions and positivity for the better. By changing your own life, you are also touching the lives of those around you. Positivity is one of those contagious feelings, and you make the world a better place by just being in it when you operate on this higher frequency with such a powerful vibration.

By taking this initiative, you have kickstarted your path to healing in the best way possible! Congratulate yourself as you continue with this journey, using this book for reference every time you feel stuck or feel like RJ is trying to get you down. Remember your soldiers, always willing and able to help you because you are never as alone as you think you are. Not only do you need to complete the steps in this book to heal yourself from RJ, but you must also continue this healing journey. Make it a priority! When you showcase how important this is to you, it will become a prominent goal in your life that you will accomplish. You can do anything.

PART III
BOOK 3: MASTERING YOUR THOUGHTS

MIND-HACKS NO ONE'S TALKING ABOUT, DETACHMENT SECRETS AND HOW TO KICK INNER EMOTIONS INTO HIGH GEAR

INTRODUCTION

For many years I lived a life of self-doubt, anxiety, regret, guilt, and helplessness. I let negativity creep in and rule every aspect of my life. I learned to smile, laugh, and portray a positive exterior, but my mind worked full time to remind me that it was all a show. In many ways, I hated myself and lived a life so much less than I knew I was capable of. Does this sound familiar?

I have a very vivid memory of being on vacation. We saved for a year to be able to go. It was a dream of ours to rent a home on the beach in California. We wanted to take the family to Disneyland, eat at amazing restaurants, and lounge on the beach. We planned the vacation for months. We packed weeks before we left, that's how excited we were!

It was our third day of vacation, and it had been the best time we ever had. It could not have been more perfect. We were upgraded to first class on our flight, our house was even nicer than we expected, and the weather was beautiful. We were laying on the beach and I should have been enjoying everything and basking in the wonderful experience. Instead, my inner thoughts were that I looked overweight in the photos. I was anxious about being a victim of a random crime. I was worried constantly about our family's safety. And I couldn't stop stressing about the finances even though I knew we had planned for it. I seemed incapable of enjoying anything and it put me in a bad mood because I was so angry at myself. What was wrong with me?

That vacation was a pivotal moment for me. I was so tired of living in a state of negativity. At home I was able to convince myself that it was normal. I was functioning on an everyday basis; I had a great career and lots of friends. I had convinced myself that I was just a negative person and that it was totally normal. If I stayed positive on the outside, it wasn't a big deal. As long as my inner thoughts weren't pushed outward, I felt like I wasn't doing any harm. I was fine.

However, when I was in paradise and unable to enjoy it, I was not able to push down my doubts anymore. I was struggling with anxiety, depression, and negative self-talk. I realized more than ever that I wanted to change this, but I had no idea where to start.

My Starting Point

When I decided to make a change for myself, I didn't realize the path I was starting down. I genuinely thought that my inner thoughts, as horrible and awful as they could be, weren't affecting my health and my life on a grand scale. I thought they were no big deal, and perhaps I didn't really need much change. I thought that if I could lower my stress levels a bit, and learn to be a bit more positive, I would be fine. I couldn't have been more wrong.

My research and journey made me aware of what my thoughts were doing to me both physically and emotionally. I had no idea that, by not taking them more seriously, I was damaging myself more and more each day. There were so many miraculous things that have changed as I have learned to master my thoughts.

Since my resolution to work on my inner self, I have seen changes within my life that I couldn't have anticipated:

1. My sleep has improved and I don't wake up tired as often as I used to.
2. I get sick much less.
3. I have lost weight.

4. I am more flexible with my schedule because I respond better to uncertainty.
5. My posture and demeanor have changed so much that I get comments on it regularly.
6. My energy levels are much higher.
7. I feel less "brain fog," and operate on a much higher level of productivity.
8. I'm more social
9. My relationships and connections with loved ones have deepened in ways I didn't know they could
10. I have a general sense of lightness. The best way I can explain it is the old standby of "a weight has been lifted off my shoulders," or, more accurately, my heart.

This list goes on and on about how much better I feel when it comes to my day to day.

My starting point when I wanted to feel better was simply by researching, "How can I make myself a more positive person?" I quickly moved onto other searches such as:

- How can I feel better about myself?
- Techniques for thinking more positively
- How can I make my inner emotions happier?
- Ways to help with anxiety, depression, and OCD.

The answers that I received were a variety of medical opinions, spiritual offerings, and emotional healing techniques that have helped transform me into a new version of myself. I feel healed and cleansed. I am living the best way I know how, and I attribute it to all of the reasons I will share with you throughout the book.

My best advice when it comes to learning new paths in your journey to self-help is to be patient with yourself. You are an amazing individual! Taking the time to read this book tells me that you are ready for a change like I was. So be kind to yourself, and give yourself time to adapt to new ways of thinking.

Each time I tried a new technique or method of mastering my thoughts, I would give myself anywhere from two weeks up to two months to really focus on how it could help me retrain my brain. And I certainly wasn't done after two months, that was just a starting point to decide if a technique was going to be beneficial to me personally. Then the ongoing work starts to make this a lifelong process. So whatever it is that you need to help get you where you want to be, take it and don't look back.

24

IS YOUR LIFE A SELF-MADE MENTAL HELL?

My vacation story is only one small example of what my life was like. I would lay in bed at night unable to sleep because I would replay situations over and over in my head. I would fixate on things that had happened that day, that month, or even years prior. I would stress about conversations I had with people I barely knew. Even worse, I would think about things I saw in the news or on TV and be terrified that horrible things could happen to me and my family. Any situation that should have been positive, I would flip to think about all the negative things that could wreck it. When I reflect back on what my daily thoughts were, I wonder how I ever justified that as normal?

Types of Negative Thoughts

Dr. David Burns discusses 10 types of negative thought in his book *Feeling Good: The New Mood Therapy* (2008). Also seen as "cognitive disorders," seeing these 10 types of negative thoughts was extremely eye opening for me. It immediately put me at ease that I wasn't alone in my way of thinking. I could put a name and an explanation to what I was doing, and also begin the process to start changing it.

I'll discuss the 10 types of thinking now as Dr. Burns describes them:

1. **All or Nothing:** This style or thinking (also referred to as "Black and White thinking") is the idea that you either do something exactly the way you expect it to happen and at full force, or you just give up. I approached everything with this mentality. I felt that if I couldn't devote large amounts of time to something, I wouldn't even bother. And then I would get upset or stressed that I hadn't done anything! It's very unrealistic and sets you up for inevitable failure. An example of this style of thinking would be if you started a new workout plan. You made a big goal of going from no workouts, to five workouts/week. If you even miss one, you just quit because either you commit fully or it's not worth it in your mind.
2. **Overgeneralization:** This style of thinking happens when one event or thought causes a person to think that's the way it always is. They create a huge generalization from one instance. An example would be if you have a really uneventful month. Work is normal, nothing too exciting happening there. You see friends a few times. You aren't too social or spending too much time alone. Your health is great. No sickness to report. Nothing is out of the ordinary except at the end of the month you receive a speeding ticket in the mail. It's going to cost you a lot of money. Your thoughts immediately start to spiral. "Of course this would happen to me, I always have the worst luck," or "What a terrible month this has been." Even though nothing bad happened all month, you overgeneralize because of one thing. Think about these statements you may have thought about:

- "Nothing good ever happens to me."
- "I never win at anything."
- "Some people have all the luck."

1. **Mental Filter:** A mental filter is when you tend to pick out and focus on the small negative details in what should be a good situation, so the entire situation is perceived as negative. An example would be if you had a great night out for dinner. The conversation was great, food was good, and the service was fantastic. As you get up to leave the restaurant, you slip and fall. No one else in your group even gives it a second thought after they realize you are okay. After you get home, the only thing you focus on is how silly you looked, and how embarrassed you feel, and you forget about the rest of the night.
2. **Disqualifying the Positive:** This type of thinking basically renders you incapable of taking compliments or positive feedback. If someone were to say to you "Wow you did a great job on that project," your response would be, "I think I got lucky." You see things that you do positively as a one time thing, or compliments as something that aren't true.
3. **Jumping to Conclusions:** This type of thinking is when we assume things about what other people are thinking, or situations that have happened, or even predict things before they have occurred. An example would be if your friend cancels plans with you at the last minute without much explanation. You assume that it must be because they are mad at you and you spend days trying to figure out what went wrong, and create a whole story in your head. Then after a few days up, they call you up to apologize for canceling but they had to go help a family member in another city with an emergency situation. You spent days of energy fretting about something that didn't even happen.
4. **Magnification and Minimization:** This type of cognitive disorder refers to our abilities to magnify situations and minimize others depending on which one will have a more negative outcome. With this type of thinking, you can take a situation and minimize something positive you did while also

magnifying one small negative detail to center that into your take-away thoughts. Let's say that you have a performance review at work. Your superior goes over all the wonderful things that you are accomplishing in your position, and references one small negative that they wish you would take more initiative to be a leader within your coworkers. In your head, you would completely minimize the twenty positive things they said, and magnify this one piece of constructive feedback to be a negative that you aren't good at your job and have no future there.

5. **Emotional Reasoning:** This is the idea that your emotions can dictate reality. You allow your emotions to cloud your ability to think rationally. An example would be if you start to get a little down about your relationship with your significant other. Rather than being reasonable, which might sound like "We haven't been getting along lately. We've both been so busy at work, we should try and make some time for each other." You might have more emotional thoughts like "We haven't been getting along for forever, we've drifted apart. What if they don't love me anymore?" You know in your mind that it's not the case, but you just let your emotions take over.

6. **Should Statements:** You give yourself orders and goals by creating "should" and "shouldn't" statements. "I should workout more." "I should be a better friend." "I shouldn't stress so much." They are statements that are usually vague, full of pressure, and set unrealistic expectations for yourself. Should statements usually set you up for failure.

7. **Labeling and Mislabeling:** This behavior is when you give labels to yourself, other people, or perhaps even situations. It makes it very difficult for you to see past the labels, and most likely the label was an unfair assessment in the first place. An example would be if you were taking a cooking class. On the first day, you burned something in the oven, so you label yourself a bad cook. You made one small mistake, and instead of recognizing that you are a good cook that did something

wrong, you add a label to all of your abilities. The same goes for other people. Maybe, because the teacher of that cooking class made a mistake and told you the wrong temperature on the oven, so you label them as a bad teacher. It's an unfair label, and then you close yourself off to fully learning from them because you have an unfair assessment of their abilities.

8. **Personalization**: This is when you make yourself responsible for external events. You will blame yourself for things that aren't your cause. An example would be if your friend invited you to grab a drink on a patio. The weather turns really badly, so you both have to cancel. Your friend seems disappointed and you blame yourself and feel really bad even though the weather is out of your control. You put the blame and guilt on yourself.

After you see these types of thoughts explained in a simple way, are there any that particularly resonate with you? Do all of them resonate with you? There's no wrong answer here. It's just being aware of those particular negative practices that you may be guilty of.

Being able to see an explanation of all these types of negative thoughts gave me instant clarity and relief. I suddenly didn't feel hopeless in a cloud of negative thoughts. I could now separate out certain recurring thoughts and recognize what they were. All of a sudden, my inner dialogue had context. If I had a thought like "This is going to be an awful week," I could immediately label it as the type of negative thought "jumping to conclusions" and try to rethink my approach heading into the week. All of a sudden it wasn't just me being a negative person anymore, it was me being able to identify my thoughts and actively label them and correct them.

Becoming more aware of what I had been doing to myself, I realized that I truly had turned my inner thoughts into a negative and emotionally draining hell. It impacted so much more of my life than I was aware of, and I was shocked that I let it go on for so long. Why on earth was I doing that to myself, and continuing to do it to myself? What was it specifically that was driving this type of behavior within me? My ongoing journey of self-improvement led me to learn about Obsessive Compulsive Disorder (OCD).

Introduction to Obsessive Compulsive Disorder (OCD)

I think everyone has heard the term OCD before. I had a misguided understanding of what it meant, and certainly didn't think it applied to me. I had only seen it referencing individuals who wanted things neat, tidy, or who obsessed over repetitive behaviors like locking doors 10 times. OCD is much more than that, and my thought patterns were very much a behavior that fell into this diagnosis.

The American Psychiatric Association defines OCD as "a disorder in which people have recurring, unwanted thoughts, ideas or sensations (obsessions) that make them feel driven to do something repetitively (compulsions)" ("What Is Obsessive-Compulsive Disorder?" 2009).

What I realized is that I associated OCD with the compulsive part, and didn't realize that my negative thoughts were a condition of the obsessive component that can affect people. I was consumed by the same types of thoughts, and patterns of responding to things, and didn't know how to break it.

People without OCD can naturally have bothersome thoughts, but the difference of how negative thinking becomes a disorder is when those thoughts disrupt your everyday life. If the thoughts prevent you from living the way you should, then you have a problem.

This was my scenario. When I was younger, I labeled myself a worrier. I would lay awake at night and worry about things that may or may not happen. If I had something due at school I couldn't relax until it was handed in. I worried about getting into trouble, getting sick and missing things. I even worried about getting into trouble because of a misunderstanding and being blamed for something I didn't do. I remember a teacher calling me a "worry wart," as if that's not the most unattractive name ever. I accepted it as who I was, and that it wasn't something I needed to change. I was a worrier, no big deal.

As I got older, my patterns never changed. The only difference now was that I had bigger things to worry about: bills, my job, relationships, and more. I would get very overwhelmed at times, and often retreat from social situations on weekends to give myself a chance to recover from the week's interactions and thoughts. Then I would worry about not seeing people. Would they be mad at me? Would they continue to keep inviting me out if I always declined? I couldn't seem to find a balance anymore between being a worrier and still being happy. The worrying took on a life of its own, and most of it became negative which led to me feeling negative about myself. Even reading back about it exhausts me when I remember how drained I felt all the time.

As I had a family, things took on a completely new level. I had to learn to function because being a parent requires a lot of different skills. I was able to put the needs of my little one's before my own when it came to retreating from situations. Being so busy at all times helped because I didn't have as much downtime for my thoughts to take over. However, when I did have time to just think, it got ugly. My worrying turned into full blown anxiety and it prevented me from sleeping. This would cause me to be less attentive during the day. Then I would feel anxiety and mild depression that I wasn't being a great parent, and that I wasn't giving a top performance at work. I had plenty of things to overanalyze because I never felt like I was doing anything right. It was an endless cycle.

I learned to put on a face, and push the thoughts down. Other areas started to fall apart instead. You know that image where you have a leak somewhere, so you cover it with a finger. It stops for a moment, but the water finds its way out somewhere else. So you cover that water with another finger, and so on. Eventually you run out of fingers to stop the water and it gets out anyway. I managed to push my negative thoughts down, or aside, and cover them up. It worked for a while, but eventually it needed an outlet and, as a result, my negative energy funneled out in the form of Binge eating disorder and I gained a lot of weight.

It took me gaining a lot of weight for my doctor to take notice that something wasn't operating right. My physical condition was now really suffering as a result of my mental struggles. My eating was a side effect of my deeper condition of OCD. The weight gain and my epiphany on our family vacation were the pushes that I needed to start exploring options to heal myself.

Although we have touched on depression, anxiety, OCD, and other emotional disorders, there is so much more to discuss in arming yourself to fight the war against them. For most of us, it will be an ongoing battle that we will fight for the rest of our lives. The exciting news is that it will get easier.

In the beginning, if you look at your disorder when it's at its most powerful moment, it is a formidable opponent. But over time as you get stronger, your opponent will get weaker and smaller. As you grow, your disorder will lose its power with each tool and skill you learn to fight them. What once was an unfair fight with you on the losing side, turns the table to give you the advantage.

Even though we may always be a little prone to suffering from these ailments throughout our lives, by taking the time to learn how to treat them you are giving yourself a lifelong gift to win.

Anxiety

Anxiety is a heightened state of stress. Our body responds to stress, fear, discomfort, uncertainty, and other emotionally charged feelings with an increased worry response. It's perfectly healthy and normal to feel anxious before events or certain situations; a job interview, or running into an ex would be good examples. It's when the level of that worry, and the frequency becomes overwhelming that it has negative consequences.

Our body's natural response to uncertainty and fear is to protect itself with hormonal and sensory reactions. You have probably heard of the "fight or flight" response that is inherent within us. When your body is pushed into this state too often and for too long, it becomes both mentally and physically unhealthy. Your body is not meant to feel that type of intensity for long durations; it needs to relax and calm itself to heal from those experiences.

There are many types of anxiety disorders that range from phobias, social anxiety disorders, to post traumatic stress disorder (PTSD). OCD falls under the category of an anxiety disorder as well, so you can see how my thoughts and cognitive behaviors are all connected.

Depression

Words that are associated with depression are sadness, unmotivated, antisocial, and down. Although these are all accurate, it doesn't fully depict the volume to which they apply. Depression is an all encompassing state of these feelings. Your emotions have spiraled so low that your physical state suffers as well. It is not just being sad and crying. Depression can be when you cry multiple times a day and are often unsure why. Your body aches with overwhelming feelings of despair. It can present itself in a variety of ways, but the one common theme is that it is debilitating to be able to enjoy your life and everything in it.

There are a lot of causes for depression, such as:

Family: Depression can be genetic and is often something seen shared between family members. It's not to say that you are guaranteed to suffer from it if a parent does, but being aware of their history can help you identify if it affects you.

Traumatic event: A tragic event such as a sudden loss can trigger depression. Coping with such events is extremely difficult and your mind can shut down without the proper tools to do so.

Childhood or ongoing trauma: Events from our childhood or ongoing exposure to a really negative source can cause depression as it manifests in us. Not coping with the source leaves us open to negative self-talk and lower self-esteem.

Negative thoughts and OCD: when your thoughts get to the level that we talked about in earlier chapters, your mindset can spiral into a place of depression in addition to your OCD and anxiety. The overwhelming thoughts that occupy every waking moment can become a lot to handle and cause grief to be added to your mental state.

There are many options for treatment of depression, and doing your research to decide what is best for you is very important. There is no one right answer in terms of a correct path to treatment of depression. My personal experience has been with anxiety and OCD, which I have always sought the natural path. My experience with depression is not thorough. It has augmented my other disorders, but I cannot say that I have been completely consumed with it the way others suffer. That being said, I am familiar with using natural methods to relieve emotional disorders and lessen the power of their grip. In the next chapter and later on in the book we will go over methods and techniques in detail to help free your mind of its cognitive disorders and reprogram your mindset to help you grow and develop into a healthier version of yourself.

The Price of Negative Thoughts

I think we underestimate the power of our thoughts both positive and negative. It affects every aspect of our lives. Our personal relationships, creativity, work, physical wellbeing, and emotional health. I've lived it and I've seen it through other people. When your systems are working irregularly or your mind is blocked with negativity, it affects you in ways you might not realize.

Relationships: Negative thoughts will spill into your relationship. Even if it's not negative thoughts directed at your partner, your ongoing negativity will wear on them. You might not even be aware of it. But if the majority of your interactions are negative, like complaining constantly, having a poor outlook on things, or upset about something that happened, then your partner will become overwhelmed and exhausted. They may not be able to handle it long-term and will withdraw to save themselves.

Creativity: Your creative light comes from within. When your meridians are all in alignment, and your energy can flow freely throughout your body without the blockages of negative thoughts, anxiety, depression, or OCD, your creativity will be in full force. The opposite will happen when you allow your thoughts to consume you. Your creative light will dim, and it can be hard to find it when you need it.

Work: Your work life can suffer due to negativity and lack of control of your thoughts. It can be hard for your coworkers to be around you and create a positive work environment. People may start to avoid you and pass you over for promotions or certain opportunities. Even if you are great at masking your negativity and staying professional, it can be hard to stay motivated when your mind is consumed.

Physical: We've discussed this a little already, but your physical body can suffer immensely due to an imbalance in your mental state. Your sleep is affected which in turn can open you up to illness. When you are tired, it can be even harder to change your thought patterns and start to heal. It's a very difficult cycle. When you are negative and suffering physically, it will start to affect your overall physical wellbeing. You may start to notice pains due to poor posture, lack of desire for physical intimacy, and ongoing sickness with a weaker immune system.

Emotional: This may be the most obvious repercussion of negative thought patterns, anxiety, depression, and OCD. With your thoughts feeling out of control, your emotions can feel like they aren't your own. I remember there being times when I felt angry or sad and I felt helpless to change it. I didn't want to feel that way, and I recognized that I had no reason to feel that way, but I was powerless to adjust it. It was horrible. My vacation story in the beginning is an example of this. I knew I should've felt blissful and happy, but was incapable of it.

If you are feeling overwhelmed at this moment, I apologize. Going through this type of information can be daunting and slightly disheartening. You can feel like it's too much to conquer when you are up against a mountain. I sure did.

But here is the GREAT news: You have the power to change it!

Repeat that to yourself again. You have the power to change your thoughts. You don't have to accept that you are "just a negative person" or "a worry wart." Your mind is the most powerful tool known to mankind. I believe that you can beat this, because I did it. I shattered my mental imprisonment of negative thoughts, destructive self-talk, OCD tendencies, and general hopelessness.

I recognized the negativity within myself as the enemy, and decided to arm myself with the weapons I needed to go to war with it, and blast it down to a presence I was comfortable with. We are about to discuss a variety of natural treatment methods to get you started on your path. As you begin your journey, try them all. Give them all a few weeks of practice because change doesn't come overnight, and you need a bit of time to decide if it's going to be effective for you. You are a powerful person, and you can master your thoughts with these tools and win the war. Throughout this book, you are going to learn about yourself, your abilities, and the potential of what you can become.

25

AN INTRODUCTION TO NATURAL TECHNIQUES FOR ENDING NEGATIVE THINKING

Treating any kind of mental illness naturally is not a path for everyone, but it was the right path for me. It takes a lot of commitment and hard work. It's a long process that can be frustrating at times, so you have to promise yourself that you will see it through to the point where you see change and progress.

We will save detailed practices and techniques till the end of the book. However, getting an introduction to these techniques provides you with a starting point, and the beginning of a plan to soak in all of the knowledge you will read throughout the book. Seeing how these natural techniques play into your development will excite and motivate you to begin your journey.

Herbal Remedies

There are a variety of herbal remedies that patients have found great success in treating OCD. As with any types of changes to supplements or diet, it's always best to talk with your doctor to make sure you have a green light to proceed with taking a new remedy.

Owen Kelly PhD sites the following options as potential herbal options to help with your OCD (2020):

- St. John's Wort: An herbal supplement used to help with serotonin levels. Quite often used to treat anxiety, depression, and OCD which are all linked to irregular serotonin levels.
- Milk Thistle: This has been used in other countries for many years in the treatment of depression.
- N-Acetylcysteine: This helps moderate glutamine production in the brain. It contributes to the overall health of your brain and can decrease the symptoms of OCD.

Diet

When it comes to your health, your diet can create issues that you didn't even realize were food based. Remember how I said my eating spiraled as a result of me ignoring my mental health? The situation got even worse because the foods that I was eating can actually exacerbate anxiety, depression, and OCD. I felt horrible, out of control, and unable to fix things. The impact of what you eat is amazing. We forget how eating healthy and nourishing our bodies moves way past physical benefits. Our brain is just as much a part of our physical bodies as our bones and muscles, and feeding it with fresh wonderful food is essential to feel good mentally as well.

Eating a well-balanced diet of healthy proteins, fruits, vegetables, low fat dairy, and whole grains will give your body and, more importantly, your brain everything it needs to operate at optimal performance.

Staying away from processed foods, sugars, high saturated fats, and alcohol will prevent your systems from becoming unbalanced and dysfunctional.

I like to think of myself as a beautiful plant. As a plant, you know the nutrients you need to stay healthy are sun and lots of clean, fresh water. If you decide to sit in the dark, and drink soda all day, as a plant you would wither away. As a person, when you don't feed your body with all the nutrients it needs, you are the equivalent of that plant. You can't be strong physically and mentally to fight off invading physical and mental ailments.

Mindfulness Meditation

Mindfulness meditation is the method of using various breathing techniques and guided imagery to be acutely aware of your feelings in the moment. It brings awareness to your deepest thoughts and emotions without judgement or analysis. It helps to lower your stress levels and relax ("Mindfulness Exercises," 2020).

There are many benefits to mindfulness meditation. What seems like a simple exercise, and may feel like you're doing nothing is wildly beneficial to your mind and body. The evidence behind meditation suggests that it lowers stress, anxiety, pain, depression, and insomnia. It has the benefits of better mental clarity, better sleep, and decreasing burnout ("Mindfulness Exercises," 2020).

There are a variety of resources to help you practice mindful meditation. There are apps on your phone, online programs, and local courses. It doesn't have to be difficult or be on a strict schedule. You just need to take time and have a quiet place to get into touch with your inner self- and emotions. As with all new skills, practice will make you better and better over time.

In the beginning, your mind will naturally wander. The practice seems easy, but letting go of your everyday thoughts can be very difficult and doesn't happen automatically. Be kind to yourself and don't get frustrated. I have dabbled in guided meditation, but I find the following technique to be the most effective for me:

1. First I pour myself a tall glass of cold water. I'll explain what I use that for later.
2. I make myself a quiet and comfortable spot to lay down. I prefer to lay down while I meditate because it calms me and allows me to fully relax. Usually I just lay on my bed with a cool fan on.
3. I set an alarm for 30 min in case I fall asleep to make sure I don't lose track of time. It happens sometimes. I might not get all the benefits of meditation every time when I fall asleep but it usually makes me feel amazing when I do. And I want to respect what my body needs, so I just let it happen.
4. Depending on how the weather is outside, I either put a hot or cold cloth on my head. I quite often put a few drops of essential oils on the cloth to create an extra level of sensory calmness.
5. I focus my thoughts on my breath. I breathe in to the count of five and breathe out for the count of five. I focus on relaxing

everything in my body. I try to sink into the bed and feel the tension go out of my hands and feet. I relax my muscles, even the facial muscles, and concentrate on breathing in and out for as long as I can.

6. If I find my mind drifting or concentrating on something other than breathing, I take a sip of water to refocus and start my relaxation and breathing all over again.

7. If I need to work through something, mediation is a time that I can calmly think things through. If I have a problem that I am struggling with, I focus my thoughts around my breathing. Let's say I am having an argument with my spouse and I find my thoughts to be spiraling in a negative direction. I can use mindful meditation to change my mindset. I will breathe in and think of something positive. I imagine that I am breathing in positive energy and thoughts about my partner. Then when I exhale I imagine myself pushing out the negative thoughts and energy. The longer I breathe positive images and thoughts in, the less upset I feel and can approach the situation more calmly and in a better head space. I find it works with all types of problems.

Mindfulness meditation is a powerful tool when it comes to mastering your thoughts, emotions and cognitive disorders. Being able to practice on a daily basis strengthens your ability to work through your negative thoughts and balance them. Meditating is comparable to exercising your muscles. The more you do it, the stronger your brain becomes.

Yoga

Many people look at yoga as a fitness option for physical health. It absolutely has physical benefits, but it is also meant to be a practice to align your physical, emotional, and mental self-through movement and breathing. Similar to meditation, it increases your ability to cope with your emotions and gain control of your thoughts. For many people, having the connection to the body and movement creates a stronger connection than mediation alone, but it's your journey and you need to decide what works for you.

I personally have always had more success with meditation alone because I find myself more likely to practice it everyday, thus getting more benefits than if I only did it a few times a week. Try each method and find what speaks to you and your needs. Try to be aware of your mental state as you come out of yoga or meditation sessions and try to see which one makes you feel like your best self.

Acupuncture

Acupuncture works amazingly for therapy as well. This ancient Chinese practice uses needles to align to different systems of the body. The acupuncturist is able to identify imbalances to restore the body back to full function. Acupuncture looks to find the root of the problem. OCD is a condition of something else that is working incorrectly, and by strengthening that system, it decreases the symptoms that accompany cognitive disorders and other emotion based issues (Molinoff, n.d.).

EFT Tapping

Emotional Freedom Technique (EFT), is quite often also referred to as "tapping." It is the practice of physically tapping along your meridians or acupressure points to restore balance to one's emotional, physical, and mental alignment. The exciting thing about EFT is that it is easy to perform and has unparalleled reported results from practitioners. This is what drew me in.

When it came to my own treatment path, I knew three things about myself.

1. My body doesn't respond well to medication. If there are side effects associated with a medication, I seem to acquire them. I

appreciate medication for having benefits of modern science, but I really prefer to use it as a last resort.
2. If a treatment requires me to go to appointments, I will eventually stop going. Time constraints and commitment are difficult for me, so to set myself up for success, I prefer to do something at home. For this reason, acupuncture did not seem like the right fit for me. I have gone in the past for other reasons and will continue to use acupuncture in the future for other things, but for regular treatment of my OCD it didn't seem like the right fit.
3. If it's something I can do in smaller blocks of time, I will have a higher success rate. For this reason, I knew yoga couldn't be my main source of treatment. I knew once I did the research that my OCD, negative thought cycles, and emotional disorders would be best treated through mindfulness meditation and EFT.

You can do EFT anywhere. If you are stuck in traffic, waiting in line, at your desk, laying in bed, or watching TV. That's one of the main reasons why it has been extremely effective for me. I found it to be very calming as soon as I started it. It was almost like it helped redirect my anxious and negative feelings into the gentle tapping I was doing to the various tapping points. I can't stress enough how much it has helped me work through my OCD and continues to help guide me on an everyday basis when I need to think through something.

There are a variety of resources that can help teach you to "tap." Below is an overview list of the tapping points and what areas they represent and can help you with (Lyons, n.d.):

Tapping Location
Meridian
What it Releases
Treatment Benefit
Top of Head
100 Meeting Point Meridian
Your Inner Critic and lack of focus

Focus, clarity, insight, emotional connection
Eyebrow
Bladder Meridian
Frustration, pain, hurt, sadness, impatience, rejection, trauma
Emotional peace and centered healing
Side of Eye
Gall Bladder Meridian
Anger, resentment, rage, resistance to change
Understanding, calmness, and empathy
Under Eye
Stomach Meridian
Worry, emptiness, fear, anxiousness, and nervousness
Safety and calmness
Under Nose
Governing Meridian
Shame, fear, guilt, embarrassment, helplessness
Self-empowerment, self-acceptance, strength
Center of Chin
Central Meridian
Confusion, indecisiveness, frustration, anxious, lack of clarity
Focus, certainty, support, and calm
Collarbone
Kidney Meridian
Stress, worry, feeling stuck, unmotivated
motivation and confidence.
Under Arm
Spleen Meridian
Obsessing, insecurity, unhappy, and worry
Contentment, calm, focus, and security

THERE ARE MANY PROGRAMS, techniques, and methods to get the most out of tapping, but in the beginning I made mine very simple for myself. I would determine something that I wanted to focus on. For example, let's say I was feeling particularly anxious one day. I find that very windy days make me anxious. I would find the tapping point that coincides with those feelings and tap repeatedly while focusing on a positive thought in regards to what bothers me. In this situation I would gently tap the center of my chin and say to myself: "Wind is beautiful, wind is powerful, wind is nature's breath, I am safe in my home."

We will cover a longer sequence and a proven tapping method in Chapter 9.

26

SELF-ACTUALIZATION AND THE PATH TO FULFILLMENT

Self-actualization is the realization of one's true potential. Paying close attention to the fact that it is called self-actualization, there is no gauge or measurement to know when you are there. It's a very personal process, and no two people are alike. There are a lot of ways to describe self-actualization, but the one that resonated with me the most was this:

"Self-actualization can generally be thought of as the full realization of one's creative, intellectual, and social potential through internal drive (versus for external rewards like money, status, or power)." (Selva, 2019, para. 8)

How amazing does that sound? Having the ability to reach your full potential on all levels? I remember always feeling held back. I knew I could do more and be more, but couldn't seem to get the traction or keep the motivation to get there. I felt like years were passing by, and I was trapped. I had so many overgeneralized thoughts all the time. "I'll never get myself organized," or I would put things off, saying "someday I will get in shape and have more time to myself." I never actually believed that self-actualization was a possibility for me anytime soon. Combine that underlying thinking with my mental illnesses, and I was really working up against a few things. I look back on myself in that state, and I completely understand why I felt so hopeless.

Preparation to Start Towards Self-Actualization

Now take that comparison of where I was and where I journeyed to and imagine how I felt when I looked around and realized that I had reached a place that I would consider self-actualization? I now feel free, accomplished, and more proud of myself than I ever have before.

On a day to day basis I am so much happier. I don't shy away from social situations, I feel more motivated to make healthier decisions, and my creative light can't be stopped.

We talked about different methods to help with cognitive disorders and negative thought patterns in Chapter 2. Working through that first is essential to get you into a head space where you are ready to progress forward into a state of self-actualization. That is a whole new level of self-reflection and happiness. Be gentle with your mental state and give yourself plenty of time to feel healthy and happy. Don't put any pressure on yourself to get to a "perfect" place. That's not what self-actualization is.

The concept of self-actualization gained its popularity through the psychologist Abraham Maslow and his theory titled Maslow's Hierarchy of Needs. His theory is that you need to take care of certain needs before you can move onto the next level of needs. If you don't satisfy all the needs of one level before you move to the next, you won't have the basic building blocks to become successful at the next point (Selva, 2019):

- At the lowest level is your physiological needs. These are the basic needs you require to survive. This would include your food, shelter, water, and rest. Only when you satisfy these needs can you move up to the next level successfully.
- The next level is safety and security.
- The third level is your belongingness and needs for love. This is having your social and physiological relationship needs met through family, romantic relationships and friendships.

- The fourth level is esteem needs. This is where you feel your sense of accomplishment and self-worth.
- The fifth and final level is our topic of conversation: self-actualization.

The theory has been popular for so long because it lends itself to understanding why sometimes we get stuck and can't move forward in our personal growth. If, for example, you lost your job and were worried about having a place to live, your focus wouldn't be able to move past that onto higher levels until you solved that problem. Once you had your shelter taken care of and you felt safe and secure, you could refocus on your psychological needs of level three and then four.

You can also see clearly now how if you are stuck on our topics in Chapter 1 and unable to move past level four, you may not have much success on our focus of level five. You don't have to be perfect at any time, but you need to feel secure enough on each level to have the head space, energy, and tools to attack the next level. When you feel strong enough and confident enough, you can begin the exciting journey of self-actualization.

The Five Points of Self-Actualization

It is commonly thought that there are five sections as a part of self-actualization. Let's get into them now.

1. Self-Awareness: This is a natural gift that not a lot of people have. It comes from being able to recognize your emotions, why you are feeling things, reasons for your behaviors, your personal traits (both good and bad), your desires, and your motivations. Becoming self-aware can sometimes come through therapy or asking for help from trusted family and friends. Sometimes it's hard for us to see certain things about ourselves, and hearing them from outside sources can help us get perspective.
2. Emotional Exploration: Trying to process your emotions, or

even recognize what your emotions are, can be very difficult. I know at times I feel very irritable and I can't figure out why. There's that old saying that "you woke up on the wrong side of the bed." Sometimes you can be angry, or frustrated, or sad and you have no idea where it came from. Try to explore the emotions by mapping them out. I like to journal them to see if over time there are patterns. I like to answer the following questions everyday to get in touch with emotions that I can't quite communicate to myself.

3. How did I feel when I woke up?
4. How did I feel when I went to bed last night?
5. How did I sleep?
6. On a scale of 1-10, how high do I rank the intensity of the emotion?
7. Throughout the day, how long did it last, and what even changed my feelings?
8. What did the weather look like?

Interestingly enough, I added that last question after a month of journaling. I was reading about other people's journaling experiences and tips, and I found one story of a gentleman who noticed his moods coincided very closely to the weather. I found that very fascinating and decided to do the same. I found that certain patterns did arise with weather changes. Obviously we can't change the weather, but by knowing that my body is sensitive to weather changes, I can coach myself through it much better. Remember my anxiousness to the wind and my EFT approach. I can do similar methods to prepare myself with other weather changes as well.

1. Emotional Awareness: The findings that I discovered through emotional exploration is what brought me to emotional awareness. Being able to link my feelings to a cause, or understand what stimulus was able to move me into a different head space was not only eye opening but incredibly freeing. I felt more in control of my emotions than I ever had

before. How exciting to not have to just throw my hands up and surrender to a bad mood, or chronic sadness, or fear, or anxiety. I was now learning tools to modify my emotions. However, the only reason these tools became effective was because I was aware of the emotions in the first place.

2. Highlighting Strengths: Make a list right now of all the things you think that you excel at. Don't be shy! No one is going to see this but you. So don't be humble. Everything you've even been proud of, write it down. After you've written your own list, ask two or three friends what their suggestions are. I would be willing to bet that they see strength in you that you have no idea about. Hearing someone say something powerful about you can bring you a level of confidence and pride that you might not feel on your own. Not that you need outside validation, but having that perspective from someone who loves you is very touching.

3. Highlighting Weaknesses: This one isn't quite as fun, but very necessary. To really get to the point of full self-actualization, you need to be aware of your weaknesses. You have to accept everything about yourself. Flaws are a part of you, and you can learn to love them, or decide you want to work on them. Either way, you are beautiful, wonderful, and incredible.

We will move onto some tips on how to achieve these five areas of self-actualization momentarily, but first I want to go over what a self-actualized person looks like.

Characteristics of a Self-Actualized Person

Everyone is going to have a different version of themselves as a self-actualized person. My best self-is not the same as everyone else's. But on a very general level, a self-actualized individual has some or many of the following characteristics (Raypole, 2020):

1. Independence: They live their lives for themselves, their own values, and their own approval. They don't look to outside sources for validation, and are confident spending time on their own.
2. A sense of happiness and humor: They find humor in most situations and don't take things too seriously. They have the ability to laugh at themselves.
3. Kindness and compassion: By being so comfortable and happy with themselves, they have the emotional availability to be patient, kind and compassionate with other people.
4. Grounded: They are realistic about most aspects of their life, and set realistic goals. They have a good grasp of their own self-awareness and different situations.
5. Creative and spontaneous: Self-actualized individuals have the ability to approach new situations with creativity and spontaneity. As well, with their meridians open and nothing blocking their creative channels, any artistic passions they have flow out of them.
6. Feel connected: They feel at peace with themselves and

connected to a greater spiritual force or the universe depending on their beliefs.
7. See the world beyond themselves: They see the world as something beyond their existence and quite often contribute a lot of their time to helping other people and different causes. They don't just focus on their own life and their own problems.
8. Compassionate: They have a longing to help other people and want to see the best for other people.
9. Enjoy the present: They have the ability to enjoy their current life and aren't always waiting for the next phase or for things to get better in some way. They can appreciate the small moments and slow down to savor little things.

Recognizing the point when you are "self-actualized" will be your own decision and feeling. When you look through the list above, you may have some of these characteristics already, but still not feel anywhere near a point where you are satisfied with who you are.

Being self-actualized for me boiled down to a few small things. And trust me when I say that I'm only partially there and it will be an ongoing journey for the rest of my life. It will be for all of us. For me, it comes down to the ability to be happy, and feel good about how I am living my life. I want to keep working towards a brighter, more fulfilled, optimistic, calm, and healthier version of my current state. I have come really far in my journey to get to a place that I would consider neutral. By working through EFT, and mindful meditation, I am not fully consumed by my OCD negative thoughts and anxiety. Now I am constantly developing myself to this dream of being a fully self-actualized person and working to stay that way.

Through my research, I've come across a lot of tips, and some of my own on how to work towards this goal.

17 Tips to Help With Self-Actualization

1. Buy a journal: I mentioned that I used a journal before for documenting my mood to help analyze my feelings and how they affected me. I also use a journal to write down a lot of what I am thinking. Each day I try to write down one thing that was great about my day, one thing I struggled with, and something beautiful that I observed that had nothing to do with me.
2. Make a list of your favorite things, small joys, and keep adding to it: I keep this at the back of my journal. I started by writing down all the little things that I can think of that bring me small joys. And then, as I experience them, I add to the list. Things like pulling warm laundry on when you are chilly, sitting and watching your child play sports, snuggling up with tea and watching the snow. All of the different things that bring you moments of pure happiness.
3. Be patient: You aren't going to reinvent yourself overnight, so if you are struggling to find your happiness, emotional awareness, strengths, and weaknesses, don't get mad at yourself. You are fully capable of this, and don't ever stop to think otherwise.
4. Try new things: Pushing your boundaries can sometimes pull down walls or open up new emotional exploration. An example would be if you don't see yourself as a spontaneous person, and you give in to a spontaneous act and have an

amazing time. Maybe you need to rethink your perception of yourself. Maybe you are a spontaneous individual!

5. Seek counseling or therapy: counselors, psychologists, and psychiatrists are all professionals trained in helping people with their self-awareness and emotional disorders. Sometimes having someone give you new terminology, or help in identifying what you are feeling, and what you are wanting to feel can be life changing. It's not for everyone, or in everyone's budget, but if you are willing and able to try it, what do you have to lose? There are also usually free services offered through local organizations and universities as well.

6. Love who you are: You have to learn to love who you are and how you act. It's so much easier said than done, but learning to care less about what people think is a big part of the self-actualization process. This is where I found my journaling to come in handy again. If I came home and was fretting about an interaction I had with someone, or upset about a situation that I was worried about what the other person was thinking, I would write it down. Similar to the idea that you've probably heard about writing out an email to someone if you are upset and then waiting a few days to send it, I would write out what I thought the interaction looked like and then I would wait a few days and reread it. It freed my mind to not think about it anymore because I knew that I would look at the writing later. It's amazing when you put a bit of space between you and what you think happened, how differently you will feel when you reread it. A few days later when I had time to distance myself, I would quite often giggle at my own writing and how silly I was being.

7. Volunteer and put yourself in new situations: Volunteering and meeting new people can sometimes make you realize how appreciative you should be of where you are. When you are exposed to situations where someone else's focus is on a different level of needs such as food and shelter, it puts into perspective how wonderful your life is. In addition, seeing

and living a compassionate lifestyle by working with those less fortunate is a part of being human that we should all strive for. By teaching yourself compassion and selflessness, it gets you to a point where you can practice it without thinking and as part of your life.

8. Recognize peak experiences: Along your journey, you will have transcendent moments where you feel something unique. These are sometimes called "peak experiences," as they represent you reaching a new peak along your path. Try to see them when they happen, or reflect back on times when you think you may have had one (Davis, 2019).

9. Be an honest person: Being honest and taking accountability for one's own actions seems like something most people do, but not always. Even if you are an honest person, you may not always behave like one. An example would be if you are upset about something and you exaggerate your point to make sure you are seen as right. Being able to be accountable for one's own actions, and be humble about your mistakes is very enlightening and beneficial to someone on the path to self-actualization (Davis, 2019).

10. Take care of yourself: As we move up the levels of Maslow's hierarchy, your needs become less about the physical, and more about your esteem and emotional. But remember if one of the lower levels falls apart, then you don't have a solid foundation to work from. So make sure to keep yourself healthy, sleep well, eat good foods, and keep yourself in good physical condition.

11. Set goals: I could talk about goal setting endlessly. Being able to set goals and achieve them is something so special. Each one of us has our own unique vision of what we want our lives to look like and the goals to get there. The goal setting process can be part of your self-actualization. If you find the task of approaching your weaknesses a little overwhelming, take it slow. Make the goal to approach one each week. Then you only have to write one thing down that week and take the

time to think about how it affects you and how you want to either accept it or change it. Only having to think about one new one each week is much more manageable then writing them all down at once.

12. Live a life of gratitude: I already mentioned how I wrote a list of my favorite things, and although there is some crossover, I also make lists of things I am grateful for. I'm grateful for my life, the food I am nourished with, my access to medical care, my family, and my home. I try every day to notice things in my life that are extra special that I need to appreciate and be grateful for.

13. Remove negativity: This might be something that you do when you are trying to meet your self-esteem needs, before you even start on self-actualization. But it's worth saying again because if you can easily remove something negative in your life, then do it. I can't tell you how many times I've said that I want to get off social media because it doesn't bring light to my life, but I've always hesitated. Don't hesitate to eliminate things in your life that are unnecessarily bringing you down.

14. Smile: Seems simple enough, but just smile as often as you can. It might even feel slightly forced at first, but it will turn into something beautiful, I promise. I sometimes try having smile days. I smile at anyone within a five foot radius, and sometimes people look at me blankly, and other times I see their faces light up and I know I've made a small connection which makes me feel great.

15. Accept spirituality: To connect with a higher power of any kind can bring a light to your life, and a bond to work towards. It can bring you purpose and direction through your beliefs. It can give you a compass that centers you.

16. Don't wait for someone else: Remember that your path to self-actualization and mastering your thoughts is your journey. No one else is going to do it for you, or start the process for you. The only person that will push you and guide

you to self-actualization and continue to keep you there is you!
17. Find your inspiration and your motivation: it can be exhausting when you are trying to analyze yourself, and complete a journey to self-actualization. You need a light that you are working towards. Find what your guiding light is and use it to motivate you to keep going.

As you start your journey to self-actualization, remember that it's going to take time, and it doesn't end. Also remember that this is a beautiful process. If you are like me, even getting to a point where I had the ability to learn the word self-actualization was a huge accomplishment. Moving from a self-made mental hell as we discussed in Chapter 1, to a point of starting self-actualization was amazing for me.

I wanted to move through the first part of my process as quickly as humanly possible. I was so tired of being unhappy, negative, self-doubting, and just a shell of what I knew I could be. If we remember the hierarchy there are the five levels, and I didn't know if I would ever have a chance to move past level three. And level five seemed like something else entirely. A world I couldn't belong to. So once I felt like I had achieved level four, I wanted to savor the process to get to move to level five. I enjoyed, and continue to enjoy the process of getting to know myself and everything that's special and beautiful about me.

27

DETACHMENT: TAKE THE BY-PASS ROUTE AND ESCAPE THE BUSY FREEWAY OF YOUR MIND

Being able to detach yourself when you need to is a skill that I did not possess, and still struggle with quite a bit. I have a busy mind and I love to analyze things. If left to my own devices, I will think about things, and then rethink about those same things, and then do it ten more times. So learning how to detach has been incredibly challenging, yet probably one of the most valuable and rewarding skills I have gained.

Detachment is the ability to remove yourself from a situation, the thoughts associated with it, and the emotions that tie you to it. An example would be if you are really upset with an argument over a misunderstanding with a friend. You keep thinking about what you could have said differently, or how you could have communicated better. The idea that a different outcome could have happened consumes you. Detaching is being able to let go. You can let go of all the emotions and thoughts that you have built up about the situation and either deal with it or move on.

Living in the Moment

Part of detaching is being able to live in the moment. When I say living in the moment, I mean living your life so that you enjoy what's happening right now. You aren't stuck on things that have happened in the past, or things that may happen in the future. Instead, you appreciate everything that is happening as you exist in this time.

When we talk about negative thought patterns, living out of the present, and all the emotional disorders that we can suffer from, they all tie together. I will demonstrate this with a personal example:

I had a job waiting tables in university. It was a really high-end restaurant and we would get a lot of very wealthy patrons. I had a lot of regulars, and dealt with mostly really nice people. Often, there would be one table each evening that was the exception. It would be either one person or a group that were rude, patronizing, and very disrespectful. After working there for four years, I had built up quite the list of stories of poorly behaved customers.

With my tendency to gravitate towards negative thinking, and no tool set to combat it, my regular thoughts would be that I would only focus on that one table each night. I would do all the 10 ways of negative thinking. I would magnify small things, I would personalize it, I would jump to conclusions, and overgeneralize. I would put my mental filter on the whole experience of being a server to focus on those negative interactions and how horrible the people were. In addition, I would rehash stories years later about these same customers. After I told the story, I would be left to replay that interaction in my head subconsciously and, again, rethink all the things I should have said.

In addition to focusing on the negative, and all the thoughts that surrounded those interactions, it affected other aspects of my life. Because I spent so much of my precious energy thinking about people that I didn't need to, I started to dream about them. I would relive rude customers through my dreams! How invasive and awful is that? I would develop anxiety if I saw those customers come in again, and would worry endlessly that a new table would be mean or rude to me. It was so unhealthy, and so exhausting.

I look back at that period of my life now, and hang my head a little. How frustrating to think about why I didn't focus on the hundreds of amazing customers I had. I spent so much time living out of the moment, that I didn't enjoy working at that restaurant as much as I should have. The people that owned the restaurant were so lovely, the other employees were fun, and most of the clientele were awesome. If I had learned to detach and live more presently, I feel like my experience over those four years would have been very different.

As I've learned more and more about self-actualization, I realize that even me looking back at this time and having regret is unhealthy. I've learned to detach from the fact that I can't go back and change that time period, and now I can just look at it through a different lens. I can use it as a learning experience and cautionary tale of what I don't want to happen again. It's now a reflection for me to remember that I don't want to miss out on current experiences, and I need to remember that to appreciate my present.

You Ego: How It's Inhibiting Your Thoughts

If you have never heard the term "ego" before, it refers to how you perceive yourself. Chitra Reddy describes it as "the feeling inside you which makes you feel different and special from everyone else" (2015, para. 6).

Every single person in this world has an ego. Some are much bigger than others. Our egos are a part of us when we are born, and then shaped and molded through our experiences the same as every other part of our personalities. By the time we reach adulthood, our egos may have developed in a variety of different ways, and most of the time we aren't even aware of the role they play in our everyday lives.

Going back to my restaurant days example, the reason so many of my rude customers bothered me so much had nothing to do with them. They probably never thought of me again after they left the restaurant. It had to do with my ego. Something they did or said hurt my ego, and it led me to ruminate on what happened. I saw myself as more important in the situation than I actually was, so I made it about me when it wasn't.

I remember one time a customer kept making snide comments about the menu. He did it over and over when I was at the table. He complained about the ingredients, the menu options, a spelling error, and the fact that we ran out of a particular item. He directed his rudeness at me because I worked there, but it had nothing to do with me. I didn't do the inventory, the menu planning, or the printing, but I still took it personally. If I had known how to detach myself from the situation, I would have recognized that he was annoyed with the restaurant, and it had nothing to do with me.

Our ego is responsible for a lot of issues in our everyday relationships and interactions. How often have you been put in a situation where it became more about you being right than actually reaching a resolution? Our ego is what makes it important to "win" an argument rather than resolve it.

How Do I Control My Ego?

The first step to ensuring that your ego isn't a source of problems is by knowing it exists and being aware of what yours looks like. Do you always feel like you are the smartest person in the room? Do you feel like you know more about most things than other people? Are you someone that doesn't listen very well because you are waiting for your chance to talk?

We naturally all have an ego. It's part of being human. We are each living our own story and part of that is focusing on ourselves and what makes us different. Earlier I asked you to make a list of all your strengths and what makes you unique. You need to recognize these special features about yourself and celebrate them. The turning point of when an ego changes from acceptable to problematic is when you start to think you are more special than everyone around you.

Thinking you are more special doesn't necessarily mean you think you are better than other people. That is definitely a feature of an inflated ego, but thinking you are special sometimes means that you think you play a bigger role in things than you actually do. If I go into a coffee shop every morning and feel that a particular employee doesn't like me I may start to focus on that. I anticipate that I will get poor service from her and replay the interaction that we have after I leave. I build a story in my head around how she doesn't like me for some fabricated reason. Over time it goes from me being annoyed while I'm in the coffee shop, to me thinking about her on my way to the coffee shop, to me anxiously forecasting her mood while I'm getting ready in the morning. These spiraling OCD thoughts make me think that she is actively thinking about the ways she can be rude to me. In actuality, she doesn't even know who I am. She's never noticed our interactions, and she's not the friendliest because she works three jobs trying to save enough money to go to school. Her story has nothing to do with me, but my ego made me think I played a role in her life.

Your ego can consume your thoughts by making you worry about how others see you, and tricking you into thinking you are more important than you actually are. That's not me saying you aren't special or hugely important to a lot of people. It's me saying that you need to focus on the roles and places where you should focus your energy. On those days that I spent so much time fretting about the coffee shop employee, did I spend that same amount of time concerned about how my significant other and I interacted over breakfast? That's the person I should be spending my mental energy on, not a stranger who doesn't even remember me.

There are many ways to center yourself and keep your ego within a place you want it to be (Reddy, 2015):

1. Try not to take things too personally

This is absolutely easier said than done. If you are a sensitive soul like I am, you take everything personally. When something is eating away at me, one thing I have found valuable is to talk it over with someone I trust to get a new perspective. It can help me detach from the situation and remember that it may not be about me at all. One time a friend told me she was visiting her sick mom at the hospital. She was distracted and almost collided with another vehicle in the hospital parking lot. The other driver got out of his car and screamed at her for a couple of minutes. She was terrified by his extreme anger and the words he was saying to her. He then ran into his car and drove off. She said she'd sat there for a few minutes, crying. She was so scared and upset that someone would yell at her on a day where she was already so stressed about her mom. At that moment it dawned on her that he was leaving a hospital, and maybe he had just gone through something even worse than what she was experiencing. She realized his yelling at her had nothing to do with her and she let go of the situation and decided to be grateful that she could be the source for him to release some of his negative energy. What a beautiful way for her to look at it. She completely detached herself and chose to not take it personally at all. I really admired her for this.

1. Own your mistakes

We all make mistakes. I'm pretty sure I've made 10 today and it's only lunchtime! Keeping your ego in check involves accepting responsibility for your mistakes. If you do something wrong, even if you don't want to admit it, you have to be humble and acknowledge that it happened. This can be harder in some situations than others, but it's crucial on your path to self-actualization. The ability to put your ego aside and admit you made a mistake is nothing short of amazing.

1. It's okay to look foolish

Being afraid to look ridiculous, foolish, or stupid can sometimes prevent people from trying things or admitting things that they've done. In a world where we are expected to present the perfect version of ourselves, everyone is afraid to look silly and be judged. It can be scary to put yourself out there and get laughed at or be seen as ignorant about something. Just remember that being able to laugh at yourself and be silly is seen as very endearing. Think about the last time you saw somebody do something silly and have a good time doing it. Or someone who was brave enough to ask a question that might be looked at as dumb. You probably didn't judge them, and mostly likely appreciated them a bit more for doing so.

1. Remember that your ego is a part of you

It will never go away, even if you are the most humble person in the world. We can't help it. But you can be proud of yourself for trying to achieve a level of self-awareness about it, and for continuing to do so in the future.

1. Acknowledge your limitations

When we look back at when we wrote down our strengths and weaknesses. Being aware of what those are is part of being graceful and humble in our everyday lives. If I wrote down one of my weaknesses as being afraid to look silly, then I can acknowledge that and try to work on it. Before, I might have put one of my strengths as communicating with other people. Now, after learning what ego is, I realize that maybe I'm just good at talking about myself. That's okay because now I can be aware of it. I can try and talk about myself less, and truly become a good communicator by learning to listen as well. Everything we are working on ties together for the same outcome and is a continual process.

1. Focus on others

Since our ego is about us, what we think of ourselves, and how we feel about ourselves, just try thinking and focusing on other people. Give compliments, ask lots of questions about other peoples' lives and talk about other peoples' interests. When you are first starting out and trying to think about what your ego is and how it exists in your life, be aware of these things as you are talking to other people:

1. How often do you take over the conversation?
2. When someone is telling a personal story, do you quickly tell one of your own just like it?
3. Do you ask a lot of questions about other people?
4. Do you remember details from your last conversation?
5. When you leave the conversation, have you learned more

about other people in the room, or are you more focused on how you came across during the interaction?

All of the above suggestions are meant to help you learn about your ego and how it plays a role in your everyday life. Being aware of it and how it affects your thoughts and interactions is the key way to not letting it consume you. Becoming wrapped up in our own thoughts, our self-importance, and just becoming overall self-absorbed is a very difficult way to live. It doesn't leave you open to learning from other people or really experiencing new things. Learning to control our ego is a way to prevent us from losing out on a whole different world.

Daily Tips to Free Your Busy Mind, Control Your Ego, and Detach When Necessary

With all of this new information, I hope you feel ready to take on your life with a new zest and appreciation for the world outside of yourself. I want you to keep that excitement and that intentional self-awareness as you move forward in life. Trying to move past our own thoughts and think beyond our own needs is a lifelong process. It's something we all need to continually work on. Below are a few techniques I have discovered to stay true to this path:

1. Journaling

I know I say journaling a lot, but it really is a gift to me. Being able to write down my thoughts has been cathartic for me in ways that other techniques haven't. For you, it might be dictation of your thoughts through an app on your phone if you don't like writing, or maybe building vision boards, or bullet points on a whiteboard in your office. Detaching and freeing my mind through journaling enables me to dump my thoughts out onto paper and not look at them for a few days. That's how it helps me with detaching myself from a problem. When it comes to helping me with my ego, it allows me to look at how I approached a situation once I've had a few days to remove emotion. I can more easily identify how my ego played a role in my perception of a situation.

1. Setting an Intention

I like to set intentions for myself on a daily basis. I may have the same intention everyday for a month, or sometimes longer. If I find that I am having trouble letting go of things, or looking beyond myself, I will set an intention in the morning and say it to myself in the mirror. An example would be: "Today I am going to make someone's day better." I choose an intention like this to encourage myself to think beyond my own life. I want to put my ego, attachments, and emotions aside so that I can be better for someone else. That's a great way to clear my mind and be a small light for someone else who might need it.

1. Admitting a mistake

If it's not in your nature to point out your own flaws or errors, it might be very daunting at first. I am a very non-confrontational person, so admitting a mistake has always been difficult—not so much because I don't like being wrong, but more so because I worry about how someone might respond. This is me making it about myself. A great example would be if you are having a really bad day and you are rude to someone who was trying to help you. It would probably be way easier to brush it off and not acknowledge that your behavior was bad because everyone has bad moods right? Just think how much better it would feel for you and the other person if you took the time to go and apologize for how you treated them and recognized that it wasn't fair.

1. Meditate

We've talked about meditation already, and I will go over more techniques in Chapter 10, but using meditation as a daily practice is as beneficial to me as journaling. Meditating will become your safe place where you can go over your thoughts with no judgement. You will learn to contemplate things patiently and remove the emotion and anxiety around topics and objectively approach thoughts without ego or attachment.

Going over the topic of ego can be difficult because we may feel like we are being reprimanded for thinking we are special or focusing on ourselves. I want to clarify and emphasize that it's not the case. You are a unique individual that isn't like anyone else on this planet. All the things that make up your personality make you special.

With the lessons involving ego we are trying to accomplish your self-actualization by understanding that although you are unique, you aren't the most important person in the world to everyone around you. As well, that you can't let a sense of self-importance cause your thoughts to spiral into negative places, or cause you to attach yourself to situations that don't concern you.

Ego can also sometimes prevent you from finding happiness because it can cause you emotions such as jealousy, sadness, anger, frustration, or disappointment. By becoming self-aware of your ego, and learning to put it aside when needed, you can free yourself of creating these emotions when you don't need to.

28

DETACHMENT FROM WHAT NO LONGER SERVES YOU

After covering what detachment is, and tactics to do it, the next thing is to learn how to identify when you need to detach yourself. In some situations, it's very clear and there's no question. Other times it can be a lot more difficult. Detaching yourself from complicated childhood experiences, personal relationships, or seemingly harmless situations are not as clear cut.

So how do you go about identifying things in your life that are creating you a lot of emotional harm? And when you do identify what they are, what are the different ways to approach them? We will talk about all these steps throughout this chapter.

I want you to practice setting an intention with this chapter. It can be very difficult to acknowledge that you have people or things in your life that are detrimental to you. It's a lot easier to think that this doesn't apply to you. Nobody wants to admit that a friend might be toxic, or that they are harboring hurtful memories about people that they love. So set the intention for yourself that you will read this chapter slowly and give yourself the chance to accept the possibility that it applies to you.

Identifying Negative Influences in Your Life

I have segmented negative influences into four categories:

1. Your Home

This may be surprising to some. Your home should be your sanctuary and a place of peace. When you look around your home, is that the feeling that you get? Do you feel calm, secure, peaceful, and relaxed in your home environment? If the answer is no, then you need to try and identify why. Is it someone that lives there (which is another source of negative influence), the home itself, or possibly the state of your home? Quite often it is cited that an organized home lends itself to an organized mind. Seeing your home as a possible negative influence can open you up to making changes to fixing that part of your life.

1. Your Career

In an ideal world, we would all work at our dream jobs, and make money through our passions. I will say though, I've known people who acquired their dream jobs and it didn't necessarily make them as happy as they thought it would. It was still work. So keeping that in mind, take an objective look at your job. If you see it as a possible negative influence, try to think about why. You may find yourself in a negative environment where there is a lot of negative energy, such as complaining. Another possibility is that you have toxic people that try to negatively affect those around them. The job itself could be incredibly stressful and emotionally draining for you. Try to recognize whether it's the job that is the negative influence, or if you just don't like the work itself. The importance of this is that if you love what you do, and can recognize that it's the environment that is creating a poor situation, then you can try and move onto another company where you can do the same thing. But if you really don't like the job itself, then maybe you need to look at changing your career options, if possible. If you can specifically identify what the negative influence is, then you can arm yourself with ways to approach the situation. When trying to identify if there is something about your job that is toxic, try to assess your feelings at work. If you notice that you start to get anxious or uncomfortable around certain people or events, try to analyze what it is you are feeling and why.

1. Your Relationships

Identifying people that are toxic or negative influences is tough. I've devoted more time to this later in the chapter. The important thing to recognize about people being a source of a negative influence is that there are a lot of different ways to deal with it. You don't have to automatically eliminate them from your life. There are a lot of steps you can do to help with relationships. Your emotional connection to another human being is something that you want to celebrate and foster as much as you can. Cutting people out can sometimes be the only answer, but we aren't there yet on an emotional level. If you are in any way physically in danger, then the relationship is toxic and you need to remove yourself from it. That moves out of your self-actualization needs, and puts you back on level two of Maslow's hierarchy because your safety is in jeopardy. I can't stress this enough that you are strong enough to leave a physically harmful situation and recognizing that it is negative, harmful, and extremely detrimental to you, is necessary.

1. How you spend your free time

When you aren't at your job, or spending time with those close to you, what do you do with your time? Where is your leisure spent? I can think of a dozen examples of people I know that spend their extra time doing things that cause them stress and anxiety. I have one friend who spends all of their free time trying to become a social media influencer. Online they look like they are living their dream life, but in person I see that they are miserable and overworked. They have become absorbed by the amount of followers they have, the comments people make about them, or their ability to stand out against other influencers. I have another friend who golfs to the point of frustration. You might think that sounds ridiculous, but let me explain. A long time ago, he was acknowledged as the best golfer that most people knew. He was constantly given recognition by people at work, friends, and family as being an "amazing golfer." It got to the point that it became synonymous with who he was. He loved golfing and everyone knew he was great at it. Unfortunately, he started to feel pressure to stay that good and fit that expectation. So now he golfs to keep up the skill level as opposed to enjoying it. It seems ridiculous, but his ego drives his need to do it. It doesn't apply to everyone, but just consider that how you choose to spend your free time can sometimes create a negative influence or source of emotional turmoil that you don't even realize.

Take some time and think about areas in your life that possibly might be a source of negative influence for you. Some of them can be very easily fixed, and other's need a more delicate approach. No matter what the outcome will eventually be, taking the time to identify what the sources might be is the first step on creating a plan to detach the areas that no longer serve you on your path to self-actualization.

Your Options to Approaching Negative Influences

At this point, you might have made yourself a list of negative influences in your life. Now what do you do with them? The answer is simple: Find a solution and fix it.

When it comes to your home and your job, it might be as simple as changing them. It can take courage to change something that is comfortable, even if it's a negative influence. If you recognize that one of these things has become a large source of negative energy and stress for you, think about how it will feel once you've moved on. Will you feel free and excited? Keep up your motivation for wanting to create this change. Be careful not to overwhelm yourself. Don't start a new job and move in a similar time frame. That can be a lot of change at once, and you want to make sure that each one is positive and puts you in a better place. You don't want to replace one source of stress with another.

When it comes to how you spend your free time and relationships, the methods to deal with them get a little more complicated sometimes.

With your free time, only you can decide if something you spend time on is worth the emotions it may create. When you think about things that you choose to spend your time on, just focus on this: Is it something that you need to do? For example, it might be hard on you, but if you regularly spend some of your free time helping a family member who relies on you, it wouldn't be easy to just stop helping them, nor would you want to. A different situation would be if you start out enjoying something but overtime it morphs into something that is more of an obligation (like my golf example). Do you have the ability to just stop doing it? Your time and energy is valuable. You probably spend a lot of time giving your energy to other people and activities, so try to engage in things that will fill that energy and life back into you.

When it comes to dealing with negative relationships, I look at the solution as a four part process.

Once you have identified someone in your life as a source of negative stress and emotion for you, ask yourself if they are a forever person in your life. What I mean by this is to evaluate how close they are to you. You're more likely to put more time and energy into your relationship with your mom than that coworker you only see on breaks. Another way to look at it is: Will you know this person a year from now? If the answer is no, then my tactic would be to avoid them and move on. Detach yourself from the relationship, and don't put a huge amount of energy into fixing something that is temporary. You don't need to create hurt feelings or anxiety for yourself or the other person if you see them as a source of negativity, but you know you will only have small interactions with them for a few months. Just do your best to place distance between you and engage in short interactions. If the person is someone that is with you for a long time, then you need a different approach.

For your long-term relationships, your next step is to identify the source within the person that is creating emotional distress for you. Are they constantly complaining? Do they tend to put you down? What is it that is affecting you, and do you play a part in it? If you have a close friend that loves to talk about other people behind their back, think about your interactions with them. Do you do it too? Try to be the change in the interactions that you are hoping to see. The next time you are with that person, try to change the subject and be more positive to see if they follow your lead. It might be easier than you think to change the negative energy your relationship has grown into. If you try this out for a while and are still not getting any sort of change, you will have to move on to having a direct conversation.

Having a direct conversation might sound like your worst nightmare. Especially if you've never had that type of conversation with this person before. Being fully honest, in my past, this is usually where I would jump ship. Rather than having an awkward conversation, I would either continue to let the relationship affect me, or just pull away to the detriment of our closeness. I really don't recommend this tactic. I am still guilty of doing it. I can't even count the amount of close relationships that I have probably lost out on over the years because of my inability to move forward on this step. What I have learned from the times I've pushed myself to approach someone I love with this type of conversation is that you eventually come out the other side closer. I would recommend going in with some sort of game plan of what you are going to say. I tend to get turned around and then spend days afterwards analyzing all the ways I could have said things better. If you go into the conversation with a plan and an intention to not attack or hurt the person, and instead aim to help them understand how you are feeling, chances are it will go well and you will be so much happier in the long run. Occasionally it can go in a different direction. The other person could feel hurt and respond in a negative way. They might not agree with your assessment, or even just dismiss it. If this happens, it's unfortunate but it leaves the door open for you to move onto the next step.

On the small chance that someone close to you is not receptive to your needs, changing your relationship can be tough. You may feel like you made things worse and you should have just left it alone. It may feel like that for a while, but I promise you it will improve over time. The person on the other side of the conversation heard you. They may not have been ready to hear what you said, but they will think about it over time and maybe come to the same conclusion you did in their own time. Or maybe they will never agree with you, but will understand why you need to set boundaries moving forward.

Setting Boundaries: Why It's Important and How to Do It Successfully

Setting boundaries is a completely natural and healthy request when it comes to your personal needs and well-being. Your focus is trying to get to a healthier and best version of yourself. You are trying to move from a place of darkness and pain to a place where you can enjoy the small things and embrace life at full force. You are trying to become a version of you that feels light with energy flowing through you on a daily basis. When I close my eyes and see that version of myself I get so excited. I am so much closer to that person than I was a year ago, and I will be even closer a year from now.

The problem with the road to self-actualization is that not everyone is going to join you along the way, or be happy for you. Someone who isn't aware of their ego, or isn't in a place in their life to welcome growth, might see your success as their failure and want to get in your way. They might be negative, hurtful, or just not connect with you the way they did before. When it comes to these situations, you will go through the four steps we just talked about, and get to the point with some people that you just need to put up boundaries. You love them, and you always want them in your life, but you just need to protect yourself from their energy for the time being.

Boundaries can be defined as both physical and emotional. With each individual that you need to set boundaries with, you need to decide what boundaries are needed to protect both your relationship and your individual needs. Next, we will go over some examples of small boundaries that can be effective.

One step you can take is to request some time apart without fearing judgement from others. Let's say that you have lunch with your sister every week. You have identified that your lunches and conversations are a negative influence for you and you have the difficult conversation to which she laughed and brushed you off. You can set the boundary by saying that you understand that she doesn't see this as a big deal, but you do, and say that you want to take a break for a while from your lunches and you need them to be okay with it. Chances are they will be hurt but they will respect your boundary and possibly take your concern more seriously.

It is important to have the courage to say no. If you mustered up the courage to tell someone you love that they are hurting you and they were not receptive, then you can protect yourself by saying no to them for a while. When they ask you for your time or energy, decline. Reassure them that you are always available for emergencies and if they really need you, but for favors and free time, you need to say no for a while. You aren't punishing them for not changing, you are just allowing yourself the freedom to work on your own needs for some time.

Learn to speak up or remove yourself when someone's behavior is negatively affecting you. If you have a conversation with a coworker that is affecting your work space and they enjoy gossiping about other people around the office, then they might apologize and promise they will be more aware of it moving forward. Then a few weeks later, they slip into old habits and start right back into the same types of interactions with you again. Don't let your intentions slide, and be sure to remind them that it makes you uncomfortable, or remove yourself from the situation so you aren't an available recipient for them.

These are just a few examples of ways that you can be clear about what you need and what your expectations are from the other person you are struggling with. Remember that the only reason you are setting the boundaries is because you want to maintain the closeness of your relationship while still protecting your needs. You love and care about this person, and the boundaries are not meant to hurt or punish them. Make sure that they understand that and that you want their support. Being able to practice setting boundaries like this will become a lifelong skill that you can use for your own health and well being when you need it.

What if You Do Everything Right and They Are Still a Negative Influence?

If you have worked your way along the steps of trying to approach a negative influence and you are still left in a place of emotional turmoil with someone you love, you might just have to approach it from a different angle and create a permanent boundary. Josh Harbinger sites these seven toxic signs that it's time to cut someone out of your life (2018):

1. They ignore and don't respect your boundaries: You've tried to maintain the relationship by setting boundaries to protect yourself from their toxic behavior but they disregard them.
2. They manipulate and control you: They use emotional tactics to control you. They can guilt you, cause you to doubt your decisions, and try to make you feel insecure to get what they want. They will do this without considering how it makes you feel.
3. They're dishonest: They don't think twice about lying to you to get what they want.
4. They will never admit when they're wrong: Dealing with a toxic person is a never ending battle that they are always trying to win. You've read threads of toxic people on social media arguing about the most ridiculous things. They argue to the point of humiliation in the quest to be "right." There's no reasoning with a person like that.
5. They judge you: When you've tried to talk with them about your needs, and your boundaries, they don't support you. Instead they judge you and try to make you feel bad about what you are trying to accomplish.
6. They play the victim: They will make you feel like you are abusing or mistreating them. That they are an innocent bystander in your attempt to be selfish. They will make this

about them no matter how hard you try to explain what you need.
7. **They take all they can, but never reciprocate:** When you have that person in your life that continues to take all the energy you give them and never offers anything in return, even when you tell them that you need it, you may need to cut them off. They will forever be a drain on you, and you can't stay healthy and keep feeding into them.

If you have exhausted all of the ways that you can comfortably approach a negative and toxic relationship and you've identified them to be someone that you just can't hold onto anymore, you may have to remove them from your life. Gently.

Approach this process with two things in mind. You want to treat them with the same love and kindness that you would want them to treat you with. Even if they are cruel and toxic as you leave them behind, don't change your tone. Be kind no matter what. Set that intention and stay true to it.

The second thing is that the way you approach it will affect how you feel about yourself moving forward as well. If you lose sight of your intention and get pulled into an ugly argument, you will set yourself back on your journey. Use the skills you have been learning to be compassionate, patient, and self-aware as you separate yourself. You will grow as a result of this uncomfortable experience.

When you make the decision to remove someone from your life, your process will be your own, but this guide can help:

- Ask them to meet you for a talk. Let them know that it's serious and that you want them to please come prepared for something big. You don't want to blindside them. They think they're meeting you for a casual meet up and you hit them with a big decision.
- Let them know it won't take long. Set the expectation that it will be a short conversation. Hashing out a long separation will not work, especially not with a toxic person.

- When they arrive, let them know in your own words that you love them, that you know they love you, but that you have grown in different directions and you can't have them in their life right now. If you feel that you are going to want to say more, write it in a letter and leave it with them.
- Make sure to bring any items of theirs that you may have so that they aren't looking for reasons to contact you.
- Ask that they not put any mutual relationships in the middle. This can include family members, joint friendships, or even acquaintances.
- Remove them from all forms of social media and general contact.

This can and will be a really hard thing to do, but remember what your reasoning is. Also remember that you've done everything you can to hold onto this person without affecting your own development and health. You are not a bad person, and you are healing yourself. You are keeping yourself healthy for the relationships that deserve you. Focus your energy on these individuals and situations. This is where you can gain new energy and grow together. These are the people that are supportive and happy that you are making changes in yourself. You sometimes have to move through some of the negatives and approach it head on to come out the other side a lighter and brighter person.

29
EMOTIONAL INTELLIGENCE AND HEALING YOUR INNER CHILD

How familiar are you with the term emotional intelligence? An American psychologist named Daniel Goleman is a leading contributor in the popularizing of the term and he describes it as having five key elements ("Emotional Intelligence in Leadership," 2009):

1. Self-awareness
2. Self-regulation
3. Motivation
4. Empathy
5. Social skills

Becoming emotionally intelligent comes through exploring these five areas and learning to be your best self in regards to each one. You will see some overlap with what we discussed in regards to the five points of self-actualization. The five points are: self-awareness, emotional exploration, emotional awareness, highlighting strengths, and highlighting weaknesses. The biggest difference is that self-actualization really focuses on understanding your emotions and how you relate to other people. It also teaches you to understand other peoples' emotions.

Self-awareness: This is understanding your emotions and being able to process them so you can understand how they relate to other people. A great example of this is being able to understand when you are not in a receptive mood. If you can identify that you are not open to a productive conversation at work because of a bad mood, you can relay that to a coworker and ask if they could set up a meeting with you on a different day so you can give them your full focus. It's not always that easy. Still, even by being aware of your emotions on that day you can try to detach from them when making work decisions that don't involve your personal feelings.

Self-regulation: This is the concept of being able to regulate your actions and behaviors. Continuing on with the previous example, if you come to work in a bad mood after arguing with your partner and a night of little sleep, you can self-regulate to not take that anger out on undeserved coworkers. Instead, you can act professional and regulate your emotions.

Motivation: Emotional intelligence involves our inner drive to succeed and develop. The fact that you are reading this book and are working on your own development means that you already have motivation for continued growth! Goal setting is a topic that has already been discussed, but it is a valuable tool to mention again. It gives us drive and a sense of accomplishment that feeds motivation and helps us want to keep moving forward.

Empathy: When we are striving towards being emotionally intelligent and learning to think outside of ourselves through self-actualization, empathy becomes a skill you will hone. With your desire to help others and connect with your relationships in a positive way, you will want to feel compassion and kindness for their emotions. If you don't naturally read other peoples' emotions well, then ask them. Ask your friends and loved ones how they're feeling and let them know that you're working on becoming more empathetic. At work, try to practice reading other peoples' emotions and asking them questions so you can be helpful when they need it.

Social skills: When you are getting to the point where you are moving into a life of thinking about others, you want to be able to develop your relationships to the best version of itself as well.

Why Is Emotional Intelligence Valuable?

Your ability to improve your emotional intelligence will weigh in on your mental and physical health the same way that your own thoughts do. When I was first starting out, I spent an endless amount of energy thinking about my interactions and how they affected me. I didn't always communicate effectively and really struggled to express my emotions and thoughts clearly. My thoughts were already spiraling and were compounded with anxiety over the fact that I didn't come away from my interactions with other people feeling positive all the time. I was quite often confused. In addition, I would sometimes be embarrassed because I realized I was so focused on myself that I didn't always ask enough questions about them or what they were feeling and experiencing.

Your emotional intelligence will aid in your work performance, your ability to gain closeness with relationships, and your overall mental health. Certain areas may come more naturally to you and you don't really have to work at them, while others will push your comfort zone. I mentioned earlier my resistance to confrontation. I have really needed to work on my ability to approach conflict and resolve successfully. My previous tactic has been avoidance, and it was very hard on my inner thoughts and emotions.

I continue to reiterate that all of these things are not an overnight process. There are so many aspects to work on, and they all intertwine. Your strengths and weaknesses when it comes to emotional intelligence are formed from both your personality and the experiences throughout your lifetime. You may have difficulty with certain aspects because you had formative situations that happened when you were younger that also need time and development to lead you to a point where you can improve your emotional connections with other people. This leads me to the topic of your inner child.

What Is Your Inner Child Saying?

When referring to your inner child, people interpret in a few different ways. Some people look at it as a concept that every mature adult has a child within that wants to be carefree and released from the responsibilities of adulthood. For others it's the reflection of themselves as a child, and specific experiences that shaped them into who they are. And finally, there are some that look at their inner child as an accumulation of all their experiences and how they play into who they are today. Realistically, I think you have to approach your inner child as all three.

When I first heard the term "Inner Child," I didn't connect with it. I had a very happy childhood, and I assumed it was going to be a development process for someone who didn't have the happiest upbringing. I thought it would relate more to traumatic experiences, and the healing that needs to come with it. I was both right and wrong.

Your inner child needs may two things:

1. Healing from specific events
2. Recognition of its experiences and how they make you who you are

Healing from a traumatic experience is not something I am qualified to guide you through. The pain, suffering, and trauma that is associated with some events during childhood need delicate and thoughtful healing with the assistance of a professional. Speaking to a therapist or someone else that you trust to help you come to terms with such an event will enable you to accept that it happened, and let your inner child start to heal from its effect. It may potentially always be a part of you, but learning to accept it will help free you of the negative and emotional turmoil that it put you through.

The other part of addressing your inner child is recognizing both the good and the bad things in your childhood that formed you into the person you are right now. This can also help you understand why you feel certain things, communicate with people certain ways, or even get triggered by certain behaviors. When I say trigger, I mean you react strongly in a way that you don't always understand. A mild example would be if you get really upset with friends that are always late. You get very frustrated and overly upset about people doing this, but when you were a child, your parents were very strict about punctuality and found it disrespectful if you were late. A stronger, second example would be if you have a trigger from childhood trauma. If you had a parent that struggled with alcoholism, you may react very strongly to overly intoxicated friends. It's something that has been formed into you. That is a small trigger. Larger and more explosive triggers can also exist which were formed from more serious situations.

When you were a child you thought certain things, dreamed about your future, and found joy from places you might not anymore. Getting in touch with that part of you is really magical on your path to self-actualization. Imagine my "peak" moment when I realized that I am so afraid of conflict because I realized I was the peacemaker when I was a child. Being the third out of four kids, I was constantly trying to diffuse sibling arguments and fighting when my parents weren't around. I then did that same tactic in school where I tried to be peaceful and friendly to everyone to avoid conflict and becoming a target of bullying. I can close my eyes and feel my younger self being terrified of people's attention and, even worse, the focus of their negative feelings. This was really enlightening for me to realize because it made me realize that I never developed any sort of conflict resolution experiences or tools because I avoided it at all costs from a very young age.

The final thing about your inner child that I want to focus on is inspiration. Remember that this whole road you are traveling is meant to get yourself to the version of you that your inner child wanted to be. Think about that for a moment. That's really powerful. When you were young, I guarantee you didn't dream about the day you could grow up and be trapped in a jail of negativity, anxiety, and distress, surrounded by toxic people and struggling to enjoy your life. That's not the version of yourself that younger you ever imagined would exist. Think back to what they thought they could be and all the things they knew they would achieve. Stay in touch with that inner part of you to remember that you are working to honor the way you anticipated your life to be. You deserve that.

Dealing with Triggers

A trigger is a complex emotional response that needs its own set of tools to be dealt with successfully. As far down the road as you come and go on towards self-actualization, a trigger will throw you into a different spot without warning.

Let me give you an example of what I mean. Let's say you have been focusing a lot of your energy on addressing and managing your ego. You know that you tend to focus too much on your role in situations when in actuality, you don't have much of a role at all. You are sensitive and make things about you a little too much. You've recognized it, you're aware of it, and you are working on changing. You are doing fantastic. Then your closest friend tells you that they are moving to another city in a month. Your immediate thought is that they are abandoning you. One of your parents left when you were young and your friend moving triggers your fear of abandonment. In your head you know that their move has nothing to do with you, but because of your trigger, your ego wins and you make it all about you and your needs. You feel angry, hurt, disappointed, and confused, when you should be feeling happy for your friend who is excited about their move. It can be frustrating because you feel set back on your journey and don't know how to handle this type of reaction.

Identifying a trigger can be pretty easy, and you may be aware of them already. Sometimes our triggers even become a source of good-natured ridicule because our emotional response is so disproportionate to the trigger itself. Maybe you become really angry when you are really hungry and it's amusing to people that you spend a lot of time with. They tease you about it, but what they don't realize is that it's a trigger for you because you had an eating disorder when you were younger. Or it can be a smell of a certain type of food that made you really sick once, and now it triggers a physical response of nausea. Triggers present themselves in a lot of different forms.

If you have a trigger that you have identified as something that is serious enough to be impeding your ability to grow emotionally, there are a number of tips to help approach them. David Ricoh PhD discusses his "trigger toolbox" containing a variety of tips to approach triggers and deal with them successfully (2020):

1. Identifying and labeling them: Giving your trigger a name helps make it real and gives you a tangible thing to focus on. If my trigger is rejection, if I say it out loud to myself that I am triggered by rejection. It can help me realize why I am so upset when something small happens, like a friend bailing on me.
2. Try to remember why: Knowing the source of your trigger can help you lessen its power. If my rejection trigger comes from an awful break up when I was a young, then I can put into perspective that those were the actions of a teenager that caused those emotions in me. This enables me to heal.
3. Be aware of who you are punishing: It can be easy to project past experiences onto new people. Let's say you had a teacher that was verbally abusive to you when you were in grade school. The emotional scarring stayed with you and you have found it to be a trigger when your own children are attending school. If a teacher disciplines them or raises their voice, you get extremely defensive and overreact with anger. Try to be aware of when you are putting your own triggers onto people who don't deserve it.
4. Stay calm: If you notice yourself having a physical reaction to a trigger, employ your calming techniques, such as meditation, to bring your physical state back to a neutral place.
5. Listen to your inner voice: If you are triggered and there is something inside of you telling you something, don't disagree or push the feelings away. Acknowledge them and try to understand why you are feeling them as opposed to dismissing them as invalid.

6. Show your emotion: When Dr. Ricoh discusses displaying your emotion, he likens them to a healthy development of any muscle. If you practice displaying your emotion regularly, your ability will become stronger. It's the same as if you use a muscle regularly. If you don't practice an emotion, such as sadness or anger, and mask them instead, then when they do come out, it will be difficult to control how you display them.
7. Step away: If the trigger is not something you feel capable of addressing when it happens, remove yourself from the situation. Promise yourself that you will come back to it when you are stronger. Don't avoid it forever, but give yourself space if you need it.
8. Laugh: If you are able to change a situation from a trigger to something you can find humor in, you've won and taken away its power.

Finding a way to respond to your triggers takes their power away and allows you to control the response that you have to them. As always, be patient with yourself and don't get frustrated if you slide into comfortable behaviors and react the next time something happens. Just remember that you are moving in an upwards direction to your self-actualized and emotionally intelligent self. Everything you are doing is providing you with the tools and weapons you need to eliminate the past behaviors and emotional disorders that have haunted you. EFT tapping is by far the most effective way to demolish your triggers in record time. It's free, easy to do, only takes a few minutes, and there are countless free videos online you can tap along to.

30

THE BEAUTY OF SELF-FORGIVENESS, SELF-COMPASSION, AND SELF-LOVE

As you have gone through this process, there have probably been some really tough moments for you. And you may be exhausted. You've been in a constant state of improvement, and trying to change. That takes a lot of work and a lot of effort. I want to devote some time for you to concentrate on what an amazing being you are. You need to spend some time falling in love with who you are and everything you have accomplished on this journey. You are incredible.

Over the past weeks, months, or years that you have been focusing your energy on this path, you have probably also had moments where you've been really hard on yourself. You might have been frustrated over things that you can't control. The negative self-talk can come out in full force when you are shining a light on all the things that you want to grow away from. This is the time where we are going to practice some compassion with ourselves and forgiveness for our past.

Self-Forgiveness: Let the Healing Begin

We have spent a lot of time healing. We have focused on healing our inner child and our wounds from past experiences. We have talked about healing from toxic relationships and emotional connections. You have analyzed your entire soul, and all the flaws that come with it. And now is the time to forgive yourself for all the things that came before.

I reflect back on my story about my time working as a server and how much I missed out on because I couldn't see the beauty of everything around me. I missed out on friendships, interesting connections with customers, and probably unique life experiences because I was so focused on the negatives. I was really mad at myself for a long time afterwards. Then, as I began to move into a more positive version of myself, I got mad all over again. I held onto so much regret on how different it could have been.

Then I stopped to think: Why was I still beating myself up over this? What good intention was I bringing to my life by reflecting on things that happened years prior with regret, shame, and guilt? I needed to forgive myself for this experience and countless others so I could fully open myself up to new ones. If I reflected back on what an "idiot" I was for wrecking that time in my life, every time I had a great night out in a restaurant and enjoyed the atmosphere and the service, then there would always be a stain on the evening in my mind. Why would I want to do that to myself? I had to find a way to forgive my former self, and release my mind of the things that didn't matter anymore.

Exercises for Self-Forgiveness

- Write a letter: By now you probably see that I am a very big advocate of putting pen to paper to voice your feelings. Write yourself a letter the same way you would write a letter to another person to show them that you care. Tell yourself that you love you, and that you want everything good to happen for you in the future. You forgive your former self for anything that you wish you could change because it's over. The only one focusing on those things is you, and with your forgiveness, they are gone.
- Recite affirmations: Every morning (or when you have time alone), stare directly into your own eyes in the mirror and confidently recite an affirmation of forgiveness. This will be personal to you, but examples could be:

- "I love you and I forgive you for the past. You did what you thought was right, and everyone makes mistakes."
- "I forgive you. You are amazing. You are older, wiser, and forgiveness sets you free"
- Recognize the good that has come out of it: There will be things in your past that have bothered you that need forgiving. Reminding myself of good outcomes that have resulted from them helps me forgive myself for what's happened. I think about previous relationships that were ruined by my inability to connect in a positive way. My insecurities were able to take over because of negative self-talk and low self-esteem. These relationships hurt at the time, and I regret hurting other people, but the result was me finding a partner that I may not have met had the other relationships worked out. That's a positive thing. And my learned experiences from that other pain prepared me to appreciate the beauty of what I have now.

Self-Love

You know what love feels like. You feel it towards other people. But have you ever stopped to direct that emotion inwards? Self-love is the practice of appreciating everything about yourself. It's taking the time to see yourself like other people do and love the things about yourself that they feel. Self-love is often overlooked because it's not a common concept. Even though it should be. You spend more time with yourself than any other person in the world, so why wouldn't you want to be in love with who you are?

Understandably, this may seem conflicting to what we talked about earlier with having an inflated ego. Being in love with yourself doesn't mean you think you are better and more important than everyone around you. It means that you can see the good in who you are and appreciate your inner beauty for what it is. So being in love with the special things about you doesn't have to mean that your ego is out of control. It means you know how to admire and cherish yourself.

Self-love also means taking care of yourself. It involves prioritizing your health and your needs to feel good about yourself. When life gets busy, taking time to look after ourselves is usually one of the first things that gets pushed to the side. We eat unhealthy foods because it's more convenient, we don't have time to stay fit, and we don't prioritize necessary relaxation. Sometimes we feel guilty and consider it selfish, but learning to detach from that thinking and show yourself self-care is necessary.

Exercises for Self-Love

- Physical care: Taking the time to nourish your body with physical care when you need it shows yourself a lot of love. Book a massage, go to a yoga class, take a nap, or partake in any other activity where you put yourself first. Ask for support and promise yourself that you will always take care of your body when you feel it's necessary. You need to be able to rely on yourself to make those calls that your health will be a priority.
- Emotional breaks: As you go through a transition of personal development, things are going to get tough and you may want to quit. Be easy on yourself and take emotional breaks if you need to. Your mental health needs to be preserved, and even the strongest muscles need rest to get stronger.
- Disconnect: Turn off the screens, turn off your phone, and just enjoy time away from the overstimulating world we live in.
- Give yourself compliments: This may sound and feel a little silly, but it works! If I love someone, I want them to be happy. If they are feeling down, I like to cheer them up, or I like to make them feel good about themselves by giving them a compliment. So do it to yourself too. Look yourself in the eye and say something nice. "You did a really great job at work today," or "Wow! Your hair looks awesome." It's a bit cheesy but it will make you smile and fall in love with yourself a little bit more each time.

Self-Compassion

I've used the phrases of being patient and kind to yourself as a theme throughout the chapters, and I sincerely mean it. We are so hard on ourselves every day. There's that saying "You are your own worst critic," and it's true! We are harder on ourselves than anybody else. So just lighten up every once in a while. We have big expectations of what we want to achieve, and putting pressure to reach our goals is a healthy attribute. But when the drive to do great things turns into negative self-talk when we have setbacks or failures, we need to show kindness to ourselves the way we would to anyone else.

Exercises for Self-Compassion

Dr. Kristen Neff is a leading expert in the area of self-compassion. She talks about practices for self-compassion (2019).

- Treating yourself the same way you would treat a friend
- Taking self-compassion breaks to make it a priority
- Writing and journaling
- Touch to calm and nourish your body and the parasympathetic system
- Moving away from negative self-talk
- Taking care of you and your caregiver

The one that resonated with me as the best way to show compassion to myself was to treat myself as a friend. For all my struggles with mental health and emotional turmoil, I can identify one of my strengths as being a good friend in a lot of ways. Definitely not a perfect friend, but I think a pretty good one. Flipping my thought process to treating myself the same way I treat my friends was really great for me. It helped me be very compassionate and kind to myself. I would never talk negatively to my friends the way I sometimes talked to myself. So why not show myself that same level of kindness?

So every once in a while, as an exercise in compassion to myself, I plan a day out. I pretend that I am planning a special day out for a friend the same way I would for their birthday. I pick my favorite restaurant for lunch, book a spa treatment, and organize meeting friends for drinks later. I show myself that I am special, and that I appreciate everything I'm capable of. I usually do this type of day at a time where I would normally be very hard on myself, like if I've had a setback or done something I regret. Showing myself compassion enables me to move on more quickly.

31

PUTTING YOURSELF FIRST IS NOT SELFISH

As we discussed the topics of showing yourself love, forgiveness, and compassion, the ability to be able to prioritize yourself was questioned. Many people have trouble putting time into themselves, and often feel guilty for trying to do so.

In some ways it can get a bit muddled, because on an ego level we put ourselves into the center of our thoughts, and in most situations we have to work on thinking beyond ourselves. In that context it sounds like we are putting ourselves first. Plus the fact that we are taking all this time to focus inwards and work towards self-actualization makes it sound like we are prioritizing ourselves. On some level it's true that you are learning to make time for yourself, but really being able to put yourself first is something almost entirely different.

In your life, you have people that depend on you. It could be children, a partner, friends, coworkers, elderly family, neighbors, and so on. It can be really hard to change expectations of your relationships when you have always been the person that is completely available and never says no. You enjoy being the one that a lot of people depend on, and you feel bad about setting aside time for yourself when you could be assisting someone else. Or you find it difficult to say no when something comes up and you already had something planned just for you. It can be really easy to tell yourself that you will reschedule your personal time, and then just help the person out who is asking at that moment. You don't prioritize yourself, and then it just becomes a habit.

Learning to Prioritize You

How do you go from being so busy and never saying no to setting boundaries and putting yourself first without guilt? It sounds like it should be simple, but something is preventing you from doing it already. Quite often we get into the habit of thinking we will have more time later, but later never comes. You just always stay busy and never learn to put you on a pedestal.

I mentioned earlier in the book that you need to have a source of light within you to keep the motivation of this process going. Your light comes from the source of wanting to be a better version of yourself. Our focus has been about you becoming this version for your own reasons. You want your life to be happier and healthier. When it comes to prioritizing yourself, it's important to remember that you are doing this journey for the people in your life too. By taking care of yourself, your mental health, and your physical being, you will be able to give more back to them and your relationship.

You should also look at it from an ego-less perspective. Are you feeling guilty about taking time for yourself because you believe everyone around you will fall apart because you are not available to be on call for them 24 hours a day? It sounds a bit silly when you put it in those terms. If you are a parent of very young children then it's probably not far off, but, even in that situation, being able to carve out at least 20 minutes a day to meditate or journal shouldn't be unreasonable.

Try these tips to begin the process of prioritizing your needs and detaching from the guilt that comes with it:

- Start small: If you feel guilty about taking time for yourself, work your way into it. Start with 20 minutes a few times each week. It can be as simple as turning your phone off, closing a door, and practicing mindful meditation.

- Ask for support: If you live in a home with other people, ask them to be respectful of your time. If you have children, ask your spouse to engage them while you have your time set aside so they don't come looking for you and interrupt you.
- Keep communication open: If putting yourself first is new, finding a balance of how much you need, and how much is too much can take awhile. If you have other obligations in your life, it might be difficult to go from no personal time to multiple hours of it a day. Keep communication open with those people in your life that may be affected. Ask them for support, but also ask them to be honest with their needs so they don't harbor any resentment if you are too absent.
- Think about what really matters: What would I do if I found out that I only had a month left on this Earth? Would I stress about all the little things that I am trying to accomplish instead of taking an hour out of my day for myself? No, I definitely wouldn't. It doesn't change the fact that I still need to get unimportant tasks done eventually, it just helps remind me that they don't have to be done right at that moment. I can put them aside, and put me first.

Defining Your Core Values

Your life is busy and you are trying to accomplish a lot with your development. You are learning to accept all the pieces of who you are, develop the weaker parts of your mind to free yourself from negativity, repair relationships, and focus on your own needs, all while learning emotional intelligence and removing negative influences from your life. You may feel pulled in many different directions, and even as you become better at prioritizing time for yourself, you may not always know how to maximize it.

Knowing your heart and what's in it will guide you to your purpose as a self-actualized person. Defining your core values will give you an inner guidance system that will help you with your decisions and help keep that inner light shining as you try to stay motivated and balanced.

Core values are the things in your life that you see as both important and necessary for your fulfillment and happiness. It's the values that you feel good about upholding and feel disappointed when you don't. They are the rules and influencers that you strive to live your life by.

There are hundreds of possibilities of what people's core values might be. Each one of us is so unique and what we hold in high regard might not have the same level of importance for someone else.

Some examples of popular values are:

1. Family: For many, their family is their main focus that drives them to be successful. Their family is their main priority because it is their primary social source and support system.
2. Achievement: Setting goals and achieving them is very important to someone who craves goal setting and reaching them. Achievement creates that inner sense of accomplishment and boosts esteem.
3. Structure: For some, having a structured schedule and being organized is calming and creates a positive environment that an unstructured environment does not.
4. Culture: Maintaining a connection to culture, family history, traditions, language, and community is very important. Preserving the culture by both practicing it and sharing it with family can be very valuable to people.

5. Laughter: Being able to laugh and find humor in everyday situations is a large priority for a lot of people who want to keep their spirit light and joyful.
6. Faith: For some, having faith is their compass for morality and finding purpose in life. Having faith provides many people with a sense of belonging and reasoning that is essential in their development.
7. Fitness: Prioritizing physical fitness is a source for many to alleviate emotional distress. It also creates a strong base to build upon.
8. Kindness: Being kind to people and treating everyone the same is a value held by many. This can mean stopping to think about others and reaching out to help when they need it.
9. Authenticity: Always being yourself. Never waver from who you are to fit other people's needs or expectations.
10. Giving Back - Being able to incorporate charity, community service, and other forms of giving back as a regular practice in life is very important to some people.

Writing down what your core values are can be a very interesting exercise. Maybe you've never put any thought into it before. Physically writing them down on paper could make you realize how important something is to you. I've always known that I enjoy creative projects, but it was only when I started writing down my values that I realized creativity is one of my core values. Not even just in an artistic sense, but also in how I approach problems and different situations. I value my creativity and use it to guide my decisions in many ways.

There isn't a correct number of values. You may have three, or you may have thirty. Think about what it is that you value and make a list for yourself so you can use it to guide you when you need it. It's also fun to go back years later and re-evaluate if your values have changed.

32

IT'S TIME TO REPROGRAM YOUR BRAIN

"Neuro-associations are the links between thoughts and emotions in your mind, which create and shape your behavior and performance results" (Girard, 2014, para. 7).

When you think about the potential of what a neuro-association is, and the abilities that we have to change them, the possibilities are endless on what we can train our minds to do. You have probably heard about simple neuro-association techniques like how chewing mint gum while studying for an exam will help you remember things if you chew that same gum later. Or maybe every time you hear a certain song it sparks a specific memory. These are all things that are associated through pathways in our minds.

We will have positive and negative associations. What we want to achieve is the ability to lessen the negative ones through neuro-association disrupting techniques and strengthen healthy ones through positive affirmations and other practices.

Liz Weighardt of the website *Happy Brain Life* discussed the example of how many people associate a dentist visit as a stressful experience and five tips to overcome that neuro-association (n.d.):

1. Find your "Why"

What is it specifically that you find stressful about the dentist? Using the calm and rational parts of your brain to try to figure out why you have this association can help you adjust and reprogram. If you had a bad experience when you were a child, you can acknowledge that it was in the past and unlikely to happen again. You can try and work on creating positive associations with the dentist now. Things like how clean your teeth feel afterwards or the sense of accomplishment you feel for taking care of yourself.

1. Understand your brain is just trying to help

Your brain isn't trying to make things difficult for you or even hurt you, it's trying to protect you. You have these associations because it's trying to protect you from having another negative experience. When you can think about it that way, it prevents you from being frustrated with your own mind. If you had a negative experience at the dentist when you were young, your brain is just trying to prevent you from having that pain again.

1. Use visualization

You can reprogram your brain with positive visualizations to create new associations in your brain. Since it only remembers the negative pain, try closing your eyes and visualizing positive images. Picture yourself relaxing in the chair, having a nice friendly dentist come in and greet you, and your beautiful smile when you are leaving. All happy, positive things. Visualize them over and over for the days leading up to your appointment to strengthen that association and weaken the other one.

1. Positive Phrases

Talk positively to yourself about the dentist. Say phrases like "I love the dentist," "The dentist keeps me healthy," and "I am fortunate to have access to a dentist." These phrases will compound with the visualization to create better associations.

1. Tell your brain to stop

After you acknowledge why you have the negative association and what it is, ask your brain to stop. When you feel yourself drifting in that direction say "stop" to yourself, and move onto one of your positive association techniques. It won't be an immediate swap of associations, but over time it will change.

Techniques for Retraining

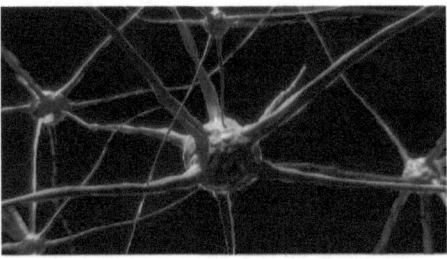

When I was young, I learned something in school about my brain. I remember a visual of pathways between connecting points in our brain. The visual showed a person thinking of something new and the pathway was a thin, tiny little line connecting to points within the brain. Then it showed them thinking about that same thing over and over, and each time they did the line or "pathway" got a little bit thicker. Then overtime, when they thought about that same thing enough, there was a thick bridge that was solid and unbreakable because it was so ingrained in their brain.

An example of this would be that 2+2=4. You have probably used that throughout your life thousands of times, so the pathway is so clear that you don't even need much energy to think about it. An example of a thin pathway would be a song that you heard when you were younger. Something reminds you of it one day but you have to think really hard about what it's called or what the tune is because the pathway isn't that strong and the line is thin.

I have no idea why this visual of our thought patterns stayed with me, but it was the first thing I thought of when I started to learn about neuro-associations. I panicked because I just kept picturing my negative associations as big thick lines that were strong and unbreakable. It was intimidating to think of how I could break them down and create new ones. What I did next has been my process for how I have changed my associations and have given new power to my mind and its abilities.

Visualization

We just spoke about visualizing with the dentist example. It is very powerful. This is how I used my pre-existing visual and started to use it to my advantage. I would label a negative association and picture it as a pathway in my brain. Let's use the example of vacation. Every time my family and I talked about going somewhere warm for vacation, my instant association was bathing suits and my poor body image. Basically it was an immediate association to "You're fat." How awful is that?

So through my visualization tactic I would:

1. Picture the pathway connecting two points in my brain with the writing on the side of the pathway as "vacation = you're fat."
2. I would then picture something coming and breaking the pathway. A rock flying right through the air and smashing it to pieces.
3. Afterwards, where the broken bridge was, I would picture my mind rebuilding the bridge with new writing. The writing would be what I wanted my brain to associate. In this situation the writing would now say "vacation = precious family time."
4. I would then picture a thought or an energy point traveling back and forth over the bridge to strengthen it and hardwire it into my system.
5. The next time I made the negative association, I would do it all over again.

Mindful Meditation

Coming back to our practice of mindful meditation, similar to its value with changing your thought process, it can be helped to reprogram your associations as well.

In our final chapters we will go over more techniques for mindful meditation and guided practices, but I often stick to a similar method to the one I discussed in Chapter 1. If you remember, I focused my mediation around breathing in the positive and pushing out the negative.

With respect to reprogramming an association, I use it in the same way.

- I breathe in the positive association that I would like to replace the negative one with.
- I breathe out the negative association and push it away from my body.

EFT Tapping

Our brief introduction to EFT tapping earlier gave a little insight into this exciting and life changing technique. I cannot say enough positive things about EFT, as it has become a regular source of relief and treatment for me in my everyday life.

I previously talked about my own methods for tapping, and introduced you to the various EFT points, and their connection to the meridians within our body. I would now like to talk more about the science behind how it affects our bodies and show you a guided technique for you to practice right away.

From a purely scientific approach, tapping affects your fight or flight response and disrupts the neural associations you've created. Your amygdala, which is the part of your brain said to be the core of your nervous system and the section responsible for our fear responses, is affected by the process of tapping. Brain scans have been said to show that the amygdala is directly affected during the tapping process. At this time, it's unclear the definitive changes that are happening, but the proof is in the thousands of people that are seeing results through its practice (Howitt, 2019).

Getting started on traditional tapping basics is not complicated:

- You will start your tapping process by creating a setup statement. We will go over the setup statement shortly.
- You repeat the setup statement slowly as you move through a sequence of tapping points, starting with the karate chop point. The entire sequence is listed below.
- You repeat the sequence over and over until you are able to let go of the negativity and harsh emotion associated with your concern and come to a neutral place. Once you have cleared your mind of negativity, you are open to repeat the sequence with a more positive statement in mind.

With this explanation you can see how wonderfully uncomplicated and freeing it is. By tapping while repeating your setup statement, you calm your body and allow yourself to accept your intention stress free.

The setup statement mentioned is the statement that you will use to define what you are struggling with and your acceptance of it. It is basically your intention for your tapping session. In our dentist reprogramming example, your statement might be:

"I am afraid of the dentist, and that's okay."

"A dentist hurt me in the past, and I forgive him."

"The dentist office makes me anxious, and I accept that."

Your intention statement allows you to acknowledge your fear and negative association. Although there hasn't been enough testing, theoretically it could be said that by acknowledging our fears and negative associations we engage the fight or flight response of our amygdala. Then, by tapping through that it causes our brain to lessen the response to that particular stimulus. By lessening the negative association it sets us up to succeed in creating the more positive associations through our other techniques of meditation and visualization.

The sequence of your tapping points are as follows:

1. Start with the side of your hand. It's called the "karate chop point." Use the four fingers from your other hand and tap the spot on the side of your hand right below the bottom/outside part of your pinky. If you were to make a karate chop motion,

it is the point on the outside of your hand that would connect. Recite your Intention Statement three times slowly while tapping this point.
2. Next tap five to seven times on each of the following points while repeating a focused word out of your intention statement. In our example it would probably be "dentist." Start at the top of the head point and work your way down to the underarm.
3. Tap Top of Head 5-7 times (TH)
4. Eyebrow Point (EB)
5. Under Eye (UE)
6. Under Nose (UN)
7. Chin Point (CP)
8. Collarbone Point (CB)
9. Under Arm (UA)
10. Repeat the process until you feel in a neutral place with your fear and anxiety dissipated.

This now leaves your brain in a neutral place to begin creating positive associations towards your negative thoughts. At this point, I find the other techniques to be more powerful for myself for positive association creation. However, the same process of EFT tapping can be highly effective with positive associations.

When you start the process, make a positive intention statement:

"I will approach the dentist without fear."

"My health is the priority and I am appreciative."

"I am grateful that I have access to dental care."

Then follow the exact same process with the intent of creating a positive association.

Self-Discipline

Moving forward, it's important to remember that these techniques are only as valuable as your resolve to use them. Their effectiveness will come through consistency and commitment. You can't reprogram a deep association with one session. It has to be an ongoing thing to strengthen what exists and build up what you want it to be.

In the beginning, don't try to reprogram every part of you that needs some change. It would be impossible both time-wise, and for your brain to take on. Chances are you don't have mass amounts of items that need to be reprogrammed, and certainly not many serious ones. Just pick one to start with. Even try something simple like a type of food.

This is actually how I practiced. For years I didn't eat a certain type of soup. I had become sick once after eating it, and every time I smelled it afterwards my stomach would do a little flip. Then as time went on, I didn't have the same physical response, but associated soup with feeling sick. I used this type of soup to practice my skills. I used all the techniques I had learned to reprogram my brain to remember that I used to like this soup and the flavors are all things I enjoy. Guess what, it worked! I don't have that association anymore, and I enjoy that soup again.

After my success with that, I was excited to move onto more reprogramming so it made it easier for me to commit to something I had actually seen work. Give yourself the gift of self-discipline to stick to these techniques. They can help you endlessly in your quest for self-actualization and ongoing growth.

33

AMAZING MEDITATION TECHNIQUES TO MASTER YOUR THOUGHTS

Meditation is a practice of calming your mind, emptying the clutter, and focusing your thoughts to a positive place. It is the one natural technique that has had extensive research and medical studies performed that prove the theory of its effectiveness. Studies have shown that it is responsible for physically changing your brain. Long-term meditators show less aging within their brain (this is displayed through gray matter volume). It decreases activity in the default mode network (DMN) section of your brain which is responsible for wandering thoughts. Those wandering thoughts in some cases are the negative, OCD, anxious, and depressing thoughts that lead to mental health issues and are associated with lower happiness. By reducing activity in this area, you are diminishing the presence of these thoughts. Through controlled testing, mediation is also shown to improve focus and concentration. Its benefits for your brain are nothing short of outstanding (Walton, 2015).

There is no correct or incorrect way to practice meditation, but there are endless resources of different ways to accomplish your intentions of what you would like to achieve. Testing out different methods will help you discover the most effective one for you. Below are some of my favorite techniques that I have found to be incredibly effective for me to reap the benefits of meditation.

Technique 1: Concentration Meditation

Concentration meditation is the practice of focusing on one thought, idea, or object for an extended period of time. It's meant to teach you to focus more intensely. In the beginning, you may only be able to maintain your focus for a minute or two, but will work up your endurance over time.

For concentration meditation, since you are going to be focusing your thoughts and energy into one spot, you can choose to concentrate on the following:

1. An object: Many people choose objects that represent nature and make them feel grounded. A candle, to focus on the flicker of the flame. A stone. A flower or a plant. You can choose any type of object. It is something for you to place in one spot and focus on.
2. A phrase or word: You don't always have to use the same phrase or word. It can be changed day to day, depending on what you would like to concentrate on for that day's meditation. You can repeat it slowly as you learn to focus your energy into the one spot.
3. Your breath: I mentioned this earlier in the book that this is something that I focus on during my meditation. Breathing in and out slowly and focusing on the sound, feeling, and duration of each breath.

With concentration meditation do the following steps:

1. Pick a comfortable spot to start. Using the same spot every day can condition your body to associate meditation and its positive benefits to that place. This can create a very special place for you in your home. But also learning to meditate in a

variety of places can be helpful to your commitment to it as well.
2. Decide the duration of your meditation practice and set an alarm. Pick a gentle alarm that will gently pull you from your meditation, rather than jolt you back to awareness.
3. When you are comfortable and ready to start, take a few deep breaths and concentrate on your object, words, or breath.
4. Continue to take deep breaths in and out while concentrating.
5. If your mind begins to wander, don't get frustrated. Feeling upset with yourself is also a distraction so don't let yourself get caught up in it. Just take a deep breath and push away distractions. Then, with your next breath, refocus back on your concentrating.
6. Lengthen your meditation over time. In the beginning, start with a few minutes, and then work your way up to 20-30 minutes.

Concentration meditation is very beneficial for teaching your mind to focus and spend less time with wandering and disruptive thoughts. It can help you in your everyday life ,at work or with relationships by giving you the skill of deeper focus.

Technique 2: Mindfulness Meditation

We discussed mindfulness meditation earlier as it is my favorite form to practice. It's the tactic of giving your mind a safe space to allow various thoughts a judgement free zone to pass through. For someone who has had trouble with OCD and negative thoughts, I think it gives me the best ability to detach and let go of my wandering and troubling emotions.

I went over my technique in detail in Chapter 2. but to summarize:

1. Find a quiet, comfortable spot away from all distractions.
2. Relax into your spot. Make sure you are physically fully

relaxed. If you are chilly, put a blanket on. You don't want physical distractions to take away from your time.
3. Slowly breath in and out to the count of five. Focus on your breath, and as thoughts enter your mind, acknowledge them without judgement or analysis. If a thought is something that you need to work through, breathe in the positive associated with the thought, and breathe out the negative.

Mindfulness meditation creates an escape for your busy mind to clear away negative thoughts and emotions. It gives you peace to know that you can go to a place to calm your emotions. For me, it took away my sense of powerlessness that I felt when I got stressed or upset. I didn't always know how to cope with it, but having a place that I know is waiting for me makes me feel safe and secure.

Technique 3: Walking Meditation

When you go for a walk, what do you think about? Even when you are walking from your car into a building, or walking around your house, where do your thoughts and focus go? If someone had asked me those questions a few years ago, I don't even know if I would have an answer. We tend to go on autopilot when we are walking, or we are busy thinking about things that need to get done.

Walking meditation is the practice of paying attention to your surroundings while walking, as well as using your natural walking rhythm as a method to maintain your focus. Similar to yoga, it uses the natural movement of your body to connect your breath, movement, and thoughts. In addition, if you are practicing walking meditation outside, you can connect your senses to the nature around you.

Perform this walking exercise as described from the online source *Headspace* ("Walking Meditation," 2020):

Do each of the following cues for about 30-60 seconds and then repeat from the beginning:

Body Check: Start at the top and sense your way down. How do you feel? Pay attention to any aches and pains, or points of tightness. Being aware of how your body feels can allow you to acknowledge your physical state. If you feel tired and heavy, then make feelings of lightness and energy part of your meditation as you walk. Adjust your posture to stand tall and feel strong.

Observe: Just pay attention to the way you walk. Maybe you've never noticed that you swing one arm way more than the other, or that your hips sway a lot. Don't try to change it, just enjoy your movement.

Tune in: Listen to everything that's going on around you. Listen to birds, music from passing cars, the wind, your footsteps, and anything else that catches your ear. Look at everything you pass in detail. Notice the bright color of flowers, interactions of people, the trees swaying, and other beautiful things you may normally have just sailed on by without noticing. Lastly, notice the smells. Breathe in the fresh air and anything else you can.

Physical Sensations: Notice the physical sensations as they happen. If it's cold, notice the wind on your cheeks. Feel the weight of your bag on your shoulder. Feel the tension in your legs. Enjoy the contact of your feet with the ground. Use these sensations to create awareness in your body.

Over time, I've created my own version of walking meditation that I call the five senses. I use each of the five sense on rotation to create a meditation sequence while I'm walking:

Taste: I always have water with me. I use a large sip of cold water as my centering and starting point to the sequence. It also provides me with a reset option if my mind has completely wandered off, or if my dog distracts me and I want to restart the process.

Sight: I take a few minutes to observe things around me and give gratitude to nature. I look at the sky and thank nature for clean air. I look at the flowers, trees, and grass, and thank nature for the healthy ground. If I am walking in the city, I observe people and give gratitude for kindness and compassion.

Smell: After sight, I take note of the smells, and connect as much as I can through familiarity of things I have smelled before.

Touch: I stop to touch something to feel more grounded. I will touch a tree, or a plant, or even stop to pet an animal. Something to engage my physical senses.

Hearing: I will listen to the sounds around me. I'm careful not to focus on words or conversations because then my mind will drift. Rather I try to find patterns in the sounds of the city of nature.

Once I'm done with the sequence, I start back to the beginning with a sip of water. The purpose of walking meditation is to maintain awareness of our bodies and our surroundings instead of passing it all by distraction in meaningless thoughts. It helps us stay present and enjoy the moment.

Technique 4: Chakra Meditation

The ancient Buddhist practice of chakra meditation focuses on seven energy points along the spine. Each energy point has a specific point, name, and color associated with it. It is believed that if any of your chakras are "blocked," it prevents you from health and wellness associated with that point.

When practicing chakra meditation, you start with the lowest energy point and work your way upwards. By focusing on the point and visualizing the color associated with that chakra, you can work on realigning its energy to bring balance to your body.

The seven chakra points starting with the base and moving upwards are:

1. The root chakra (red color): Located at the base of the spine near your tailbone. A blocked root is associated with anxiousness of finance, basic needs, arthritis, constipation and bladder ailments. A balanced root brings feelings of stability, grounding, and calmness.
2. The sacral chakra (orange color): Located just below the belly button and above the pubic bone. A blocked sacral is associated with lack of creativity, sexual impotency, and urinary infections. A balanced root brings creativity, sexual confidence, and self-worth.

3. The solar plexus chakra (yellow color): Located between the rib cage and the navel. A blocked plexus is associated with digestive issues such as ulcers and heartburn. A balanced root brings high self-esteem and confidence.
4. The heart chakra (green color): Located in the center of the chest. A blocked heart is associated with heart attacks, weight issues, selfishness, loneliness, and low self-esteem. A balanced root brings love, and the ability to communicate with others.
5. The throat chakra (blue color): Located directly in the throat. A blocked throat is associated with throat problems, dental issues, negative communication, and dishonesty. A balanced throat brings strong communication and a healthy smile.
6. The third eye chakra (indigo color): Located in the space between your eyebrows. A blocked third eye is associated with headaches, poor hearing, and foggy thinking. A balanced third eye brings clarity and imagination.
7. The crown chakra (deep purple): Located at the top of the head. A blocked crown can be associated with brain function and nervous system issues. Since it is connected to the entire body through the brain, it can affect all organs negatively. It is also associated with narrow minded and negative thinking. A balanced crown brings balance to the entire body, kindness, compassion, and intelligence.

To practice the chakra meditation, simple breathing and visualization techniques are effective. There are two methods:

1. Follow the seven chakra points from root to crown. Take slow, deep breaths while visualizing each point. Picture the associated color and breath into the energy point. Visualize your breath giving energy to the point and making the color brighter and full of energy. As you exhale, push out the negative energy manifesting itself in that energy point. Spend a few minutes on each point.

2. Concentrate on one chakra that you feel is out of alignment. For example, if you have been getting a lot of headaches and can't seem to focus, spend time on your third eye chakra to bring balance and alignment back.

Chakra meditation is a powerful method of bringing a sense of calm and alignment to the body. It can be used to compliment your other types of mediation by adding a unique and effective method of visualizing positivity into your various energy points.

Whatever your method of choice for meditation is, remember to be consistent and try to do it every day. The purpose is to create a clearer, healthier, and calmer version of your brain to help you with your journey to self-actualization. It's an extremely valuable tool and I am so grateful I am able to share it with you.

34

THE 10 STEP DAILY EMPOWERMENT RITUAL FOR MASTERY OF YOUR THOUGHTS

You have experienced so much growth during our time together. I hope you have learned everything that I have poured from my heart in the hope to help you grow. I feel so blessed in my life to have come across so many profound and wonderful people who share their wisdom with love and acceptance. I want you to feel that same level of support from me as you continue on your path.

I have spent years developing a routine that works for me on a day to day basis to maintain my ongoing commitment to self-actualization. Getting comfortable within my own skin and accepting every aspect of who I am has been the journey of a lifetime. I want to share my routine with you so that you have a starting point of creating the perfect life for yourself.

This routine is something I do each and every day. When I am struggling or going through some extra emotions, I will add time to the routine to get through everything I need to, but I will put my extra care tips in here as well. By keeping this routine up, I feel like my mind is lighter, more free, and clearer than it's ever been in my life.

My 10 Step Secret Routine for Success:

Step 1: Each evening before I go to sleep, I write a phrase or word on a chalkboard hanging by my bed. When I awake in the morning I look to the board and see what I have written. Some days it will be something specific for that day such as "You are brave, and your interview will go great." On other days it will be something I set as a general intention, like "Love freely today, show the world your heart." I used to wake up and reach for my phone. I would check emails and read the news, which set my mind racing for the day. Now I wake up calmly and with a great start.

Step 2: I take five minutes to stretch and breathe. I do a few stretches to wake up my body and get myself connected before I start my day. I reach to the sky and breathe in, and then reach to the ground as I breathe out. If you are familiar with sun salutations in yoga, it is a similar concept.

Step 3: As I get myself ready I say positive affirmations to myself in the mirror. Staring directly into your own eyes is a very powerful experience. I had never noticed it before, but I think I always avoided eye contact with myself before. I was always looking at my hair, or focused somewhere else on my face. It's a very different feeling when you stare deep into your own eyes and recite something positive. It makes you feel supported, strong and focused as you start your day.

Step 4: As I eat my breakfast, I write in my journal. I will write an intention for the day as well as something I am excited about or grateful for. It focuses my energy for the day to a positive place.

Step 5: I walk to work, or on my days off, I go for a recreational walk. I practice walking meditation.

Step 6: Throughout the day my time gets pulled in a lot of directions, and focusing inwards isn't my priority. To stay focused, I practice tapping at my desk one or two times each day to distract my mind from any negative thoughts or out of control emotions.

Step 7: Each day I have a goal to compliment three people. I make a point of creating conversation to improve my emotional intelligence by complimenting someone and creating a conversation around that compliment.

Step 8: Each day I set aside 10-15 minutes no matter what for meditation or visualization. Whether I am working through a specific goal of retraining a neuro-association, meditating over something that is bothering me, or practicing concentration meditation to improve my focus, I dedicate that time for my brain's health. This is my mental workout and I never miss it.

Step 9: At the end of the day I go back to my journal and write the three things I mentioned when we were talking about tips for self-actualization. I write one thing about my day that was great, one thing that I struggled with, and one thing that I observed that had nothing to do with me.

Step 10: I reflect on my day and decide to set my intention for the next day. I firmly believe that if I go to sleep visualizing the words I just wrote down for the next day, my mind marinates them all night, and the next day I live by them authentically. It's stunning to realize how much power our thoughts have to set the tone for a day full of experiences.

By following these ten steps each and every day, I have found myself to be happier, calmer, and emotionally healthier. The difference is so huge, I struggle to find words to display the difference between who I was and who I am now. I feel completely different, and approach life in an entirely different mindset.

Follow these 10 steps like I do, and make them your daily practice. You will feel empowered, free, and fully in control of your own thoughts and emotions.

AFTERWORD

When we started out on our journey together, I told you that you would learn more about your mind and its abilities than you ever thought possible. Your brain holds possibilities to give you the life you've always dreamed of.

When I started my path years ago, I didn't even realize I was in such a dark place. I genuinely thought I would lower my stress and increase my positivity and I would be fine. Even looking at that and seeing that my goal was to be "fine" is heartbreaking to me. I am so grateful that I came to know all these wonderful methods and knowledge that have enabled me to strive for more.

More is what I want for you too. I know that you are capable of great things. You too can connect to your emotions and master your thoughts. By doing this you will see benefits pop up in all different facets of your life.

Staying You

The theme of mastering your thoughts and living a path to self-actualization is one of change and growth. But a concern that some may have is: Do you lose who you are along the way? Do you spend so much time trying to focus inward, that you forget who you are in relation to the rest of the world? Do you change so much that your connections with other people change and dissolve as a result?

We talked about finding and clarifying your core values. This will act as a guidance system so that you don't ever lose focus on who you are deep down. The point of self-actualization and growth is not to lose what makes you unique. Self-actualization is meant to accentuate your favorite and most positive parts of yourself, and cope with the negative and turmoiled parts you've been living with. None of this will change the things you laugh at, your favorite foods, or the way you smile. You will still be you, only a healthier and happier version.

Along the way, you might have relationships that don't like this version of you. There's the old saying "misery loves company." It's unfortunately true. If someone in your life is also unhappy, but not open to a new path, they may be angry at you for moving forward. They won't have the mental capacity at this time to be happy for you and your relationship may suffer.

Get excited about your future. You have now armed yourself with a toolbox bigger than most people on this planet have. You understand your thoughts and emotions with more awareness than most people you know. You have abilities to control your mind. Now remember how powerful your brain actually is, and think about how profound that is.

My Ending Point

Do you remember my stories about my vacation, and the time I worked as a server? Do you remember my mindsets for each of these stories? Now listen to one that happened to me about a month ago.

Last month I was quickly running to the mall to grab a gift for a child's birthday party. I was in a rush leaving the house so I wasn't looking my best and I ran into someone that I worked with at that restaurant! What happened next for me was nothing short of a miracle. I was nothing but happy to see them. I excitedly told them about things happening in my life and eagerly asked about theirs. I genuinely enjoyed our interaction and walked away feeling energized.

What made me even more happy is what I would have done in that situation a few years earlier. I would have immediately been embarrassed about how I looked and been self-conscious the whole time. Now I didn't even care. I'm so much more confident that it didn't phase me. Plus my ego is smaller so I realized that they weren't super dressed up either and it didn't matter to me, so I know they would be thinking the same thing.

I would have been frantically trying to think of things going on in my life that they would care about and not listening to what they were saying. Or even worse, I might not have even asked because I was so self-absorbed. Now I genuinely have things I'm excited to share and really want to know about their accomplishments.

I would have been distracted trying to remember things that I had to get done, or worried that I wouldn't have enough time to get my errands done that I wouldn't have been very engaging. Now because I'm more focused, my schedule is better organized and I'm not always rushing and feeling frantic. I was able to relax and enjoy the conversation.

I would have walked away stressed about what they were thinking. I would have made up stories in my head about how they thought I looked heavy, or seemed rude, or any number or negative thoughts. Now I walked away thinking how great it was to see them, and didn't put any thought into what they were thinking about me.

This small interaction was a peak moment for me. Look how far I had come and what I was able to do. I felt a sense of accomplishment walking away from that person that it almost brought me to tears. It was in that moment that I had my first inkling that I had reached some level of self-actualization. I know that the growth never stops, and I will continue to practice my 10 steps daily and work on other areas as well, but I felt pretty great that day. This is the peak moment that I want for you, and that you will experience over time.

Thank you for sharing your time with me and giving your energy to this book. Your devotion and passion towards yourself will create a new future for you. Remember to be kind to yourself, be patient, and enjoy the journey.

REFERENCES

All photos sourced from pixabay.com

American Psychiatric Association. (2008). "What is obsessive-compulsive disorder?" Psychiatry.org. www.psychiatry.org/patients-families/ocd/what-is-obsessive-compulsive-disorder.

Burns, David D M.D. (2008). Feeling good: The new mood therapy. Harper.

Davis, Matt. (2019, August 20). "8 ways to achieve self-actualization." Big Think. bigthink.com/personal-growth/achieving-self-actualization

"Emotional intelligence in leadership." (2009). Mindtools. www.mindtools.com/pages/article/newLDR_45.htm.

Girard, Joe. (2014, March 3). "3 ways to be memorable using neuro-associations." Joe Girard. joegirard.ca/neuro-associations/

Harbinger, Jordan. (2018, March 5). "7 signs it's time to cut a toxic person out of your life (and how to do it)." Jordan Harbinger. www.jordanharbinger.com/7-signs-its-time-to-cut-a-toxic-person-out-of-your-life-and-how-to-do-it/

Howitt, Nigel. (2019, February 6). "EFT (Tapping): Healing through reprogramming the subconscious mind." Lawful Rebel. lawfulrebel.com/eft-tapping/

Kelly PhD, Owen. (2020, March 8). "Could an herbal remedy help relieve your OCD symptoms?" Verywell Mind. www.verywellmind.com/herbal-remedies-for-ocd-2510631.

Lyons, Deanna. (n.d.). "EFT handouts." Deanna Lyons. deannalyons.com/eft-handouts/

Mayo Clinic Staff. (2020, September 15). "Mindfulness Exercises." Mayo Clinic. www.mayoclinic.org/healthy-lifestyle/consumer-health/in-depth/mindfulness-exercises/art-20046356.

Molinoff, Mark. (n.d.). "Raleigh acupuncture obsessive compulsive disorder treatment." Raleigh Acupuncture Associates. raleighacupunctureinc.com/raleigh-acupuncture-obsessive-compulsive-disorder/.

Neff, Dr. Kristen. (2019). "Self-compassion exercises by Dr. Kristin Neff." Self-Compassion. self-compassion.org/category/exercises/.

Raypole, Crystal. (2020, February 27). "Self-actualization: What it is and how to achieve it." Healthline. www.healthline.com/health/self-actualization#characteristics.

Reddy, Chitra. (2015, October 14). "How to control your ego problems: 10 best tips." WiseStep. content.wisestep.com/control-ego-problems/.

Ricoh PhD, David. (2020, September 20). "13 strategies to deal with your emotional triggers." Experience Life. experiencelife.lifetime.life/article/13-strategies-to-deal-with-your-emotional-triggers/.

Selva, Joaquin. (2019, June 26). "What is self-actualization? A psychologist's definition [+ examples]." Positive Psychology. positivepsychology.com/self-actualization/.

"Tapping 101." (n.d.). The Tapping Solution. www.thetappingsolution.com/tapping-101/

"Walking meditation." (2020). Headspace. www.headspace.com/meditation/walking-meditation.

Walton, Alice G. (2015, February 9). "7 ways meditation can actually change the brain." Forbes. www.forbes.com/sites/alicegwalton/2015/02/09/7-ways-meditation-can-actually-change-the-brain/?sh=53c1df521465.

Weigardt, Liz. (n.d.). "5 steps for rewiring negative associations." Happy Brain Life. www.happybrainlife.com/blog/2019/2/21/5-steps-to-rewiring-negative-associations.

PLEASE LEAVE A REVIEW

From the bottom of our hearts, thank you for reading our books. We truly hope that it helps you heal from Retroactive Jealousy and live a more empowered and happy life. If it does help you, then I'd like to ask you for a favor. Would you be kind enough to leave a review for this book on Amazon? It'd be greatly appreciated and will likely impact the lives of other Retroactive Jealousy sufferers across the globe, giving them hope and healing.

They are suffering like you and I have and we can help them move past this together.

We read **EVERY** review we receive and each one helps us to become a better writer to serve you more.

www.ingramcontent.com/pod-product-compliance
Lightning Source LLC
Chambersburg PA
CBHW021438070526
44577CB00002B/215